GERMANY IN THE AGE OF TOTAL WAR

Germany in the Age of Total War

Edited by
VOLKER R. BERGHAHN AND MARTIN KITCHEN

CROOM HELM LONDON
BARNES & NOBLE BOOKS
TOTOWA, NEW JERSEY

©1981 Volker R. Berghahn and Martin Kitchen
Croom Helm Ltd, 2-10 St John's Road, London SW11

British Library Cataloguing in Publication Data

Germany in the age of total war.
  1. Germany – History – 1918-1933 –
     Addresses, essays, lectures
  2. Germany – History – 1933-1945 –
     Addresses, essays, lectures
  3. Germany – History – Allied occupation,
     1945- – Addresses, essays, lectures
     I. Kitchen, Martin
     943.086   DD235

ISBN 0-7099-0119-4

First published in the USA 1981 by
Barnes & Noble Books
81 Adams Drive,
Totowa, New Jersey, 07512
ISBN 0-389-20186-3

Printed and bound in Great Britain by
Biddles Ltd, Guildford and King's Lynn

ESSAYS IN HONOUR OF FRANCIS CARSTEN

CONTENTS

1 FRANCIS CARSTEN: POLITICS AND HISTORY IN TWO CULTURES

Volker R. Berghahn*

The essays in this volume were written by friends and pupils of Francis Carsten in honour of his seventieth birthday this year. In these seven decades he has personally witnessed the upheavals which resulted from two total wars and revolutionary crises. These events have had a profound effect on both his personal life and his scholarly development. His biography, as recounted below, is thus of considerable interest in itself.

However, the introduction to this volume also seemed to be the appropriate place to set Francis Carsten's work into the broader context of what might be called the Anglo-German historiographical relationship. Although his biography reflects the upheavals which German society experienced in the period up to 1945, he was among those British historians who wrote widely about Germany after the defeat of the Third Reich and who, through his books, articles and lectures, tried to contribute to the inevitable reappraisal of German history. The second part of this introduction will therefore examine how Francis Carsten's writings were received by his colleagues in the Federal Republic in the 1950s and 1960s. Although this would seem to be a worthwhile exercise in itself, it also raises, indirectly at least, broader questions concerning differences between the historiographical traditions and academic cultures of Britain and the Federal Republic.

Francis Carsten was born on 25 June 1911. On his mother's side, his family belonged to the Jewish upper middle class of Berlin with many connections to the commercial and academic world. His father was a well known eye specialist at the Charité Hospital and an honorary professor at the Humboldt University. His family originated from Silesia. Both parents strongly identified with German culture and the two sons were barely aware of their Jewish background. The atmosphere at home was staunchly conservative and monarchist. There was a picture of the Kaiser on the wall in the lounge and Francis's father was deeply grieved not merely by the sight of horrifyingly mutilated soldiers who were sent to his hospital for treatment, but also by the course of the war.

* The evaluation of Francis Carsten's work on the early modern period was written by Henry Cohn.

After primary school, his second son moved to the Königliches Wilhelms-Gymnasium and later to the Mommsen-Gymnasium which he remembers as having been scarcely less 'horrible' than the KWG. The political atmosphere at both schools was firmly *deutschnational*, though not anti-Semitic. Francis Carsten's reaction to this kind of upbringing was a 'classic' one: he rebelled against it. At the age of fourteen, he proclaimed himself an atheist and refused to participate in religious instruction. A year later he joined one of the youth organisations of the Communist Party, the Sozialistischer Schülerbund; his parents were, predictably, appalled. With a number of like-minded fellow pupils he edited a magazine, *Der Schulkampf*, which published, *inter alia*, anonymous reports on the political views of the teachers. Not surprisingly, these activities did not go down very well, and there was trouble when Francis Carsten took his *Abitur* (A levels) in 1929. In History, for example, his examiners awarded a 'B', although his History teacher thought the performance had been genuinely first-class.

In the autumn of 1929, he began to study law at Geneva University. At the beginning of his second term he was back in Berlin. He moved to Heidelberg in the following year and back again to Berlin where he passed his *Referendar* examination early in 1933. At Berlin and Heidelberg he attended lectures by famous lawyers like Gustav Radbruch, Hermann Heller and Martin Wolff. But legal studies occupied barely more than half of his time. For much of the rest, he was active in politics. It must, of course, be remembered that these were the years of a disintegrating Weimar Republic and the rise of National Socialism. After 1930, the universities became centres of Nazi agitation and fights between political opponents among the student body became a daily occurrence. Several times Francis Carsten found himself in the midst of such brawls and on one occasion had to have several stitches.

During his schooldays he had been a faithful adherent of Communist orthodoxy. But with the Stalinisation of German Communism progressing and under the influence of Richard Löwenthal who, three years his elder, was a well known student leader, he became increasingly critical of the Thälmann course. Above all, his group disagreed with the 'Social Fascist' strategy of the Party; to Francis Carsten and his friends the real enemies were the Nazis, not the Social Democrats. By 1931 he found himself involved in the creation of cadres which, operating secretly inside the SPD and the KPD, simply called themselves Die Organisation, later known as Neubeginnen.[1] It is through this underground work that he met a number of young Social Democrats, among them Fritz Erler.

None of this hectic political activity was, of course, able to change the course of history. The split between the two working-class movements remained unbridged and in January 1933 the Nazis finally came to power. Neubeginnen never shared the illusions of the KPD leadership that Hitler would only last for a short while. On the other hand, as Leninists they did believe that Fascism – that product, as they saw it, of the crisis of capitalism – would collapse eventually and that this would be the hour of Die Organisation. While continuing to be involved in conspiratorial work, Francis Carsten, having passed his first law exams early in 1933, outwardly maintained the life of an ordinary citizen. Having passed his law examination at the Berlin District Court (Kammergericht), but unable to find a *Referendar* position because of the anti-Semitic policies of the new regime, he joined the Bleichroeder Bank for a year. In 1934, he opened a bookshop together with Norbert Elias. At the same time he acted as an occasional courier between Berlin and Prague. By 1935, the Nazis began to introduce economic discrimination against Jews and the bookshop on Kurfürstendamm was closed. For Francis Carsten it was high time to leave the country. He received a tip-off that the Gestapo were after him. Basle was his next stop, then London and finally Amsterdam.

His career as a lawyer lay in ruins, but there had always been his interest in history, now intensified by the fact that so much had obviously 'gone wrong' in his native Germany. At Amsterdam he became a serious scholar of early modern Prussian history, as his three articles in *Tijdschrift voor Geschiedenis* and *International Review of Social History*, all of them published in 1938, testify. Yet Holland was not a safe place to stay and in April 1939 Francis Carsten sailed to Britain. In October he was accepted at Wadham College, Oxford, to do his doctorate which, interrupted by internment in 1940, he completed in June 1942. At Oxford he became instrumental in establishing the Social Democratic Club, a student society of moderate left-wingers, and he also met Ruth, later his wife, fellow historian and collaborator. He spent the rest of the war at the Political Warfare Executive, first with Sefton Delmer's propaganda unit and, subsequently, with Duncan Wilson, when he was involved in the preparation of handbooks on various aspects of German life for use by the Allied Occupation authorities in Germany after VE-Day.

When that day finally arrived, Francis Carsten's interest in German history was undiminished. In 1947 he obtained a post as lecturer at Westfield College, London, and thus launched himself into a university career which ultimately took him to the Masaryk Chair of Central

European History at the School of Slavonic and East European Studies. Nor did his attitudes towards Germany undergo a marked change. He was, it is true, no longer a Marxist. On the other hand, he always saw himself as a refugee for political rather than racial reasons, and his experiences before 1933 and later in the underground never led him to adopt the kind of indiscriminate anti-Germanism which could be found, for perfectly plausible reasons, among other refugees after 1945. As a young activist he had met too many anti-Nazis and as a trained social historian he had learned to differentiate sociologically when looking at the basis of Nazi support in Germany. Above all, it appears he had never lost a belief in the positive force of enlightenment. Accordingly we find Francis Carsten travelling to Germany soon after the end of the war to give lectures on German history under the auspices of the British re-education programme.

Not all his encounters with German audiences were encouraging. In 1947, for example, he found himself locked in a violent argument with middle-aged Germans during a residential course at Rendsburg. Evidently few of the students liked his views and interpretations of German history and at one point he was even branded a 'Bolshevik'. Although it is not altogether easy to reconstruct the political atmosphere in early post-war Germany, the tenacity with which many people continued to adhere to certain notions of the course of German history can hardly be exaggerated. Barbara Marshall's article below[2] deals with these problems as seen by the British Occupation authorities and, at least indirectly, also with the emotional obstacles which Francis Carsten encountered during his lecture tours through North Germany. In a more subdued way it was much the same with the reception of his books by the older generation of German historians in the 1950s. As one of the most prominent among them once remarked, these writings did not belong to the 'mainstream of German historiography'. In what ways, then, did Francis Carsten's books diverge from the mainstream? It was this question that made it tempting to take a closer look at his reception among the West German historical Establishment.

The first twenty-five years of his historical scholarship were largely devoted to the social and political history of the German principalities in the medieval and early modern periods. Norbert Elias, then preparing his own seminal study on *The Civilising Process*, had not only influenced him to become an historian, but suggested that it would be worth his while to find out what had gone wrong in earlier centuries of Prussian and German history. Intensive work on Prussian history also allowed him to purge his own Prussian background. A dozen articles published between 1938 and 1951 paved the way for a major study of *The Origins of Prussia*, based on the thesis for which he had received his Oxford doctorate. It broke new ground in eschewing narrative political history for a structure carefully designed 'to describe the growth and the decline of the classes and the institutions which formed the basis of the later Prussian state'.[3] Because the Hohenzollern state remained unaltered in its fundamentals during the eighteenth century, as a later article on Prussian despotism at its height was to show, *The Origins of Prussia* was restricted to the period up to the end of the seventeenth century. The colonisation of Brandenburg, Pomerania and Prussia in the thirteenth and fourteenth centuries had resulted in a society in which the nobles enjoyed no overwhelming advantages over the peasantry and towns. This balance gave place to the ascendancy of the Junkers in the fifteenth and sixteenth centuries, as the towns declined economically and politically and the peasants gradually lost the legal safeguards of their position. After the Thirty Years War, when the majority of these territories as well as Cleves and Mark in the Rhineland were consolidated in the possession of the Hohenzollerns, Frederick William the Great Elector largely eliminated the political power which the nobles had exercised through the Estates. The introduction of the excise and stricter administrative control further weakened both the economy of the towns and their self-government. The Great Elector launched the process whereby the Junkers became by the mid-eighteenth century a service nobility forming the backbone of the Army and the civil service. The price of their co-operation was heightened control over the peasant serfs. Thus the baneful influence of the Junkers over the Prussian state was established which lasted until the early nineteenth century and beyond. In this Prussian variant of a common Eastern European development, the monarch worked closely with the nobles to place insuperable barriers in the way of the growth of a strong middle class, such as emerged in most Western European states.

Francis Carsten's broad perspective on Prussian history was too novel to win immediate acceptance from traditionally-minded German historians. The few academic reviews which appeared at the time, while recognising the thoroughness of his research, regretted the deliberate neglect of political history and insisted that developments in the separate Hohenzollern territories were more differentiated than he had allowed.[4] Gerhard Oestreich's contributions to Prussian history in successive revisions of Gebhardt's handbook of German history until 1963 took no account of *The Origins of Prussia*, although this omission was partly remedied in the 1970 edition.[5] No German publisher was prepared to back a translation until 1968, when the author was already well known for his book in the Reichswehr. Only then did *The Origins of Prussia* receive general acclaim in German-language daily newspapers, weeklies, radio reviews and academic journals,[6] although Gerd Heinrich still rejected the whole approach outright for thinking in terms of classes and placing too much blame on the Junkers for the course taken by Prussian history.[7] Otto Büsch was exceptional among German historians when he adopted Francis Carsten's methodology for his searching analysis of the Army's place in eighteenth-century Prussian society.[8]

Reviewers had criticised Francis Carsten's first book for failing to draw on comparative material from other German principalities. In fact post-war German historical writing on the origins of the early modern state itself consisted either of panoramic and derivative textbooks or of regional and local studies of limited chronological scope and historical vision. This barrier was first broken by *Princes and Parliaments in Germany from the Fifteenth to the Eighteenth Century*, in which the author took issue with the prevailing view among German historians that the Estates had been a conservative force putting obstacles in the way of the constructive state-building policies of the princes. The more favourable view of the Estates that had characterised the earlier work of Georg von Below, Otto Hintze and the Swiss historian Werner Näf[9] had been relegated in favour of the negative verdicts of Fritz Hartung and Gerhard Oestreich.[10] Carsten's was the first major book-length comparative study of this subject, which gave the fullest and most reliable account hitherto of the varied reasons for the rise and subsequent decline of representative institutions in the German principalities. It was also based on the intensive use of archives. He had already used manuscript as well as printed sources for his work on Brandenburg-Prussia. No scholar working in the Anglo-Saxon world had previously done more than rely mainly on printed materials when writing about German history. In future the path to the well organised German archives would increasingly be followed by those who were stimulated by his example.

From a survey of Hesse, Saxony, Württemberg, Jülich-Berg, Cleves and Mark, the Palatinate and Bavaria, *Princes and Parliaments* concluded that the Estates at the height of their power, which in most places was during the sixteenth and early seventeenth centuries, did in some senses represent the interests of the 'country', especially when princes were prone to sacrifice them to a costly foreign policy. However self-seeking the noble and urban oligarchies may have been, they also on occasion contributed to both the strength of the state and the liberty of its subjects by introducing new financial institutions and opposing dynastic partitions, high taxation, forcible recruiting and other petty tyrannies. Even after being deprived of many of their powers by the absolute rulers of the seventeenth and eighteenth centuries, the Estates in Württemberg and other parts of south-west Germany preserved a spirit of constitutionalism which later helped nineteenth-century liberalism to strike roots.

The first response of the majority of German academic historians was even more hostile to *Princes and Parliaments* than to *The Origins of Prussia*. In 1961 Fritz Hartung explained that for the 1959 edition of his German constitutional history he had not been persuaded by Carsten's book to alter the opinion of the Estates which he had held unchanged since the first edition of 1914.[11] In a widely influential review article Peter Herde not only reaffirmed the purely reactionary role of the Estates but took issue with Carsten's comparison of them with the English Parliament. The grounds for doing so were that *Princes and Parliaments* failed to note the differences between the two sets of representative institutions, although in fact most of the distinctions made in the review are drawn from the very book it criticises.[12] During the following years many German scholars in the field only consulted the two short summaries of the book available in German translation. In time Gerhard Oestreich came to take a more favourable view of the contribution made by the Estates to the development of the modern state, without however acknowledging that it was Francis Carsten's book that had compelled German historians to rethink their position.[13] Only ten years and more after its appearance has a mostly younger generation expressed their full appreciation of its main thesis and added further evidence to emphasise the continuing importance of the Estates in later German history.[14]

In Britain Francis Carsten's seminal work on early modern German history won widespread recognition as soon as his first book was published. Evidence for this comes not only from the numerous favourable reviews in weekly periodicals and academic journals, but his choice as editor for volume 5 of the *New Cambridge Modern History*, covering the period of European history coterminous with the Great Elector's reign.

Francis Carsten was no man to rest on the laurels which his first two books had earned him. However, his next study was on a topic of twentieth-century German history. Psychologically it was not altogether easy for him to move into a period which he had lived through himself, first as a teenager in Berlin and later as a student at Heidelberg and at

the Humboldt University. Moreover, he disagreed with the older generation of German historians whom he had met repeatedly during the
1950s and who had linked the collapse of the Weimar Republic and the
rise of National Socialism with the 'demonic' qualities of Hitler and the
impact of mass politics.[15] Francis Carsten was more inclined, in line
with his earlier beliefs, to argue that there existed a close connection
between National Socialism and the old elites of Germany which had
throttled the genuinely democratic aspirations of the so-called masses
and of the working class in particular. Both aspects of the Weimar
tragedy were to preoccupy him in his research during the following
decade.

What probably made the shift towards the inter-war period easier
was that West German colleagues like Karl Dietrich Bracher had meanwhile begun to cast doubt upon the interpretations of the generation of
Gerhard Ritter. In his study on *Die Auflösung der Weimarer Republik*,[16]
Bracher had pointed to the structural and institutional weaknesses
inherent in the 1918/19 settlement and had consciously abandoned the
earlier concentration on personalities and the plebeian 'gravediggers of
the Republic'. Furthermore, a debate also started in the 1960s on the
character of the Council Movement during the German Revolution and
on the chances that it could have produced a more thoroughgoing
democratisation of society and politics than was ultimately achieved.
It would be interesting to speculate why, in joining the ranks of those
scholars engaged in a critical stocktaking of Weimar history, Francis
Carsten first concentrated on the right and why it took him much
longer to begin work on the extreme left which had once been his
intellectual and emotional home territory.

Looking back upon this phase in his research work, it appears that
he was partly hoping to clarify his own mind about the history of his
generation. However, there was also a pedagogical impetus which
impelled him, as he once put it, to help destroy the legends which had
grown up in the Federal Republic about the origins of the Third Reich.
One of the institutions which had indeed become the subject of a good
deal of myth-making was the Army.[17] Certainly by the late 1950s the
notion had found widespread public acceptance that the 'shield' of the
Wehrmacht had remained untainted during the Nazi period. It had, so
the argument went, not been involved in any of Hitler's crimes and its
ideological Nazification had been minimal. Much work had also been
done on the active military resistance to Hitler and the existence of a
conservative 'Other Germany'. This positive record had been extended
backwards into the Weimar period and various authors had cast the

Reichswehr in a most favourable light. General Hans von Seeckt, the 'founder of the Reichswehr', was portrayed as the saviour of the Weimar Republic in troubled times;[18] General Wilhelm Groener, Reichswehr Minister from 1928 to 1932, had been turned into a Republican 'democrat'.[19] The English-language books by Gordon Craig[20] and John Wheeler-Bennett[21] had, by and large, done little to dent this image, while in West Germany the field was dominated by memoirs, biographies and monographs on the military resistance to National Socialism before and after 1933. Nor had a comprehensive treatment of the Reichswehr yet been produced which made full use of all available primary sources and which tried to take a critical look at the Army's role between 1918 and 1933.

These historiographical realities and the fact that the Bendlerstrasse, the seat of the Reichswehr Ministry, had been just around the corner from where he grew up, tempted Francis Carsten to think of writing on the subject and of doing so in his mother tongue — again something which he had not done for many years. In the end, he wrote the manuscript in both languages, with the German version of his political history of the Weimar Reichswehr appearing before the English one. The book made an immediate impact both because it contained much new material presented in a very readable form, and because of its critical overall assessment of Reichswehr politics which culminated in the concluding sentences:

> If the republic after 1930 had possessed an army entirely loyal to it, the great crisis would have taken a different course. A Reichswehr which in the hour of peril would have cooperated with the Prussian police and the republican organizations, instead of intriguing against them, could have been the rock on which the waves broke. But the policy of the army command prevented such a cooperation and led to the weakening of the republic and the organizations willing to defend it. In so doing, however, the army command also undermined the foundations of its own power.[22]

This being the general theme of the book, Seeckt was bound to be taken off his pro-Republican pedestal. But there are also smaller revisions to be found in the book's footnotes, as for example the discovery of the doctoring of the published version of the Stieff letters. These and other discoveries in the archives convinced Francis Carsten that it was time to set the record straight. Thus, although much of the book is concerned with the presentation of empirical material and lacks systematisation and theorisation, as Karl Rohe pointed out in his criticism,[23] its overall message is profoundly political and committed. It was published at a time when the critical evaluation of modern German history had begun on a broader front. The Fischer Debate on the origins of the First World War was in full swing,[24] and it had become more generally accepted that the destruction of the Weimar Republic had been the work of forces other than 'Hitler and Stalin'. The reception of the book in West Germany was therefore much more favourable than that of Francis Carsten's first studies. Most of the many reviewers, while perhaps objecting to points of detail, approved of the overall analysis. Thus Bodo Scheurig wrote in *Frankfurter Allgemeine Zeitung* that this history of the Reichswehr would remain the standard work for many years to come and praised the author's circumspect and sober judgements.[25] Heinz K. Wendland expressed the wish that the book would gain a wide readership.[26] Above all, he added, 'it is to be hoped that [it] will soon be available in all Bundeswehr libraries.'

It is unlikely that this suggestion was adopted very quickly in view of the fact that all reviewers with Bundeswehr connections found the book objectionable. Comparatively mild criticism came from Lieutenant Colonel Wolfram von Raven, one-time Deputy Press Officer of the Federal Defence Ministry and a military journalist.[27] He believed that Carsten's book lacked balance because it had failed to treat the attitude of the left to the Reichswehr and to recognise the psychological significance of the Versailles Treaty. Although he found the volume worth reading, Raven nevertheless left little doubt that it had raised questions without answering them. Friedrich Ruge, a retired admiral, honorary professor at Stuttgart University and jack-of-all-trades among West Germany's military historians, was much less generous.[28] He thought the work was full of contradictions, adding that he had seldom read an author who had so little sensitivity for what he was writing about. Carsten, he charged, had minimised the threat of Communism and made no mention of the Reichswehr's educational work in democracy. Poor judgement, tendentiousness and 'a certain superficiality' were the criticisms made by Michael Salewski, a pupil of Walther Hubatsch and an enthusiastic naval historian.[29] Like Ruge, he, too, engaged in a vigorous defence of Seeckt's politics which, he argued, had never violated the Weimar Constitution.

All in all, the book's reception in West Germany enables us to gauge its impact on two levels. The large number of favourable reviews in the daily press demonstrate how far an understanding of the structural and institutional 'faults' of the Weimar Republic had advanced since the early post-war period. In these quarters, the book aroused little controversy. It was a different matter in Bundeswehr circles which had been reared on the interpretations of the 1950s and which found it very difficult to accept Francis Carsten's view of the Reichswehr. The reception of the volume in the ranks of the West German officer corps therefore tells us something about the political and historical consciousness not merely of some of Francis Carsten's colleagues, but also of the Bundeswehr. The author gained first-hand experience of this when he was invited to lecture before the officers seconded to the Schule für Innere Führung at Coblence. His talk was so deeply upsetting to those present, and the subsequent discussion became so emotional, that General Ulrich de Maizière, who had introduced the speaker, felt obliged to apologise to his guest.

By the time Francis Carsten's next book appeared, the West German historiographical scene had undergone a further shift. Its topic – Fascism – was a problem which preoccupied many historians of the younger generation. In fact it had become a major industry. But they tended to find *Der Aufstieg des Faschismus in Europa*, an enlarged translation of a manuscript originally written in English, too descriptive and empirical. If German scholarship had had a world-wide reputation for being excessively concerned with abstract ideas, the younger generation of West German historians appeared to have inherited this tradition from the 'Neo-Rankeans', however much they differed from the latter in other respects. During the late 1960s, the search was on for a comprehensive theory of Fascism, with Marxist interpretations enjoying considerable popularity, not least because they were deemed to provide a framework of analysis of the 'Fascistic' tendencies of capitalist societies like the Federal Republic. Yet Francis Carsten's study, written in the tradition of British empirical social history, was concerned with something much more mundane and, one might add, less sweeping. As he, who had physically experienced Fascism and worked underground against it, put it in the introduction to the German edition:

Above all it is the author's heartfelt need, to explain to the younger generation of today how fascist movements became possible, how they grew into mass movements and how they gained power – in countries with a very ancient culture, very high educational levels and a civilised life of long standing . . . The author grew up in Berlin during the rise of National Socialism. Chapter 4 therefore describes events which he was able to observe himself and which may have influenced his judgment. It is still possible for him to relive the political atmosphere of those years, the endless discussions with Nazi students, their enormous influence in the universities, the mass meetings at which Hitler, Otto Strasser and other Nazis spoke, the perennial battles in the assembly halls and street-fights, the political unrest that permeated Berlin and the terror of 1933. This chapter tries to give the reader an impression of the atmosphere which forms so enormously important an element of the rise of National Socialism.[30]

To the extent that it is possible to gauge the impact of this paperback, it is probably safe to say that the West German generation of the 1960s, though agreeing with the author in their rejection of an approach to the problem through the history of ideas, was looking for more fundamental explanations.

A similar shift of interest towards abstraction and theorisation occurred in the late 1960s with reference to work on the Revolution of 1918/19 and the Soviet Movement in Germany and Austria, the subject of Francis Carsten's next book, *Revolution in Central Europe*, first published in London in 1972 and translated by him into German a year later. Like his volume on Fascism, this is a detailed and *comparatiste* analysis of the problem; yet, once again, it appeared at a time when West German experts in the field debated the role of the Workers' and Soldiers' Councils in much more abstract terms than Francis Carsten would have considered wise. He merely wished to investigate how it happened that a series of outwardly successful revolutions 'failed in their principal objective: to bring about a "democratization" of state and society'. There was no doubt in his mind 'that "democratization" was a real possibility'.[31] Yet, as in 1848,

the forces of conservatism and of social inertia prevailed; in the end parliamentary institutions were destroyed and the limited gains made in 1918 wiped out. Parliamentary democracy in central Europe suffered from weaknesses which marred its birth. I have described some of them in an earlier volume, *The Reichswehr and Politics, 1918-1933*. This volume is a further contribution to the subject.

It was more than this; for it was now, in the 1970s, that Francis Carsten finally began to turn to an examination of his own intellectual roots. What he found was a record of defeat by the stronger battalions of the right which he had fought as a young man. Not surprisingly therefore, the Workers' and Soldiers' Councils of 1918/19 are painted by him in warm and positive colours, and looking at the historical balance-sheet and at what came after, he was no doubt right in doing so. However, for the younger generation of West Germans this was not enough and it is no coincidence that the reviewer of his book in the *Stuttgarter Zeitung* should, at the end of her piece, enquire after the author's *Demokratieverständnis*:

> Nowhere in his empirical examination which is undertaken with the greatest care, but which unfortunately rarely moves beyond pure description, does the author explain how a democracy of councils, which were neither Bolshevik nor liberal democratic, might have worked. It thus remains unclear whether Carsten is an advocate of a direct or a liberal democracy.[32]

No doubt he would have reacted in bewilderment that such a categorical statement should have been expected of him and no doubt he would have replied that historical time and place must be taken into consideration. Yet this was a kind of pragmatism which his younger readers found most difficult to accept. Unlike the critics of his own generation, they had come to value the methodological questions which he had raised in his books on early modern German history. But they remained dissatisfied with the political answers which he provided in his studies on twentieth-century Central Europen history.

Taken as a whole, Francis Carsten's biography and *oeuvre* point not merely to the 'outsider' problem in a personal sense, but also to that of the Anglo-German relationship after 1945. It has been observed before that this relationship was highly problematical for historical reasons.[33] Having experienced severe strains well before 1914, it never again normalised during the inter-war period. The number of professional historians with a scholarly interest in Germany declined. This trend continued after 1945 and although most British historians had their own and no doubt firm views on the course of German history, few of them actually did their research in this field. It is difficult to see how two historians who had worked on the other country's history – say A. J. P. Taylor and G. Ritter – could have had a relaxed conversation on problems of mutual interest. In short, after 1945 the political and cultural divide was deeper than ever. In this situation it may be legitimate to ask if refugees from Nazism in British history departments could have played a role similar to that of their counterparts in America who acted as important bridges between the two professional establishments and kept an interest in German history alive in the United States. Yet, for a reason which it would be interesting to explore, most refugees who stayed in Britain turned to other areas, above all English history. They wrote in English and some of them became so well integrated into the British university system that their writings have had a major impact on the study of English history here.[34] It seems also that most of them adopted a method of historical empiricism which was certainly very different from the German tradition.

Francis Carsten, although he too adopted the empirical method, was one of those who retained a scholarly interest in Germany and transmitted it to the next generation. After his lecturing experiences in the late 1940s and through his work in West German archives in the 1950s, he also became an important contact in a growing network of academic exchanges between Britain and Germany which was extended to Austria and East Central Europe when he moved to the Masaryk Chair in 1961. Many German academics who passed through London in the 1960s and 1970s were guests at his house in Hampstead. The younger generation also came either singly or in larger numbers on an *Oberseminar* excursion, headed by their professor. If they stayed on to study at London University, they attended Francis Carsten's postgraduate seminar in German history and met his own pupils. It was, in view of his bridging role, not surprising that he should be among the founder members of the German Historical Institute which is now trying to provide a fixed meeting point for historians from both countries. All this has meant that there has been an appreciable growth in the number of historians of Germany at British universities. Inevitably their research takes them to the Federal Republic where they are exposed to the methodological arguments among their German colleagues. Their response has frequently been quite critical, although they are often more profoundly influenced by approaches on the Continent than they are prepared to admit.[35] Conversely, German historians have become more interested in historiographical work in Britain than ever before. This appears to be particularly true of a social history 'from below', whose tools of analysis are now being brought to bear on the study of popular history in the Federal Republic. Some of this work is concerned with the early modern period, so that it is only now that Francis Carsten's work of the 1950s is being recognised. This is at any rate a better outcome than would have been instant appreciation followed by long-term neglect. But it also provides us with an insight into the evolution of the Anglo-German historical relationship.

Anyone who has been involved in the preparation of a Festschrift knows how difficult it is to give a volume of this kind thematic cohesion, the more so when the scholar to whom these essays are presented has written on a wide range of topics. In order to obtain a closer focus the editors were forced to restrict the scope of this book and to concentrate upon the twentieth century in their attempt to give this collection a measure of unity.

It is hoped that the following ten essays by friends and pupils of Francis Carsten represent not merely important and useful contributions to their respective field in their own right, but also fit the volume's title. Above all, it is hoped the reader will agree that the contributions reflect, in different ways, the concerns and experiences of Francis Carsten as a scholar and politically committed intellectual in a period of great upheaval.

Notes

1. For general background on *Neubeginnen* and other left-wing splinter movements in the early 1930s see: H. Drechsler, *Die Sozialistische Arbeiterparti: Deutschlands* (Meisenheim, 1964); K. H. Tjaden, *Struktur und Funktion der KPD-Opposition (KPO)* (Meisenheim, 1965); W. Link, *Die Geschichte des Internationalen Jugend-Bundes (ISB) und des Internationalen Sozialistischen Kampfbundes (ISK)* (Meisenheim, 1964); R. Zimmermann, *Der Leninbund* (Düsseldorf, 1978).
2. See below, pp. 218ff.
3. F. L. Carsten, *The Origins of Prussia* (Oxford, 1954), Preface.
4. W. Hubatsch in *Historische Zeitschrift*, 179 (1954), pp. 121-3; E. Maschke in *Deutsches Archiv für die Erforschung des Mittelalters*, 11 (1954), pp. 278-9; H. Beyer in *Historisches Jahrbuch*, 75 (1956), pp. 390-2.
5. G. Oestreich, 'Die Errichtung des absoluten Staates in Brandenburg-Preussen' in B. Gebhardt, *Handbuch der Deutschen Geschichte*, vol. II, 8th edn, 5th revised printing (Stuttgart, 1963), pp. 353-5; 9th edn (1970), pp. 414-19.
6. See, e.g., M. Schlenke in *Die Zeit*, 6 Dec. 1968; H. R. Guggisberg in *Neue Zürcher Zeitung*, 13 Sept. 1968; F. Gause in *Das Ostpreussenblatt*, 8 Mar. 1969; P. G. Thielen in *Zeitschrift für Ostforschung*, 18 (1969), pp. 342-3; W. Abel in *Zeitschrift für Agrargeschichte und Agrarsoziologie*, 17 (1969), pp. 123-4.
7. G. Heinrich in *Jahrbuch für die Geschichte Mittel- und Ostdeutschlands*, 18 (1969), pp. 369-70.
8. O. Büsch, *Militärsystem und Sozialleben im alten Preussen, 1713-1807* (Berlin, 1962).
9. G. von Below, 'System und Bedeutung der landständischen Verfassung' in *idem, Territorium und Stadt*, 2nd edn (Munich-Berlin, 1923), pp. 53-160; O. Hintze, 'Typologie der ständischen Verfassung des Abendlandes' (1930) in *idem, Staat und Verfassung*, vol. I, 2nd edn (Göttingen, 1962), pp. 120-39; W. Näf, 'Frühformen des modernen Staates im Spätmittelalter' in *Historische Zeitschrift*, 171 (1951), pp. 225-43.
10. F. Hartung, *Deutsche Verfassungsgeschichte vom 15. Jahrhundert bis zur Gegenwart*, 6th edn (Stuttgart, 1950); G. Oestreich, 'Landständische Verfassung' in Gebhardt, *Handbuch*, vol. II, pp. 345-8.
11. F. Hartung, *Staatsbildende Kräfte der Neuzeit* (Berlin, 1961), p. 63, n. 4.
12. P. Herde, 'Deutsche Landstände und englisches Parlament' in *Historisches Jahrbuch*, 80 (1961), pp. 286-97; see, in similar terms, S. Skalweit in *Historische Zeitschrift*, 193 (1961), pp. 661-5; G. Birtsch, 'Die landständische Verfassung als Gegenstand der Forschung' in D. Gerhard (ed.), *Ständische Vertretungen in Europa im 17. und 18. Jahrhundert* (Göttingen, 1969), pp. 34-5. Slightly more

receptive to Carsten's interpretation were H. Helbig, 'Fürsten und Landstände im Westen des Reiches im Übergang vom Mittelalter zur Neuzeit' in *Rheinische Vierteljahrsblätter*, 29 (1964), pp. 33-4, 72; K. O. von Aretin, *Heiliges Römisches Reich, 1776-1806*, vol. I (Wiesbaden, 1967), pp. 26-34.

13. G. Oestreich, 'Ständetum und Staatsbildung in Deutschland' in *Der Staat*, 6 (1967), pp. 61-73; *idem*, 'Landständische Verfassung' in Gebhardt, *Handbuch*, 9th edn (1970), pp. 400-4.

14. H. Lehmann, 'Die württembergischen Landstände im 17. und 18. Jahrhundert' in Gerhard, *Handbuch*, pp. 183-207; K. Bosl, *Repräsentation und Parlamentarismus in Bayern vom 13. bis 20. Jahrhundert*, vol. I (Munich, 1972), pp. 8, 227, 238; P. Blickle, *Landschaften im Alten Reich* (Munich, 1973), pp. 44-5; R. Vierhaus, 'Land, Staat und Reich in der politischen Vorstellungswelt deutscher Landstände im 18. Jahrhundert', *Historische Zeitschrift*, 223 (1976), pp. 40-60.

15. Among the most prominent advocates of this interpretation were F. Meinecke, G. Ritter and L. Dehio. For a detailed discussion see G. G. Iggers, *The German Conception of History* (Wesleyan University Press, 1968), esp. Ch. 8.

16. K. D. Bracher, *Die Auflösung der Weimarer Republik* (Villingen, 1955).

17. For a recent critical assessment see, e.g., K.-J. Müller, 'The Army in the Third Reich', *Journal of Strategic Studies*, 2 (1979), pp. 123-52.

18. See esp. H. Meier-Welcker, *Seeckt* (Frankfurt, 1967).

19. D. Groener-Geyer, *General Groener. Soldat und Staatsmann* (Frankfurt, 1955).

20. G. Craig, *The Politics of the Prussian Army, 1640-1945* (London, 1955).

21. J. Wheeler-Bennett, *The Nemesis of Power* (London, 1953).

22. F. L. Carsten, *Reichswehr and Politics, 1918-1933* (Oxford, 1966), p. 405.

23. K. Rohe in *Government and Opposition* (Winter 1968), pp. 123-7.

24. For a summary of this controversy and its implications see, e.g., J. Moses, *The Politics of Illusion* (London, 1975).

25. B. Scheurig in *Frankfurter Allgemeine Zeitung*, 30 Aug. 1965.

26. H. K. Wendland in *Berliner Stimme*, 9 Jan. 1965.

27. W. von Raven in *Die politische Meinung*, 103 (1965), pp. 88-90.

28. F. Ruge in *Wehrwissenschaftliche Rundschau* (May 1966), p. 298.

29. M. Salewski in *Historisch-Politisches Buch* (Feb. 1965).

30. F. L. Carsten, *Der Aufstieg des Faschismus in Europa* (Frankfurt, 1968), p. 6.

31. F. L. Carsten, *Revolution in Central Europe, 1918-1919* (Berkeley, 1972), p. 9.

32. B. Adolff in *Stuttgarter Zeitung*, 28 Nov. 1973.

33. See, e.g., V. R. Berghahn, 'Looking Towards England' in *Times Literary Supplement*, 5 Nov. 1976, p. 1404.

34. Names like G. R. Elton, S. Pollard, J. Grenville and H. Hearder come to mind.

35. See, e.g., R. J. Evans (ed.), *Society and Politics in Wilhelmine Germany* (London, 1978).

2 THE TOPOS OF INEVITABLE WAR IN GERMANY IN THE DECADE BEFORE 1914*

Wolfgang J. Mommsen

A historical analysis of the causes of the First World War and the factors which determined it must, in my opinion, proceed from a fundamental presupposition, namely that in a period of accelerating modernisation and democratisation, combined with increasing political activity amongst broad sections of the populace, all the traditional political systems in Europe had, though perhaps to differing degrees, been caught in a crisis of adaptation which was increasingly restricting the traditional elites' ability to lead. In particular the military elites were under the impression that the social pre-conditions for the maintenance of a powerful army were beginning to erode. Throughout Europe the traditional ruling elites harboured increasing doubts as to their ability to govern effectively under the conditions of mass politics.

What follows is an attempt to analyse more closely a factor which can be considered as an essential component of a more general explanatory model of a structural-functional kind, namely the transformation in public opinion in the last years before 1914 as regards expectations and fears of an imminent war in Europe. In this analysis we are limiting ourselves to the German Reich, but are assuming that comparable tendencies, if not always equally strong, can also be found to have been at work in other European countries.

We are working on the assumption that precisely those political systems which can be characterised by Max Weber's term 'semiconstitutional' tended to be particularly dependent on fluctuations in public opinion, or to be more precise, dependent on the opinion of the politically active groups or strata within that system. Their position of authority was no longer sufficiently strong for them to be able simply to ignore public opinion on questions of foreign policy. On the contrary, they had no firm basis of legitimacy and consent amongst the parties and amongst the population at large, as do functioning parliamentary systems; nor did they have the institutional implements for effectively guiding public opinion on issues of foreign policy. They tried continually to manipulate public opinion, or at least those sections of the press under their control, but all the same they were always

* Translated by Jane Williams.

helpless when public opinion happened not to be on their side.

After the great wars of national unification in the middle of the century, culminating in the Franco-Prussian War of 1870, Europe had enjoyed a period of uninterrupted peace. Admittedly there had always been warlike incidents, but these were invariably peripheral and the powers had been able to keep the repercussions of such conflicts on the system of European states to a minimum. The war-in-sight crisis of 1874 and the war hysteria, to a large degree artificially aroused, over the Boulanger crisis in 1887 had, in fact, done little to destroy the conviction that at least as long as Bismarck was Chancellor there was little danger of a major European war. Even the problem of Alsace-Lorraine had gradually lost any immediate significance. Faith in the fact that governments would be able to solve regional or peripheral conflicts by diplomatic means, or at least without war, had always been justifiably strong. Since the mid-1890s, however, with the onslaught of the second, final wave of the scramble for overseas territories, this faith was gradually lost. The construction of the German battle fleet awoke fears of a 'Copenhagen' of the German fleet; repeated incidents in the relationship with France aroused new worries on both sides of the Rhine. But above all the view gained ground that the inevitable imperialist expansion of the major states into the still undeveloped areas of the globe, regarded as indispensable for the survival of the homeland in future eras, could not be carried out without severe warlike encounters between the rivalling major powers. Under the influence of these developments a tendency emerged, fostered by imperialist enthusiasm, towards the use of violence and war. Violence was increasingly regarded as an essential element in international relations and indeed positively welcomed. On the other hand, as a sort of reflex to these ideas, a basically fatalistic attitude developed which began to see a world war as sooner or later inevitable. Initially introduced by interested parties as a highly effective rhetorical argument, this attitude increasingly detached itself from such clearly propagandist connotations and finally became, in the face of mounting tension in many international relationships, a sort of independent factor in its own right. This weakened, from a formal point of view, resistance to aggressive tendencies. The widespread assumption that war would come sooner or later, whatever particular policies might be pursued, had, in the final analysis, the effect of a 'self-fulfilling prophecy'.

It is, of course, extraordinarily difficult to filter out as independent elements from the multiplicity of historical factors enthusiasm for war on the one hand and fatalistic expectation of war on the other. This is precisely because they extend into the realm of the 'unspoken assumptions',[1] but more particularly because models of argument of this sort have usually been reflexes of the most diverse political and social interests. In the meantime a multitude of studies on public opinion in the last decade before 1914 have been published, predominantly based on an assessment of quite inexhaustible newspaper material, for example the works of E. M. Carroll, O. Hale, K. Wernecke and, for a specific sphere, A. Jux and R. Ropponen.[2] However, the validity of the results of such studies is limited since ultimately they have never been able to shake off their largely impressionist nature. So, continued investigation into the syndrome of the inevitability of the coming war should serve here rather as a *Leitmotiv* for an analysis of the attitudes of the major social groups, and in particular of the 'strategic cliques' in the years before the outbreak of the First World War. We are not attempting to single this factor out as the decisive one which caused the war.

It is, in any case, difficult to define a suitable point of departure. In Germany, as everywhere in Europe, the bourgeois and aristocratic strata accepted war, at least in principle, as a necessary political expedient. When Treitschke, in his famous political lectures, characterised war as a 'God-given thing', and regarded recourse to war as a natural political expedient of any state, he was merely giving expression to a popular opinion of his time.[3] On the other hand, in the wake of the emergence of the modern state, with the masses increasingly participating in the political decision-making processes, and the simultaneous breakthrough of liberal principles, the psychological threshold for war had become considerably higher. Even if pacifist attitudes met with little response in the German public, though not in the working class, the ruling elites were prepared to accept that the age of cabinet wars was gone and that adequate justification of war policies before the public had become a real problem. Amongst the military and political elites there was complete unanimity concerning the necessity of 'so formulating the *casus belli* that the nation will take up arms enthusiastically and with one accord' (Moltke).[4]

In partial contradiction to the attitude of the broad masses, who overwhelmingly abhorred the prospect of an impending war, the idea that the war would represent a health-cure for the satiated bourgeois culture, obsessed with its materialistic rat-race, gained a good deal of support. Such ideas regarding the revitalising effect of a war on German society were current largely in conservative circles, but also amongst sizeable sections of the intelligentsia. It was, for instance, the conservative newspaper *Die Post* which willingly gave space to such ideas in its columns. In its edition of 28 January 1912 it published an article by a Medizinalrat named Fuchs, who pleaded for a war of aggression on the basis that the 'disruptive influences' of a long period of peace 'could have a detrimental effect on the body and soul of the German people'. The *'Post'* justified this in the following terms:

> If, generally speaking, we consider war, the greatest exertion of national strength that a nation is capable of, as being in the interests of our people, it is simply because this is, at present, the only means by which we, as a nation, can be saved from the physical and psychological lethargy and emasculation which are relentlessly threatening.[5]

Even the Chancellor, Bethmann Hollweg, sympathised with the idea 'that the [German] people were in need of a war'.[6] These ideas were echoed in vulgarised language in the organs of the nationalist associations, above all the Pan-German League and the 'Wehrverein'. The latter had been conducting a wide-ranging agitation campaign since 1912 under the leadership of General a. D. August Keim, with the object of increasing the nation's willingness to take up arms, and at the same time of counteracting the 'physical and moral emasculation' to which it would otherwise become prey.[7] A particularly spectacular example of this sort of thing was an article published in 1912 by the Pan-German agitator Schmidt-Gibichenfels entitled 'Der Krieg als Kulturfaktor, als Schöpfer und Erhalter der Staaten'. In this he put forward a vulgarised version of Treitschke's arguments, couched in the language of a pathological nationalism.

The connection between such patterns of argument and the sectional interests of the conservative classes is all too obvious in the majority of cases. The leader of the Prussian Conservatives, Heydebrand von der Lasa, gave expression to a widespread belief when he said in 1914 that 'a war will lead to a strengthening of the patriarchal order and mentality.' And Bethmann Hollweg himself testified that there were at that time 'circles within the Reich which expected the war to make the internal situation in Germany more healthy — in the conservative sense', a view which he tried in vain to counteract.[8] Indeed the conservative press organs considered it just as likely as did the numerous conservative politicians that a war would be a convenient opportunity to suppress social democracy and to apply an effective brake to the general decline of German politics into democratic parliamentarism. Another factor also fits into this context, namely the complaint about the lack of an 'undisputed leader' who would be powerful enough to pursue a decisive foreign policy that did not shy away from war – in stark contrast to Bethmann Hollweg who was disparaged as being weak and supposedly lacking the determination necessary not only to get German interests accepted, but also to keep the Social Democrats under control. Occasionally this argumentative pattern was even turned around, for example when the *Post* wrote on 5 January 1913: 'Bethmann Hollweg's weakness makes it particularly necessary to prepare public opinion for the war which his attitude makes inevitable.'[9] Here the argument that war was a means of putting back the clock in internal politics, i.e. re-establishing a sound basis for conservative policies, was linked in an extremely effective rhetorical way to its opposite, namely the topos of the inevitability of an impending European war.

Parallel to this, the syndrome of militarism should be mentioned. This viewed war as a natural element in the conflicts between nations and was at pains to encourage aggressive tendencies and the upholding of militarist values amongst the population. The traditionally prominent social position enjoyed by the officer corps within German society guaranteed the ideals of the military a high priority in that society's consciousness. This position was, however, increasingly threatened by the process of modernisation that resulted, for the time being, in a stiffening of the attitudes of the military establishment.

The indirect link between military attitudes and agrarian interests is so well known that any further comment on it here would be superfluous. However, it should be noted that the actually aggressive varieties of militarist thinking, often connected with the propagation of a preventive war or alternatively of a war of aggression, did not primarily originate from the officer corps or from the landowning Prussian aristocracy. In this respect the opposition to a dramatic increase in the strength of the German Army which, it was feared, would tend to undermine the conservative-monarchical inclinations of the officer corps, deserves some consideration. It is no pure chance that a bourgeois social climber, Erich Ludendorff, who in 1912 made himself the spokesman for an unrestricted increase in the Army's strength, without regard to the delicate question of the repercussions which this might have had on the *esprit de corps* of the officer corps, subsequently fell from grace and was only restored to a position of command after the outbreak of war, having been given the rather unattractive job of regimental commander in Düsseldorf. In the last decade before 1914 it was sections of the intelligentsia and the higher bourgeoisie who identified particularly strongly with the demand for a powerful foreign policy supported by the strongest possible armaments, even though well tried generals such as Friedrich v. Bernhardi, v. Freitag-Loringhoven and Keim readily served this wave of opinion as experts and propagandists. The Alldeutsche Verband and other *Agitationsverbände* formed the spearhead of a new, potentially anti-conservative nationalism which favoured an open, aggressive foreign policy.[10] As the international situation deteriorated these groups began openly to agitate for war if the other powers would not give proper consideration to what they held to be the legitimate and vital interests of the German nation state.

The extremely voluble propaganda of the *Agitationsverbände* and the extreme right in favour of increased armaments and an openly aggressive foreign policy did not, however, find such a positive response in German society as has frequently been argued. Enthusiasm for war in any real sense was by no means widespread. It has to be admitted, however, that broad sections of the middle classes were convinced that a powerful German world policy of the type needed to secure the future interests of the German nation must include a willingness not to shy away from armed confrontation if the other European powers failed to give adequate consideration to legitimate German interests. In particular the National Liberal Party, under the leadership of Rudolf Bassermann and his political adjutant, Gustav Stresemann, made itself the mouthpiece of such a policy — as they would have it, a 'realistic world policy', but one which at the same time made full use of the military strength of the German Reich. Bassermann's attitude can best be summed up in the following formula: German policy should not seek war, nor provoke it by ill-conceived, menacing policies, but on the other hand it should not shy away from war if it became unavoidably necessary in order to secure vital German interests. Full exploitation of Germany's armament potential, combined with a thorough modernisation of the army and diplomacy, seemed to be the logical consequence of such a view.

This amounted to a fatalist acceptance of war as the ultimate means of implementing a successful world policy, if all other less radical means had failed; in the event that German foreign policy encountered insurmountable obstacles, the idea of war was found to be acceptable. In this a not insignificant role was played by the expectation that as long as it was made clear to the opponent powers that the Germans really meant business, they would withdraw and give proper consideration to the so-called legitimate interests of the German Reich. The mentality of 'cold', or as Hans Delbrück has put it, of 'dry' war, i.e. offensive diplomacy on the very brink of war, was widespread. In a much acclaimed book published in 1913 Kurt Riezler, Bethmann Hollweg's private secretary, developed the view that the threshold at the door of the temple of Janus had become higher under modern conditions, i.e. that it had become more difficult than ever before for statesmen to take the first step towards war. The bold conclusion he drew from this was that such a rising of the threshold beyond which lay the decision for war could be diplomatically exploited if only one calculated one's own strategy and the positions of the rival powers with sufficient astuteness.[11] This theory had a most unfortunate influence on German policy decision-making during the July crisis of 1914.

In contrast to Riezler's somewhat naive optimism, Bethmann Hollweg was almost over-sensitive to the fact that under the prevailing conditions it had become very difficult to pursue a rational foreign policy. He considered that the far-reaching dependence of the governments of the major powers, namely of Russia, on an enormously fluctuating public opinion had made international relations increasingly incalculable and thus considerably heightened the likelihood of war.[12] This complaint must be considered a mere symptom of a far more fundamental fact, namely that with the emergence of popular politics the traditional political elites had lost a great deal of their ability to lead and were subjected more than ever to pressures from influential social groups and 'public opinion'. It is no coincidence that this was particularly marked in the German Reich and in Tsarist Russia. In both these cases the governments, before 1914, were under increasing pressure from influential groups who accused them of conducting their foreign policies poorly and of failing to see their own national interests respected by third parties.

Much the same can be said of the military elites. In military circles the idea that they had been cornered by events gained increasing ground. On the one hand the officer corps saw their own privileged position within the political and social system progressively undermined by advancing modernisation. This had manifested itself in the numerous suggestions for reforms put forward by the majority parties of the Reichstag during the parliamentary proceedings concerning the rearmament Bills of 1912 and 1913. The behaviour of v. Falkenhayn and the officer corps in the Saverne Affair can be regarded as symptomatic of the feeling that the Army was rapidly losing out on all counts. To fight back and dig their heels in, in order to defend their positions, seemed to them perfectly justified. On the other hand the deteriorating military situation required a substantial expansion of the Army; this, however, carried with it the danger that the officer corps would become increasingly bourgeois in its social composition, a process that was bound eventually to destroy its special bond with the throne. All this raised doubts as to their ability to overcome the growing military and strategic problems without resorting very soon to the extreme solution of a major war, all the more so since any feeling for the political dimension of war, which had been so emphasised by Clausewitz, had largely been lost as a result of the growth of an overwhelmingly instrumental mentality as regards strategic planning. This increased the willingness of the military establishment to accept a solution to the problems in the form of a preventive war.

Even in the camp of the socialist left the fundamental opposition to war increasingly dissolved into an attitude that was either fatalistic or moderately positive. Admittedly a strong basic mood of pacifism continued to exist, but on the other hand the 'secondary integration' of social democracy had been successful enough to give more and more ground to the idea of the workers supporting a war of self-defence. Certainly there was a strong pacifist current amongst the working class, but there was little opportunity to give it politically effective expression. Even confirmed opponents of war, such as August Bebel, were pessimistic about the prospects of being able to prevent war as things stood. In 1910 Bebel had expressly warned Britain, through the British Consul-General in Bern, against disarmament for the time being, since a war of aggression on the part of the German Reich was on the cards at some stage — probably 1912. 'Before the great war has taken place in Europe, I do not encourage the idea of general disarmament in Europe.'[13] On the socialist left there were only gloomy expectations. In his book *Das Finanzkapital*, written in 1909, Hilferding had already predicted with some precision the outbreak of a world war resulting from the increasing rivalries between the capitalist states.

Hence all the pre-conditions necessary to establish the topos of the inevitability of a major European war firmly in the minds of the German public did in fact exist. Indeed it is apparent that the rhetorical figure of the inevitability of a future war or, as Oron Hale has called it, 'the cult of inevitability',[14] gradually found support in ever wider circles. In this respect the Agadir Crisis of 1911 signified a decisive caesura. The crisis and its outcome left deep scars on the political landscape of the German Reich and in some respects altered it fundamentally. After the meagre outcome of the diplomatic offensive on the brink of war with France, planned so carefully by Kiderlen-Wächter, had been exposed, the nationalist enthusiasm amongst the public which had alternated with a fear of war bordering on panic, was transformed into deep resentment. As far as the bourgeois press was concerned, condemnation of the compromise and the government's willingness to concede was virtually unanimous.[15] Contrary to their previous line, the conservatives now did everything possible to join the phalanx of bourgeois nationalist imperialism led by the National Liberals. Bethmann Hollweg tried in vain to counter this phalanx of nationalist critics: 'To bring national passions to boiling point for the sake of utopian plans for conquest and of party objectives, that is to compromise patriotism.'[16] At that time he wrote privately to Eisendecher: 'This summer the German people have toyed so readily with war . . . I had to oppose them.'[17] On the other hand, August Bebel analysed the situation after Agadir in words whose prophetic quality cannot, in retrospect, be denied:

> So there will be armament and rearmament on all sides until one day one or other side will say: rather an end in horror than horror without end . . . they might also say: listen, if we wait longer, we are the weaker side instead of the stronger. Then comes the catastrophe. Then the great general march will be embarked upon in Europe, in which 16-18 million men, the blossoming male youth of the different nations, equipped with the best murder weapons, will turn against one another as enemies in the field. . . . The twilight of the gods of the bourgeois world is in prospect.[18]

Under the influence of the Agadir Crisis of 1911 which he saw as the prelude to an impending war, Spengler conceived his book *Der Untergang des Abendlandes* with which he intended to confront his critics at the moment of the German victory he expected. But at the same time he also expected that as a consequence of this the face of Western culture would undergo a fundamental change, initiated by a caesarian German regime over central Europe.[19] And the young Moltke who, unlike the vast majority of the German officer corps, regarded German involvement in the Morocco Question as a shameful retreat, came to the following conclusion in his major memorandum on the military situation at the end of December 1911:

> There can be no doubt that the tension between Germany and France which has existed for years and periodically intensified, has given rise to increased military activity in almost all countries. All are preparing for the great war which all expect sooner rather than later.[20]

These testimonies, to which many more could easily be added, speak for themselves. From 1911 onwards, the idea increasingly took root in German public opinion that Germany had no prospect of realising her global political ambitions without a major European war, because no kind of co-operation was forthcoming from Britain or France. Against this background nationalism spread, sparked off by the competitive struggle between the Conservatives and the National Liberals for whatever voters were left to them.

The topos of the inevitability of an impending major war was propagated most effectively a short time later in General Friedrich v. Bernhardi's book *Deutschland und der nächste Krieg*, published in the spring of 1912, and greatly acclaimed by the national press. The level of argument in Bernhardi's book differed considerably from that of other publications of this kind. It described the supposed future dangers, while at the same time invoking the great German cultural tradition of Weimar, and thus appealed very successfully to the educated bourgeoisie. Bernhardi's argument was

> that there is no way in which we can avoid going to war for the sake of our position as a world power and that we should not be concerned with postponing it for as long as possible, but rather should concentrate on bringing it about under the most favourable conditions possible.[21]

The response to this book was extraordinary and its effect was multiplied by reviews of the book in numerous right-wing newspapers. However, it would be a mistake to consider this as an expression of the dominant opinion at that time. The major liberal newspapers, no less than those of the social democrats, condemned Bernhardi's war propaganda in the strongest terms. Even the government mobilised those means available to it to influence the press to oppose Bernhardi's dangerously provocative theses.[22] Not long afterwards Hans Plehn, commissioned by Richard Kühlmann, published under a pseudonym a brochure *Deutsche Weltpolitik und kein Krieg*, which presented Kühlmann's concept of a policy for acquiring colonies in co-operation with Great Britain. However, one can assume that attempts to counteract the propagation of these dangerous views among the German public were only partially successful.

One reason for this was, of course, the increasingly tense international situation after the first Balkan war, during which the Wilhelmstrasse, in the interests of Germany's partner Austro-Hungary, had turned unexpectedly harshly on Russia, though with the ultimate objective of collaborating with the British government to find a solution to the crisis that was as satisfactory as possible for Austro-Hungary. At the peak of the crisis early in December 1912, Bethmann Hollweg gave an unusually vehement speech in the Reichstag, in which he gave Russia a scarcely concealed warning against an attack on Austro-Hungary, and made it clear that in such an event Germany would be prepared to go to war.[23] The British government replied to this through diplomatic channels with a warning that Great Britain would be obliged to enter the war, with the immediate aim of making the German government abandon its incautious identification with the interests of Austro-Hungary. This news gave rise to a 'war scare' at the court. Wilhelm II immediately summoned his military advisers to what has since become known as the 'Council of War' of 8 December 1912, behind the backs of the Chancellor and the Foreign Secretary.[24] At this memorable meeting, at which Wilhelm II was in a state of great agitation, and which was directly influenced by the possibility of a war in Europe arising from the Balkan question, clear warlike inclinations emerged for the first time at the highest level. Fritz Fischer, and more recently John Röhl, have argued that at this 'Council of War' it was decided to go to war, and that, though the outbreak should be delayed until July 1914, everything should, in the meantime, be geared to this purpose, including the preparation of public opinion for war.[25] It is fairly easy to demonstrate that such conclusions are wide of the mark.[26] Even so, the fact cannot be overlooked that on this occasion the possibility of solving Germany's political and strategic problems by means of a preventive war against Russia and France was discussed very seriously indeed. Moltke declared categorically that he considered 'the war to be inevitable', and his advice was that it should be conducted 'the sooner the better'. However, his suggestion of immediately going to war cut little ice with his colleagues, least of all with Tirpitz. In this connection it was further agreed to 'prepare the people better for a war against Russia' by means of a press campaign.

However, the immediate repercussions of this conference were minor, apart from the decision to introduce a major new Army Bill (and originally also a Navy Bill) as soon as possible. In any case preparations for the former were already in full swing. The decisions taken at the so-called 'Council of War' therefore, had an influence only as far as the scope of this Bill was concerned; when the Bill was eventually introduced in the Reichstag in April 1913 it envisaged a massive increase in the armed forces far beyond what had been considered acceptable only a few months earlier by the Ministry of War or the Treasury. On the other hand, the press campaign to prepare the people for a war with Russia, which had been the only point agreed upon on 8 December 1912 that was actually transmitted to the Chancellor for implementation soon fizzled out again. Wilhelm was successfully calmed down when it was pointed out that adequate measures to this end had already been carried out by the Foreign Office.[27] In fact the Chancellor and the Foreign Office did all they could to suppress all press agitation by the other government departments in connection with the Army Bill, even though they rightly suspected that it had been instigated by the Emperor himself. But the idea of the inevitability of a future world war now took firm root in Wilhelm's mind, in the particular form of an inevitable conflict between the Germanic and Slavonic peoples.

Wilhelm II's attitude in all this was, of course, little more than a reflection of similar arguments put forward in the right-wing press. For example a leader article in the *Hamburger Nachrichten* had, on 3 December 1912, already spoken of the 'sooner or later unavoidable clash between the Germanic and Slavonic peoples'.[28] None other than Friedrich Meinecke ridiculed the use of such clichés as an 'effect of that trivial philosophy of history with which the German petty bourgeois disparages world events'.[29] Subsequently, however, this became a slogan which the right-wing press did all it could to exploit, since it seemed to correspond only too well to the gloomy prognostications of Danilewski, one of the fathers of panslavism.

Unfortunately, this topos of the 'final battle between the Germanic and Slavonic peoples' received renewed and serious attention among the public — and this was partly, though inadvertently, Bethmann Hollweg's own doing — during the Reichstag negotiations on the scope of the Army Bill. In presenting this Bill to parliament and to the public the government had tried to steer a middle course which stressed the need to prepare for a possible European war, but at the same time avoided adding more grist to the mill of the right-wing press such as the *Post*, which was eagerly stirring up a war hysteria. In his speech in the Reichstag on 7 April 1913, in which the Bill was introduced, Bethmann Hollweg tried to deal a blow to the widespread view of an 'unavoidable' clash between the Germanic and Slavonic worlds.[30] But he did so in such an unfortunate manner that everyone understood the exact opposite of what he had intended to say. And indeed none of his assurances could remove the impression that the Reich government was very close to the view that a future war with Russia, and consequently also with France, had moved into the realms of possibility.

In the public debates on the international situation and the dangers of a future war, nationalist enthusiasm had thus far been primarily directed against Great Britain, and to a lesser degree against France. The latter now no longer escaped invective either. She was now accused of systematically preparing for a war against the Central powers. The so-called 'Störenfried' article in the *Kölnische Zeitung* of 10 March 1913 was a particularly blatant example of this. It attracted particular attention because this newspaper was considered the mouthpiece of the Foreign Office. In the article attention was drawn to the imminent introduction of three-year conscription in France and the accusation made that she was preparing for a war to re-conquer Alsace-Lorraine:

So whichever corner of the world catches fire, there can be no doubt that we shall be crossing swords with France. When this will happen, no one can know, but it is certain that the French will use any opportunity to march against Germany, since they can reasonably hope to be victorious, either through the superiority of their own weapons, or with the help of Russia.[31]

However, the fears expressed in the heated public debates on the possibility of a future war concentrated increasingly on Tsarist Russia, although France still remained in the picture in so far as she financed Russia's armament and thus made it at all possible. At the same time the topos of inevitable war was now no longer only repeated in right-wing nationalist papers such as the *Post*, the *Berliner Neuste Nachrichten* or the *Rheinisch-Westfälische Zeitung*, but was also taken up by leading bourgeois papers such as the *Kölnische Zeitung* and the *Germania*, the latter being the semi-official organ of the Centre party. The *Germania* wrote on 8 March 1913:

When the great world war finally comes, and all the major powers think it will, then the Triple Alliance will have not only Russia, France and England against it, but also the Balkan League. . . . Hitherto the feeling in Germany has largely been that we must prepare ourselves in the first instance for a more or less inevitable war with England, but what seems nearer, far nearer since the events of the last months, is conflict with Russia. The oriental question has taken on a different shape and is now quite simply: *Germanic or Slavonic*.[32]

Fritz Fischer and Klaus Wernecke have argued that the so-called 'Russian threat' was systematically 'built up' by the Reich leadership in order to justify their own aggressive intentions in the public eye.[33] Formulated in this way this is, of course, not accurate. Admittedly, within the ruling cliques of the German Reich there were groups in whose interest it was to paint the threat from Russia in the most vivid colours, in particular the military and to a certain extent the National Liberals. But even if a certain manipulative influence by certain quarters on anti-Russian propaganda cannot be ruled out, this was by no means decisive. Rather, popular agitation had its effect on the ruling circles themselves; it established itself as a determining factor in its own right in the behaviour of the politicians and the military establishment, even if it was originally instigated by interested parties. In any case the fear of Russia was very real in broad sections of the population.

Within this syndrome of the Russian menace, which increasingly determined the discussion within Germany, subjective and objective factors merged into a mixture that cannot easily be defined. The military were seriously concerned about the extent of Russian armament and above all about the completion of Russia's Western railway lines which threatened to do away with the pre-conditions of the Schlieffen Plan. Wilhelm II was not to be deflected from his notion that an ultimate showdown between the Slavs and the Teutonic peoples was pending. In the late autumn of 1913 he maintained to Graf Berchthold that 'the war between East and West ... is, in the long run, inevitable.'[34] Even Bethmann Hollweg, though he was convinced that the leading statesmen wanted to do everything possible to avoid a European war, suspected that they would have to give in sooner or later to aggressive panslavonic feelings in their own countries:

> Russia is a cause for concern. Her policy is quite impenetrable, because one does not know whose influence is at present decisive and because this influence fluctuates rapidly. None the less, I hope that reason will, after all, be able to temper the panslavonic attitude which is so strong at the moment. Fortunately France is now peace-loving.[35]

But there were now concrete reasons for regarding the developments in Russia with growing concern. The brusque intervention of Russian diplomacy against the promotion of General Liman von Sanders, head of the German Military Mission in the Ottoman Empire, to a senior command position in Constantinople, showed that Russia was not inclined to accept Germany's comparatively modest efforts towards an indirect economic penetration of Asia Minor, involving avoidance, as far as possible, of concrete collisions with the interests of Great Britain and France. What is more, anxieties began to develop that Russia was actively working towards the destruction and division of the Ottoman Empire. This would have destroyed all German aspirations to an informal imperialist position in the Near East. A division of the Ottoman Empire amongst the powers without Germany having an adequate share in the booty would force her into a position where she had to take up arms. There is evidence to suggest that maintaining the political pre-conditions necessary for an informal German imperialism in the Ottoman Empire was the only political objective that the German government before 1914 considered worth a world war!

After critical weeks of extreme tension in the capitals of Europe, it was finally possible to resolve the Liman von Sanders Crisis relatively painlessly by means of a tactical concession on the part of Germany. But bitterness remained on both sides. In German military circles, presumably on the basis of fragmentary information on Russian military conferences during the Liman von Sanders Crisis, the assumption gained increasing ground that Russia was planning a war of aggression against the German Reich after the armament measures in progress at that time had been completed – probably in 1916/17. Concrete evidence for such an assumption was, of course, not available, apart from the fact that Russian armament, when compared with the stage it had reached at the time the Schlieffen Plan had first been formulated in 1905, had indeed advanced dramatically.

Despite intensive efforts by researchers, it is still impossible to determine whether (as would appear most likely) the famous 'war-in-sight' article of 2 March 1914 by the Russian correspondent of the *Kölnische Zeitung*, Oberleutnant a.D. Ulrich, was written at the instigation of the military circles in order to test these suspicions and put Russian armament, as it were, under the spotlight.[36] However that may be, the article maintained in scarcely concealed terms that Russia was arming against Germany and suggested that she was probably intending to launch an attack in three years' time, after her armament programme had been completed. This provided the impetus for a hectic German-Russian press feud which was further fuelled by the fact that the Russian War Minister, Suchomlinov, published a denial of these allegations in a St Petersburg financial paper – although this was, admittedly, primarily addressed to the French public.[37] On the one hand it said that it was not Russia which harboured aggressive intentions, but on the other hand it emphasised strongly that Russia was ready for war, and that if there should be one, the Russian Army would wage it offensively. It is easy to see why this declaration was received extremely negatively in Germany, not least in military circles. It seemed to confirm the general staff's secret fears that the essential premisses of the Schlieffen Plan were about to disappear, namely that Russia would mobilise only slowly and hold back strategically in the initial stages of the war.

Attempts by the semi-official press to counter this 'war scare' were virtually ineffective. So were the submissions of Graf Pourtalès, the German Ambassador in St Petersburg, who tried in vain to convince Wilhelm II that Ulrich's assumptions about Russia going to war within a few years were completely unfounded. Wilhelm II, who in this matter as so often before, was merely the mouthpiece of the dominant trends in public opinion, had only this to say to Pourtalès: 'As a military man, I have not the slightest doubt, from all my reports, that Russia is systematically preparing for war against us; I conduct my policy accordingly.'[38]

In the wake of the 'war-in-sight' crisis of March 1914 a mass anti-Russian hysteria developed which released aggressive energies and subsequently proved to be uncontrollable. At the same time the idea gained ground, not only in military circles, but also amongst the public, that the opportunity to forestall Russia while her armaments were still incomplete should be seized upon. In one particularly flagrant case of public agitation in favour of a preventive war Bethmann Hollweg intervened personally (if one is to believe Bernhardi's testimony). In March 1914 the *Post*, expressly quoting Bernhardi, pleaded again for German policy to be such 'that if a war is necessary we ought to start it as aggressors under the most favourable general conditions possible', instead of waiting for the Entente to attack. But Bethmann Hollweg defended his wait-and-see policy in an article – written anonymously – entitled 'Ist die Zeit für oder gegen uns'.[39] By trying to influence those press organs receptive to governmental suggestions the Foreign Office, however, ran into serious trouble with the *Kölnische Zeitung* because of the latter's obstinacy on this issue. Semi-official statements also appeared in the *Norddeutsche Allgemeine Zeitung*, by which the government tried to assuage public outrage over the alleged Russian menace. But all these efforts were essentially unsuccessful, not least because they were carried out in the most clumsy and indiscreet manner.

The idea of a war with Russia, in which France would inevitably participate, had now entered the realm of probability and gained increasing ground in public opinion. Even the propagandists of a 'Liberal Imperialism' now joined the chorus of the prophets of doom. In the spring of 1914 Paul Rohrbach and Ernst Jäckh founded a new weekly paper, *Das größere Deutschland*, whose aim, as the former later explained, was 'to prepare the German people for the impending war'.[40] Russia, according to Rohrbach, 'was in fact the greatest danger to peace in Europe'.[41] He accused the Russian statesmen of regarding a victorious war as a way out of their own internal difficulties and argued that the current financial crisis could provoke the Tsarist government to attack virtually overnight. France, he said, was also interested in an early start to the impending clash between the nations and would, therefore, hardly hold Russia back:

> Any intelligent person must realise that France cannot bear this burden [i.e. the three-year conscription] for long and that the adoption of such a measure can only be comprehensible if those involved say: this will be the last great strenuous effort before the decision. The most the French can bear is a few more years of three-year conscription and when this period is over the acceleration of Russian deployment will also be complete. And what will happen then? Does anyone believe that after the great sacrifice she has made France would draw the line by reverting to two-year conscription and Russia would let the grass grow on her new railways? Or should we perhaps let Austria or Turkey be sacrificed for us.[42]

The anti-Russian campaign, in which the topos of the inevitability of war played an important part, was conducted during those months by the right-wing press and agitational organisations with scarcely diminished vociferousness. There were countervailing forces; notably the *Berliner Tageblatt* and the *Vossische Zeitung* continued to denounce the folly of such an irresponsible, extremist agitation, not to mention the Social Democratic press. But the 'strategic cliques' within the political establishment now turned more and more to the opposite stream of thought. In the end this had serious repercussions on the course of action of the influential circles within the German Reich, however much the Chancellor and the Foreign Office tried to erect dams against it. Bethmann Hollweg had always pursued a gradual *rapprochement* between the German Reich and Britain as the best solution to Germany's diplomatic problems. For with British assistance the critical period ahead, of which he was very much aware, could be overcome without a major war. But since 1913 it had obviously become increasingly difficult for him to convince the rival strategic cliques within the government that this was still a viable political option.

As for Moltke, the head of the General Staff, he had, as we have seen, declared himself as early as 1912 in principle in favour of an early war. Hitherto, however, in accordance with the policy of the Foreign Office, he had resisted the overtures from his Austrian colleague, Conrad v. Hötzendorff, who urged him to subdue the hated Serbia by a surprise attack, in order to create acceptable conditions for Austro-Hungary in the Balkans. But now he made it known that he would welcome military action by Austro-Hungary against Serbia that would set the ball rolling. On 12 May 1914 he complained to Hötzendorff that, unfortunately, the Reich leadership was still hoping that England would remain neutral, even though this would never happen. In the spring of 1914 Moltke had evidently come to the definitive conclusion that Russia, according to plan, was preparing for a war of aggression against the Central powers and that it would, therefore, be better to forestall her by a preventive war as soon as a suitable opportunity arose.[43] According to the scanty sources available on this issue, Bethmann Hollweg seems for the time being to have taken a firm stance against the demands of the military that in the foreseeable future – Moltke appears to have reckoned with 1916 or 1917 – the anticipated war with Russia ought to be countered preventively. At the end of May or the beginning of June 1914 Moltke confronted the Secretary of State at the Foreign Office, v. Jagow, with the concrete question as to whether, in view of the fact that Russia 'will have completed her armament in 2-3 years', it would not be better 'to wage a preventive war, in order to strike the opponent while we are still in a position to retain the upper hand, even if only marginally'.[44] He pressed Jagow to orientate German foreign policy in such a way that Germany would at least no longer try to avoid war, should it become imminent. But at this stage Jagow and Bethmann Hollweg still refused to engage in a preventive war. On 4 June 1914 the latter curtly told Lerchenfeld: 'the Kaiser has never waged a preventive war, and will not do so.'[45] At this stage, however, Wilhelm II was no longer certain whether it would be better to follow the advice of his Chancellor or that of his generals. On 21 June 1914, only a few weeks later, he put the question to his friend, the banker Warburg, as to whether, considering Russia's war preparations suggesting a Russian attack in 1916, 'it would not be better to attack rather than to wait'.[46]

All this leads to the conclusion that the possibility of a preventive war was seriously discussed at the highest government level in June

1914. The disquieting news of British-Russian negotiations on a naval agreement, which reached the ears of the German government in those very weeks, and which Sir Edward Grey unwisely tried to deny publicly, must have further weakened the position of the Chancellor and the Foreign Office, since any hopes of improved relations with Britain, always a factor in the Chancellor's deliberations on a preventive war, now appeared to be destroyed. For years the right-wing press had maintained that an attack by the Entente would be an absolute certainty once it could be sure of England's support. This very situation had, it seemed, at last arisen. The basic fatalistic attitude revealed in statements by the government, primarily by Bethmann Hollweg himself, may be considered as a reaction to this situation. Bassermann, leader of the National Liberal Party, reported at that time to his party colleague, Schiffer:

> Things are not going well. The anti-German movement in Russia is becoming stronger, the French are getting more and more cocky . . . Bethmann said to me with fatalistic resignation: 'if there is a war with France, the last Englishman will march against us'.[47]

And from this he drew the conclusion: 'We are drifting towards the world war.'

The topos of the 'inevitability' of a great European war had now finally transcended the level of biased propaganda and nationalist agitation. It had acquired the quality of a 'self-fulfilling prophecy'. Bethmann Hollweg's statements during the weeks immediately preceding the July crisis show with great clarity the effectiveness of this principle even at the highest level. A fatalistic attitude, which no longer believed in the possibility of being able to control the course of events, overshadowed the decisions of the Reich leadership in the days and weeks following the murder at Sarajevo. In July 1914 this must have made a significant contribution to overcoming any remaining reservations about adopting a course which involved the highest possible risk of war. This course consisted, in fact, of unreserved support for Austro-Hungary in her desire to strike out at once against Serbia, despite the enormous risk, and indeed included the probability of thereby initiating a general European war. According to Kurt Riezler, Bethmann Hollweg himself called this decision a 'leap in the dark . . . and the hardest duty'.[48] Admittedly the German Chancellor hoped that contrary to all predictions Russia would be forced, as in 1908, to retreat by Britain and France, who had no interest in the Serbian question nor in war, and thus make a restructuring of the system of alliances in Europe possible. However, as far as he was concerned the only way of attaining such a solution was unequivocal and unrestricted support of Austro-Hungary, even if the General Staff, not to mention quite a few Conservatives as well as bourgeois politicians, were inclined to regard the war as a welcome release. 'A fate greater than human power', he said on 27 July at the height of the July Crisis 1914, 'hangs over the situation in Europe and over the German people.'[49] This was the abdication of politics in the face of circumstances which the leading statesmen no longer appeared able to master. Yet in the final analysis this fatalism was home-made. It was a consequence of two decades of nationalist agitation which official policy had never been capable of keeping in check.

Notes

1. J. Joll, 1914. *The Unspoken Assumptions* (London, 1968), p. 24.
2. E.M. Carroll, *Germany and the Great Powers 1866-1914. A Study in Public Opinion and Foreign Policy* (New York, 1940); K. Wernecke, *Der Wille zur Weltgeltung. Aussenpolitik und Öffentlichkeit im Kaiserreich am Vorabend des Ersten Weltkrieges* (Düsseldorf, 1970); A. Jux, *Der Kriegsschrecken des Frühjahrs 1914 in der europäischen Presse* (Berlin, 1929); R. Ropponen, *Die russische Gefahr. Das Verhalten der öffentlichen Meinung Deutschlands und Österreich-Ungarns gegenüber der Aussenpolitik Russlands in der Zeit zwischen dem Frieden von Portsmouth und dem Ausbruch des Ersten Weltkriegs* (Helsinki, 1976); J.F. Scott, *Five Weeks. The Surge of Public Opinion on the Eve of the Great War* (New York, 1973).
3. Heinrich v. Treitschke, *Politik. Vorlesungen gehalten an der Universität Berlin*, 3rd edn (Leipzig, 1911), vol. 2, p. 553.
4. See also Ludendorff's major memorandum of December 1912, quoted in W. Kloster, *Der deutsche Generalstab und der Präventivkriegs-Gedanke* (Stuttgart, 1923), p. 48: 'In spite of this we shall, if we can, so formulate the *casus belli* that the nation will enthusiastically take up arms with one accord, and under the prevailing circumstances we shall still be able to carry out the most difficult tasks in a reliable fashion.'
5. Quoted in O. Nippold, *Der deutsche Chauvinismus* (Stuttgart, 1913), p. 14.
6. K. Riezler, *Tagebücher, Aufsätze, Dokumente*, intr. and ed. by Karl Dietrich Erdmann (Göttingen, 1972), p. 180, entry for 30 July 1911.
7. See A. Keim, 'Ein Wehrverein' in *Tägliche Rundschau*, 15 Dec. 1911, reprinted in *idem, Erlebtes und Erstrebtes. Lebenserinnerungen* (Hannover, 1925), p. 167.
8. See Lerchenfeld's report about a conversation with the Chancellor on 4 June 1914, in P. Dirr (ed.), *Bayrische Dokumente zum Kriegsausbruch und zum Versailler Schuldspruch*, 4th edn (Munich, 1928), pp. 111-12.
9. Quoted in Nippold, *Deutsche Chauvinismus*, p. 13.
10. See the recent work by G. Eley, *Reshaping the German Right. Radical*

Nationalism and Political Change after Bismarck (New Haven, Conn., 1979).

11. K. Riezler, *Die Erforderlichkeit des Unmöglichen* (Berlin, 1913). On this, Andreas Hillgruber, 'Riezlers Theorie des kalkulierten Risikos und Bethmann Hollwegs politische Konzeption in der Julikrise 1914', *Historische Zeitschrift*, 202 (1966).

12. See Bethmann Hollweg to Eisendecher, 19 February 1913, Eisendecher Papers, 1/1 – 7, Politisches Archiv des Auswärtigen Amtes, Bonn (hereafter PAAA); see also Bethmann's Reichstag speech of 7 April 1913, *Stenographische Protokolle der Verhandlungen des deutschen Reichstags*, vol. 289, p. 1413C and p. 4513 C and D.

13. D.J. Crampton, 'August Bebel and the British Foreign Office', *History*, LVIII (1973), pp. 219-20.

14. O.J. Hale, *Publicity and Diplomacy* (London, 1940), p. 445.

15. Carroll, *Germany*, p. 682. The *Berliner Neueste Nachrichten*, for example, demanded that henceforth the Reichstag should make it quite clear that it disapproved of the current policy of peace at any price.

16. *Stenographische Protokolle der Verhandlungen des Reichstags*, vol. 268, p. 7756C.

17. Bethmann Hollweg to Eisendecher, 16 November 1911, Eisendecher Papers, 1/8, PAAA.

18. *Stenographische Protokolle der Verhandlungen des Reichstags*, vol. 268, p. 7730C-D.

19. A.M. Koktanek, *Oswald Spengler in seiner Zeit* (Munich, 1968), pp. 137, 140-1.

20. H. v. Moltke, *Erinnerungen – Briefe – Dokumente* (Stuttgart, 1922), p. 362.

21. Quoted in Kloster, *Generalstab*, p. 48.

22. Ibid., p. 212.

23. On 2 December 1912; see *Stenographische Protokolle der Verhandlungen des Reichstags*, vol. 286, p. 2472A-B.

24. See W. Görlitz (ed.), *Der Kaiser. Aufzeichnungen des Chefs des Marinekabinetts Admiral Georg Alexander v. Müller über die Ära Wilhelms II* (Göttingen, 1965), p. 124, and for vital passages omitted by Görlitz, J.C.G. Röhl, 'Admiral v. Müller and the Approach to War 1911-1914', *Historical Journal*, XII (1966). Müller's report on the conference is now reprinted in full in J.C.G. Röhl (ed.), 'An der Schwelle zum Weltkrieg: Eine Dokomentation über den "Kriegsrat" vom 8. Dezember 1912', *Militärgeschichtliche Mitteilungen*, 1 (1977), p. 100. For an analysis of the context in which this 'Council of War' has to be interpreted see W.J. Mommsen, 'Domestic Factors in German Foreign Policy before 1914' in J. Sheehan (ed.), *Imperial Germany* (New York, 1976), p. 231.

25. F. Fischer, *Krieg der Illusionen* (Düsseldorf, 1969), p. 231; Röhl (ed.), *Schwelle*, p. 77; see also *idem*, 'Die Generalprobe. Zur Geschichte und Bedeutung des "Kriegsrates" vom 8. Dezember 1912' in Dirk Stegmann, Berndt-Jürgen Wendt and Peter-Christian Witt (eds.), *Industrielle Gesellschaft und politisches System* (Bonn, 1978), pp. 366ff.

26. Thanks are due to Röhl, inasmuch as he has carefully edited all the documents relevant to an adequate assessment of the 'Kriegsrat' and its immediate consequences. But contrary to his own repeated assertions, his own account lends support to the view that the 'Kriegsrat' cannot be seen as a turning point in German foreign policy in any concrete sense. Röhl's argument is confused insofar as he fails throughout to distinguish between a war that might arise as an immediate consequence of the Balkan crisis, which at that very moment was at its climax, and a European war deliberately prepared over a period of one and a half years. The circumstantial evidence assembled by him in order to

substantiate his, or rather Fischer's, argument, that from 8 December 1912 onwards the German Empire deliberately headed for war, or, more precisely, for a war with France, Russia and Britain, does not convince anyone who does not approach the issue with the pre-conceived idea that there was a carefully thought-out plot to launch this war by June or July 1914. In November 1913, on the occasion of an attempt by Constantin v. Gebsattel to bring about his downfall, Bethmann Hollweg declared: 'In einem zukünftigen Krieg, der ohne zwingenden Anlass unternommen wird, steht nicht nur die Hohenzollernkrone, sondern auch die Zukunft Deutschlands auf dem Spiel' (quoted in H. Pogge-v. Strandmann and I. Geiss, *Die Erforderlichkeit des Unmöglichen. Deutschland am Vorabend des Ersten Weltkrieges* (Frankfurt, 1965), p. 36). He found Wilhelm II to be in full agreement on this point. How could this have been possible if the Emperor had long since decided to bring about the war deliberately in June or July 1914? If Röhl had argued that there had been a growing tendency in court circles to consider war, and for that matter preventive war, as a way out of the present troubles, rather than claiming that there had been a deliberate policy to launch the war on the part of the government at a specific moment in time, his interpretation might be more credible.

27. The only new piece of evidence of major significance brought to light by Röhl is the letter by Bethmann Hollweg of 10 December 1912, in which he sent a copy of an article, 'Um Durazzo', to Wilhelm II, and a parallel letter by Kiderlen-Wächter to Admiral v. Müller, written on the following day. They show that the Chancellor and the Secretary of State had taken heed of the advice by Müller, that the public should be better prepared for the eventuality of a major war with Russia, should the negotiations between the powers break down, and they were quick to satisfy Wilhelm II's demand in this respect. The text shows without doubt that the article had little to do with preparing the public for war in a general sense, rather – and this it shows most clearly – it tried to explain why it might be necessary to go to war in the event that the present diplomatic activities in support of Austria-Hungary failed, though this would be much against the intentions of German diplomacy. This article does not make any sense at all if one assumes that its author (Kiderlen-Wächter) was acting on the assumption that henceforth everything had to be geared towards the preparation of the public for a major European war. Rather it presented the issue in a very tentative manner, not likely to arouse any war fever whatsoever.

28. Quoted in Wernecke, *Wille*, pp. 185-6.
29. Ibid., p. 184.
30. *Stenographische Protokolle der Verhandlungen des Reichstags*, vol. 289, p. 4513A-B.
31. Quoted in Nippold, *Chauvinismus*, p. 90.
32. Quoted in ibid., pp. 67-8.
33. Fischer, *Krieg der Illusionen*, p. 542; Wernecke, *Wille*, p. 249, who argues in a much more restrained way.
34. Berchthold's notes on his conversation with Wilhelm II on 26 October 1913, *Österreich-Ungarns Aussenpolitik*, vol. VII, no. 8934, pp. 512.
35. To Eisendecher, 19 February 1914, Eisendecher Papers, 1/1-7, PAAA. See also Bethmann Hollweg's statements in his Reichstag speech of 7 April 1913:

I have every reason to believe that the present French government would like to co-exist with us as peaceful neighbours. What changes, if any, the future may bring, no one knows. Compared with 25 years ago, I believe that the likelihood of aspirations to war centering around the cabinets of the major Powers is not greater, but less. No one can have any conception of a world war, of the misery and destruction that it would bring to the nations. It would probably make all previous wars look like a childish game. No responsible statesman will be eager to set the match to the powder. Inclinations in this direction have diminished. What has increased, however, is the power of public opinion and within public opinion that of those who make the most fuss about things. The more democratic the system is, these tend, in times of unrest, to be not royal persons, but minorities (*Stenographische Protokolle der Verhandlungen des Reichstags*, vol. 289, p. 4513C, D).

36. See Wernecke, *Wille*, pp. 249-50.
37. See Jux, *Kriegsschrecken*, pp. 140-1.
38. Wilhelm II to Pourtalès, 6 March 1914, in *Die grosse Politik der europäischen Kabinette*, vol. 39, p. 554.
39. F. v. Bernhardi, *Denkwürdigkeiten* (Berlin, 1927), p. 387; the article is dated 9 March 1913.
40. P. Rohrbach, *Zum Weltvolk hindurch* (Stuttgart, 1914), p. 4.
41. *Preussische Jahrbücher*, 15 June 1914, quoted in ibid., p. 12.
42. *Das Größere Deutschland*, 19 Apr. 1914, quoted in ibid., p. 61.
43. Lerchenfeld was able to report to Munich on 5 August 1914 that Moltke had declared: 'I am quite certain that Russia, France and England have decided and are ready to wage a war of aggression against Germany in 1917.' Quoted in Dirr (ed.), *Bayrische Dokumente*, p. 557. See also Bethmann Hollweg's testimony to Friedrich Thimme in 1919:

He also admits that our military are quite convinced that they could *still* be victorious in the war, but that in a few years time, say in 1916 after the completion of Russia's railway network, they could not. This, of course, also affected the way in which the Serbian question was dealt with (Thimme Papers 62, PAAA).

44. Quoted in E. Zechlin, 'Motive und Taktik der Reichsleitung 1915', *Der Monat*, 209 (1966), pp. 92-3.
45. Lerchenfeld's report of 4 June 1914 in Dirr (ed.), *Bayrische Dokumente*, pp. 111-12.
46. Quoted in Vagts, 'M.M. Warburg & Co. Ein Bankhaus in der deutschen Weltpolitik', *Vierteljahrsschrift für Sozial- und Wirtschaftsgeschichte*, 45 (1958), p. 353.
47. Bassermann to Schiffer, 5 June 1914, Schiffer Papers, Geheimes Staatsarchiv, Berlin.
48. Riezler, *Tagebuch*, p. 185.
49. Ibid., p. 192.

3 WALTHER RATHENAU — INTELLECTUAL OR INDUSTRIALIST?

James Joll

The biographical approach is unpopular with many serious historians today; and to attempt to use some reflections on a single individual as a contribution to the study of the Wilhelmine Empire will seem to some more shocking still. It is not, we are constantly reminded, the intentions or actions of individuals which are important, but rather the whole structure of the society in which they live. Still, however attractive the idea of a blinding neo-Hegelian vision of the world may be — a vision of a totality in which everything interconnects with everything else and in which no detail is ever irrelevant, and which at the same time reveals to us the vast inexorable laws of the historical dialectic — we must start somewhere; and the life of an individual is as good a point at which to begin as any other. Actually, as a point from which to view the complexities of Wilhelmine Germany, the life of Walther Rathenau — a complicated and contradictory man in a complicated and contradictory society — is not perhaps a bad beginning.

However, before we look at the relations of Walter Rathenau with that society and at the paradox of this ambitious social thinker who was at the same time an ambitious, successful and ruthless financier and industrialist, we must outline the external framework of his career.[1] Walther Rathenau was born in 1867, the son of Emil Rathenau, who, by acquiring Edison's patents for the production of electric light bulbs, was able to found what was to become one of the biggest concerns in Europe, the *Allgemeine Elektrizitäts Gesellschaft* (AEG), and to become one of the pioneers in what is sometimes called the 'second industrial revolution', the new technological developments based on electrical engineering and the electro-chemical industry and, in conjunction with the internal combustion engine, a new and revolutionary system of transport. Walther was sixteen years old when his father founded the AEG; and it was several years before the financial success of the firm was established. His university career — and this perhaps makes a notable contrast with what the education of a young Englishman in a comparable position would have been — was devoted to the study of mathematics, physics and chemistry, and, although he attended philosophy lectures by Dilthey, which do not incidentally seem to have left

46

much impression on him, he emerged as a qualified electrical engineer and specialist in electro-chemistry with a thesis on the absorption of light by metals. On the face of it, then, Walther Rathenau was a good example of the new technocratic managerial class, to whose development Eduard Bernstein was shortly to point as one of his examples of the falsification of Marxist predictions about the squeezing out of the middle class in capitalist industrial society.

Rathenau, however, although he spent an apprenticeship working in metal and electro-chemical factories, soon showed that he had other ambitions, even though these pushed him in contrary directions. On the one hand, he rapidly became a director in his father's firm and branched out from that into becoming a banker as well as a member of the boards of many other companies. (It has been calculated that he was more or less permanently associated with 86 large concerns.) He was launched on a career as what Hartmut Pogge von Strandmann, whose researches have thrown so much light on his activities as an industrialist and financier, has called a 'grand master of capitalism'.[2] But at the same time he was beginning to write essays and aphorisms and to find an outlet for these in the pages of that remarkable periodical, notable both for its pungent political criticism and its literary contributions from many of the best-known writers of the day, *Die Zukunft*, edited by Maximilian Harden, with whom Rathenau established a deep, though uneasy and edgy, friendship.[3] From 1895 onwards Rathenau was both increasingly successful as a capitalist and increasingly ambitious as a writer, philosopher and social thinker.

At the same time he was, in spite of the difficulties which his Jewish origins created for him — difficulties of which he was very much aware and which he took an almost masochistic pleasure in emphasising — moving in the highest ranks of Berlin society, including visits to the Kaiser's court. It was typical of Rathenau that although associating himself with some of the bitterest criticisms of the Kaiser such as those voiced by his friend Maximilian Harden, he nevertheless felt a certain awe in the presence of the monarch; and it was equally typical of him that when he described the Kaiser he was in fact describing himself:

A true prince; conscious of the impression he was making, forcing his nature so as to give it dignity, strength, mastery. There was scarcely an unconscious moment; the only unconscious thing, and that was when he began to be a touching human being, was the struggle with himself; a nature set against itself without its knowledge.[4]

Rathenau's social and financial success led many people to expect that he would also have political ambitions. Emil Ludwig, for instance, wrote of him in 1913:

> Here is a man with whom not more than a dozen creative men can be compared in his combination of qualities; by position, education and independence, in every way he is practically superior to others. Why does this man withdraw from public life?[5]

In fact, Rathenau seems to have preferred the great but not directly political power which he was exercising as a financier; and the extent of his political influence over the statesmen with whom he was on terms of personal friendship, Bülow and especially Bethmann Hollweg, remains uncertain. In 1907-8 he accompanied Bernhard Dernburg, the State Secretary for the Colonies, on a visit to Africa and in 1910 he was entrusted by the government with the task of acting as intermediary in complicated negotiations between rival German firms and the French government about the exploitation of the mineral resources of Morocco.[6] There seems to have been some discussion of the possibility of his being a candidate in Reichstag elections of 1912 but nothing came of it; and Rathenau's first experience of an official position came at the start of the war in 1914 when he was put in charge of organising the Kriegsrohstoffabteilung, the department responsible for securing stocks of vital strategic raw materials. Although he made a major contribution to Germany's war economy by his work in the department, he did not stay in the job for more than a few months, and in March 1915 he returned to his business activities, with responsibilities that increased with the death of his father in June of that year. Nor did his brief period of working for the government go uncriticised. He was held responsible for the inevitable muddles and shortcomings in mobilising the economy for an unexpectedly long war; he was accused of favouring the interests of his own firm, and conversely he was also attacked by some of his business associates for not doing enough for the companies with which he was himself connected. As at every point of his career, as David Williamson has shown in his study of Rathenau's period at the Raw Materials Department,[7] he made enemies and irritated people by his alleged arrogance; and he himself emphasised the difficulties which his Jewishness caused with the military authorities. The reasons for his resignation remain obscure: Gerald Feldman has suggested that there were disagreements of principle:[8] David Williamson believes that Rathenau was worn out by the months of hard work and was anxious to get back to his own business interests and above all to his writing. Perhaps he preferred to be an adviser behind the scenes rather than having direct responsibility for a government department: and it would be in keeping with much of his career if he preferred to surround his activities with an air of mystery. Not for nothing did he suggest to Robert Musil many of the traits the novelist gave to his character Dr Arnheim in *The Man without Qualities*.

At the end of the war, Rathenau found himself rather more involved in public life, though not very rewardingly. He was an unsuccessful candidate for the Democratic Party in the elections for the National Assembly, and there was a humiliating episode in February 1919 when the secretary of the newly convened National Assembly read out telegrams proposing names for the office of President of the Republic. A group of German residents in Sweden put forward Rathenau's name, with disastrous results. Rathenau wrote a few months later:

> The parliament of any other civilised state would have shown sufficient respect for a man of recognised intellectual standing to have passed over in silence this act of bad taste. But the first Parliament of the German Republic, assembled in the darkest and most solemn hour and destined to set the seal on Germany's ignominy, greeted it with shouts and roars of laughter. The papers talked of merriment lasting for several minutes and eye witnesses related how men rocked in their seats with delight at the idea. This was their way of greeting a German whose intellectual achievement they either did or did not know, as the case may be.[9]

We shall return later to the reasons — mainly arising from his published writings — why Rathenau was an object of scorn and dislike both on the right and the left, and why these setbacks to his short-lived political ambitions did not interfere with the pursuit of his far-reaching business schemes and the effective reorganisation of his industrial empire after the disruption of war and revolution. It was indeed the success of the reconstruction of his own enterprises that made it natural for him to be called in by the government in July 1920, first as a technical adviser to the German delegation to the Spa conference on reparations, and then, in May 1921, as Minister of Reconstruction. At the end of January 1922 he was appointed Foreign Minister — with characteristic misgivings: 'I stand before this task in deep and earnest doubt. What can a single individual do in the face of this torpid world, with enemies at his back and conscious of his own limitations and weaknesses?'[10] His

appointment was partly due to the skill he had already shown in international negotiations, partly due to his personal friendship with the
Chancellor Wirth and largely to the fact that he was without political
affiliations, so that his appointment did not affect the delicate balance
between the parties on which the survival of the coalition government
depended. These last months are, of course, the best known of
Rathenau's career. He led the German delegation to the Genoa conference, during which he drove over to Rapallo and inaugurated a new
Ostpolitik by signing the famous treaty with Russia. Within two months,
on 24 June 1922, he was murdered by a group of young nationalist
terrorists.

Rathenau's business and public career itself contained enough
ambiguities and paradoxes, successes and failures to make it clear that
he was by no means a typical tycoon of the Wilhelmine epoch. Throughout he remained an outsider, as a Jew, as a writer, as an individualist
impatient of the routine of government. He was a man who stood apart
from his fellow members of boards of directors because he moved in a
higher social and intellectual sphere than many of them. 'His personality
itself,' one of his colleagues wrote, 'his place in the social and business
world give him a definitely independent standing in every sphere of
activity.'[11] But it was his activity as a writer and the kind of books he
published which more than anything else set him apart from his colleagues and aroused their suspicion and hostility. 'Do you really understand our Minister's books?' one of the members of the Foreign Office
asked anxiously when Rathenau took over the post of Foreign Minister.[12]
So, if we are to try and situate Rathenau the intellectual in relation to
Rathenau the capitalist, we must now look at the kind of books he was
writing and his own conception of what was − or so he sometimes
claimed − his main role in life.

From the mid-1890s onward Rathenau was writing essays and pam-
phlets and he continued to do so until he joined the government in
1921. Although many of the occasional articles are empty and pre-
tentious examples of *belles lettres* at their worst, some of his later ones,
notably *Die neue Wirtschaft* of 1918, throw light on his vision of what
a reformed and rationalised capitalist society might be like. However,
he himself believed that his three larger theoretical works were a major
contribution to twentieth-century philosophical and political thought.
These were *Zur Kritik der Zeit* (1912), *Zur Mechanik des Geistes oder
vom Reich der Seele* (1913) and *Von kommenden Dingen* (1917).[13] It
is hard, at least for an English reader, to take the first two of these
works very seriously. They do not indeed seem to be in any very

different category from the philosophical writings of two of Rathenau's near contemporaries who were also men influential in political life: A.J. Balfour's *Foundations of Belief* or J.C. Smuts's *Holism and Evolution* — works which do credit no doubt to the intellectual earnestness of their authors but which add little to our philosophical understanding. Rathenau was himself dissatisfied with the reception of his works, though in fact they did surprisingly well. *Zur Kritik der Zeit* sold 7,000 copies in the first month and had sold some 20,000 copies by the time of Rathenau's death. *Zur Mechanik des Geistes* was from this point of view a disappointment: only 3,000 copies sold in the first four years.[14] The reviews were respectful, though most of them stressed, as one would expect, the surprising contrast between the worldly success of the author and the plea for unworldly values which he makes in his books. As Stefan Zweig wrote of the first book, 'It is with amazement that one perceives a strong conservative current, a violently antimaterialistic *Weltanschauung* coming out of this book by a businessman.'[15] Indeed what makes the books difficult to evaluate is the extent to which they seem to reflect directly the opposing aspects of Rathenau's character.

Rathenau was, as we have seen, a successful technocrat, a qualified chemist and a professional engineer as well as a successful financier. He was well aware of the process of mechanisation which so appalled him, but to which he was contributing directly himself through the activities of the AEG and the other firms with which he was associated. Almost the only moments when his stilted and conventional prose style, with its abstract nouns and lack of any precise detail, seems to come alive are in those passages in which he describes with horror aspects of life in the great city made possible by the electrical power stations such as his own firm had constructed in Manchester, Amsterdam, Buenos Aires and Baku. Rathenau writes:

The traveller from the depths of the country who approaches the city at dusk experiences the descent into the land of unhappiness. When he has traversed the atmosphere of the sewers, the hutches where people live open like dark rows of teeth and shut out the sky. Green flames line the street, illuminated iron ships carry their cargoes of men over the smooth asphalt. From the courtyards stream exhausted men and women who fill up the space behind the plate-glass windows with signs which are pale blue arc lamps flashing '*Gross-distillation*', '*Frisiersalon*', '*Bonbonquelle*', '*Stiefelparadies*', '*Lichtspiele*', '*Abzahlungsgeschäft*', '*Weltbazar*'.[16]

It is a scene which recalls cityscapes of Macke or Kirchner or the other Expressionist painters whom Rathenau hated so deeply. What does not emerge is any sense that Rathenau as industrialist and purveyor of electric power might have some responsibility for the state of affairs he is attacking, unless the bitterness of the attack itself is evidence of a feeling of guilt.

It is only in occasional passages such as the one just quoted that Rathenau in these two earlier works shows any signs of contact with the real world. For the most part, in a phrase from a review by Robert Musil which gave great offence, Rathenau was content 'to suspend the discarded skin of experience from the stars'.[17] One of the personal tragedies of Rathenau's life was his intellectual isolation. He longed for close friendship with writers — *Zur Kritik der Zeit* is dedicated to Gerhard Hauptmann — but when he met them they often found, like Rilke whom he met on a walk in the Tiergarten, that he did not let them get a word in. At the same time, he mistrusted academic intellectuals and professional philosophers or sociologists for what he regarded as their pedantic approach and lack of instinctive insight and feeling. While it is possible to detect the influence of earlier writers — Fichte, Schopenhauer and especially Nietzsche — and while he seems to have known the writings of the Chassidic Mystics to whom he may have been introduced by Martin Buber, he showed no awareness of how unoriginal much of his writing is and little sign of any contact with those thinkers among his contemporaries such as Max Weber, for example, who were also concerned with the development of the mass mechanised society.

Both *Zur Kritik der Zeit* and *Zur Mechanik des Geistes* start from an analysis of the effects of mechanisation on human society and on the human spirit. The former is one of those essays in cultural pessimism popular in Germany in the late nineteenth and early twentieth centuries, a work which owes something to prevailing theories of the master race as expressed in the writings of Houston Stewart Chamberlain or Julius Langbehn. It already affirms what was to be a consistent theme in Rathenau's writing, the conflict between the soul and the materialism of contemporary society, and it suggests that there are only a few people capable of preserving spiritual values in a decadent world. *Zur Mechanik des Geistes* is a more ambitious work which sets out to be a major treatise on metaphysics, but its message is much the same. Here again the ambiguity of Rathenau's own position emerges in the ambiguity of his thought. On the one hand, the chosen few seem to be those who are ready to abandon the world and live wholly in the realm of the spirit, the *Reich der Seele*. On the other hand, like his predecessors among the German *völkisch* writers who speculated about the course of history, and like his contemporary Oswald Spengler, Rathenau was also worried about what was to happen in this world. In the past ruling classes had risen from below, had established their power and then lost it. He writes:

> This law works inexorably, for what made the conquerors the masters, what made the few capable of subduing the many was fearlessness, toughness and a purer spirit; and there is no way of preserving these advantages during periods of tedious inaction or of protecting the nobler blood against interbreeding. . . . Thus has the earth squandered its noblest racial stocks and we are faced with the terrifying question: is it really the goal of tens of thousands of years of effort to brew a grey decaying mixture out of all the colourful-ness and individuality of the races of mankind?[18]

The solution, Rathenau believed, lay both in a return to older spiritual and artistic values and in an economic and social reorganisation of society which would give the ruling elite the power to enforce its puritanical and ascetic values on the masses. This is the theme of *Von kommenden Dingen*. The book was written against the background of the increased government and business activity in which Rathenau was involved because of the war. He had begun to sketch it just before the war broke out and had taken it up again on resigning from the Raw Materials Department. When the book appeared it was an immediate success: 65,000 copies were sold in just over a year. It was seriously and on the whole favourably reviewed by well known writers and political scientists, including Hermann Hesse, Ferdinand Tönnies and Ernst Troeltsch.[19]

In the introduction to this best-selling blueprint for a capitalist Utopia, Rathenau claimed that 'it strikes dogmatic socialism to the heart.'[20] In fact, however, he at no point makes any serious examination of Marxism nor does he attempt any analysis of the workings of the capitalist economy. Capitalism is taken for granted — as is perhaps right in a book dedicated to the memory of Emil Rathenau — though it was not a capitalism to which all capitalists were prepared to subscribe. On the one hand Rathenau seems to uphold a system of free enterprise in the face of socialist planning, as when he writes:

> Our task is neither to even out the inequalities of human destiny and human claims nor to make all men independent or prosperous or

equal or happy; our task is to put in place of blind and impervious institutions self-determination and responsibility to oneself, not to force men to be free but to open the way to freedom for them.[21]

But on the other hand many who might have responded to Rathenau's contemptuous dismissal of socialist ideas were horrified by what he proposed instead as a means of rectifying the manifest evils of capitalist society. Inherited wealth should be abolished. Conspicuous expenditure of luxury goods should be heavily taxed, not in order to raise revenue but to reduce consumption of worthless objects. Wasteful business methods should be controlled:

Every widow who owns a wool shop demands that fifty times a year young representatives of her preferred wholesalers should call on her, chat with her for a few hours and show her novelties while she makes up her mind whether to place an order. Millions of working days are lost each year on so-called business trips.[22]

The profits produced by the newly reorganised and rationalised firms will be ploughed back into them or used to set up foundations for public, educational and artistic purposes. Society will consist of a small number of what Rathenau called 'autonomous undertakings', run by a specially selected elite chosen from an educational system which will have given every individual the chance to develop his abilities. An inflexible class system will be replaced by one in which there will be a circulation and renewal of the elites. (Since Rathenau hardly ever acknowledges that he has read anything by his contemporaries, it is hard to know how much he was aware of the writings of Pareto.) This vision of a technocratic world in which production and consumption are controlled by selfless sages has much in it of the Saint-Simonian tradition, and as a forecast of capitalist society as it was to develop in the later twentieth century it contains some perceptive ideas. Its weakness is that of Rathenau's earlier works, a lack of concrete details or examples and a tendency for the discussion of economic organisation to be pushed aside in favour of high-minded but empty philosophising. Some of his shorter works from this period − notably *Die Neue Wirtschaft* − describe more accurately, though still in general terms, the actual decision-making processes of the great financial and industrial concerns with which Rathenau was involved, but often these are not developed very far and we are soon back at declarations that all this high capitalist activity is intended to serve 'the transfiguration of the

Divine out of the human spirit'.[23]

There are a few points in *Von kommenden Dingen* at which reality breaks in: in a moving passage, for instance, written on 31 July 1916, where Rathenau contrasts the calm and beautiful view of the summer landscape from the window of his country house with the bloody battles on the Eastern and Western Fronts, but he soon returns to his personal position and his personal problems: 'Today it is two years since I felt myself so painfully cut off from the way of thinking of my people in so far as they saw war as a liberating event.'[24] In fact his reactions to the war were more ambiguous than this suggests. He had, unlike many of his contemporaries, from the start seen that the war would be a long one; but he had written in August 1914: 'The new life which it fell to us to proclaim is dawning, a life which will be stronger and deeper than the lamentable end of the old life. But this birth is a hard one and will take a long time.'[25] And, at the end of the war in 1918 he was still able to look back on August 1914 as 'great and unforgettable. It was the ringing opening chord for an immortal song of sacrifice, loyalty and heroism.'[26]

More serious than the egocentric, self-pitying and sometimes self-deceiving tone of much of Rathenau's writing is the absence of any clear account of what the institutions of the future society would actually be like. He seems to be about to enter on such a discussion when, for example, he attacks vigorously and trenchantly the rigidity and inequity of the existing German and, especially, Prussian state. But he then goes on to dismiss as unimportant the constitutional forms of the state and simply talks of the future *Volksstaat* as 'a living organism drawing the noblest strength from every level of the body of its people',[27] and he gives as an example of such an organism, of all things, the Prussian officer corps; and even this discussion is soon put on one side in favour of more about the '*Werden, Wachsen und Leben der Seele*'.[28]

Yet for all their pretentiousness and ambiguity, the message of *Von kommenden Dingen* and *Die neue Wirtschaft* seemed unequivocally shocking to Rathenau's fellow industrialists. Works which to Rathenau seemed to be striking a mortal blow at socialism were taken by many of his colleagues to be pleas for the introduction of dangerous socialist measures involving the abolition of inherited wealth, the limitation of personal consumption and a strict and compulsory rationalisation of economic and industrial activity. While his business associates had been prepared to overlook his earlier work as the harmless philosophising of a sophisticated man who had taken up writing as a hobby, his writings of 1917-18 seemed to represent a direct threat to their interests. And the more concrete suggestions they contained, the more dangerous they were. 'In my view this is the first time Rathenau has his feet on the ground,' Gustav Krupp von Bohlen wrote of *Die neue Wirtschaft*, 'even if the structure he has invented is quite incapable of realisation.'[29] Krupp was to some extent a business rival of Rathenau; but as Hartmut Pogge von Strandmann has shown in his fascinating study of the management of the Mannesmann concern of which Rathenau was a director,[30] his own associates were equally, if not more, worried by what one of them called 'the very dangerous cloud-cuckoo land which Dr Rathenau has constructed'.[31] Or again, 'The poison of his publication has filtered through to the lowest circles. The author must, I assume, realise with the deepest regret that he envisaged things quite differently from what they turned out to be.'[32] The suggestion that workers might have a say in the running of enterprises – the *Mitbestimmung* which has become one of the sources of strength of German capitalism in the second half of the twentieth century – was enough to make some of his fellow capitalists urge a boycott of Rathenau. 'Dr Rathenau has done us immeasurable harm with the ideas he has launched on the world; I do not understand how he could still talk of such things in the shareholders' meeting of the company without meeting with vigorous contradiction.'[33]

But of course Rathenau's writings had not endeared him to the left any more than they had to the conservatives. He was genuinely worried by the rigid class structure of imperial Germany: 'The separation of classes is so sharp with us,' Rathenau wrote to a Swedish friend, 'that in thirty years I have only once known of the case of a worker, the son of a worker, who has risen to a high position in the bourgeoisie.'[34] One of the main purposes of the capitalist Utopia he sketched in *Von kommenden Dingen* was to remedy this; but because he preached his doctrines while continuing to operate effectively and ruthlessly as an industrialist and businessman it is not surprising that his ideas did not sound very convincing to a working class which, in the early months of the German revolution, was still hoping for the introduction of genuine measures of workers' control in industry and for a thoroughgoing socialism based precisely on the expropriation of the fortunes of men like Rathenau.

Here we come to what is perhaps the most fundamental of the many paradoxes of Rathenau's career and the basic contradiction between his activities as an intellectual and his activity as an industrialist. He was often personally generous as well as personally austere in his tastes –

although his home, which he claimed to be 'bürgerlich anständig', was in
fact an example of that carefully cultivated simplicity and restrained
elegance only available to the very rich — and his vision of one of the
future roles of capitalism as being the establishment of educational and
cultural foundations was both genuine and prophetic. Yet the fact
remains that as a businessman he was just as tough and ruthless as any
of his contemporaries. However, the application of his considerable
intellect to industrial and financial problems was genuinely selfless. He
had a vision of a new rationalised capitalism from which waste would
have been eliminated and anomalies abolished. His tireless efforts to
make his own factories independent of others for their raw materials,
to produce an interlocking network of specialised concerns, were based
on a vision of the world in which rational organisation had an intrinsic
value of its own. It was also a world in which power was as important
an incentive as money: 'I pay my people according to their work in
office hours and base their promotion on their overtime.'[35] And it is
possibly this desire to impose rational structures on industry that
underlies not only his Utopian vision, but also his long struggle to end
the influence of the great steel barons, Krupp, Thyssen and the others,
over the electrical industry and other branches of industrial production
in which Rathenau was involved. 'The restoration of the health of
German industry,' Rathenau said in 1920, 'is only fully possible when
in place of an unregulated and unbridled economy based on monopolies
and illegitimate competition, an orderly organic economy based on
clear fundamental conceptions is introduced.'[36]

Rathenau once wrote of imperial Germany:

> It will be difficult for future writers of German history to under-
> stand how, in our time, two class systems could penetrate each
> other; the first is a survival of the feudal system, the second the
> capitalist class system .... But it will strike him as even odder that
> the newly arisen capitalist order has first of all to contribute to the
> strengthening of the feudal order.[37]

It was one of those extremely perceptive remarks which Rathenau
often made; but in fact there was a similar contradiction between rival
value systems going on within himself. On the one hand he was a
technocrat, interested in the introduction of new industrial processes
and new forms of economic rationalisation. 'I consider,' he wrote, 'that
mechanisation is one of the great movements of history, comparable
to the introduction of agriculture in prehistoric times and the great

discoveries of primitive times – weapons, fire and clothing.'[38] And elsewhere he said, 'It is not just crass materialism if I believe that in the new city there will be more dynamos than pearly gates.'[39] Yet on the other hand in his books, with their reiterated assertion of the superiority of the *Reich der Seele* over the *Reich der Zwecken*, he again and again comes back to a vision of the pre-industrial past which has a great deal in common with that, say, of Julius Langbehn's *Rembrandt als Erzieher*. (Rathenau did in fact contrast the spiritual qualities of Rembrandt with the worldliness of Manet.) His longing for old traditional values, for the lost skills of vanishing craftsmen, for a society in which everyone had his place and knew where he belonged, his deep feeling for regional differences and unpolluted landscapes – these are themes to which he returns again and again. He had a profound hatred for many aspects of contemporary life, for its frivolous materialism – he particularly despised women and especially fashionable women who seemed to embody all the wasteful squandering of resources which he detested; and he seems to have held women largely responsible for the corruption of twentieth-century taste. (One cannot help thinking of Antonio Gramsci's belief that the wives and daughters of American businessmen were becoming a useless class who undermined the strength of primitive American capitalism.) He hated modern art, even the works of respectable post-impressionists such as Vuillard, which his mother collected, or those of his cousin Max Liebermann, though he did allow himself to be painted by Edvard Munch. He was prepared on technological grounds to hire one of the pioneers of modern architecture, Peter Behrens, to work for the AEG, but his own taste was for the late-eighteenth-century Prussian neo-classicism of Schinkel and Gilly who had built his country house, Schloss Freienwalde. (It is typical, perhaps, that he defended his purchase of the house by saying he was only concerned to save this historical and artistic monument from the speculative builders.) But his contempt for the vulgarity of contemporary society was genuine enough: 'Anyone', he wrote, 'who sees a lawn desecrated by the trivial humour of clay gnomes, hares or toadstools may well reflect on this symbol of the misdirected economy of our time.'[40] Indeed readers of Rathenau today will find in his works, as in those of Oswald Spengler, support for our contemporary ecological and environmental causes, but they may not like Rathenau's conviction that the only way to save the values he admires is by creating a society governed by an austere elite of far-sighted capitalists steeped in the ideology of the German *völkisch* movement. As one contemplates Rathenau's vision of the future one wonders whether there may not be worse things in the world than garden gnomes.

David Williamson has called one of his articles on Rathenau 'Realist, Pedagogue and Prophet'.[41] And there are many other epithets, most of them contradictory, which could be applied to this visionary capitalist metaphysician, this Jewish Prussian patriot who published in 1913 a romantic poem to mark the centenary of the battle of Leipzig. It would be tempting, too, to write a psycho-biography of Rathenau in an attempt to explain some of the contradictions of his nature in terms, for instance, of his uneasy relationship with his father, always suspicious of Walther's intellectual pretensions and whose judgement on his son's publications — 'Walther's books are far easier to write than to read'[42] — remains one of the best criticisms of them. Such a biographer would go on to interpret Rathenau's close relationship with his mother, his deep grief at the early death of a much loved younger brother, his close and intense friendship with Lili Deutsch, the wife of one of his closest professional colleagues, the high-flown romantic language of his correspondence with his male friends. And such an analysis of Rathenau's character would need also to take account of the fatalism of his last weeks when warnings of his forthcoming assassination had already reached him.

But fascinating as such a study of a remarkable and in many ways mysterious individual might be, it is even more interesting to see in Rathenau's character some of the contradictions of the society in which he lived. He embodied some of the problems of 'modernisation' in Germany which preoccupy many German historians and social scientists today. He was, that is to say, on the organisational and technological level personally very much involved with the modernisation of German industry. Yet he brought to this a set of values based on a romantic admiration for a pre-industrial age which. as with so many of the social values of Wilhelmine Germany, could never be fully integrated with his activities as an industrialist and the society in which he lived. His solutions to the social and economic problems which he believed to confront him foreshadowed some of the best and the worst in twentieth-century capitalism. His vision of the role of vast cultural and educational foundations financed by industry both recalls the ideas of Saint-Simon a century earlier and looks forward to the activities of, for example, the Ford or Volkswagen Foundations in our own day. His organisation, while at the Raw Materials Department during the war, of a new type of company under public control which would combine state direction of commodity supplies with the freedom of capitalists to make money — something, as he put it, 'between a joint stock company which embodies the capitalist form of private enterprise and a bureaucratic organisation' – was, he believed, 'an industrial form which perhaps foreshadows the future'.[43] And indeed it certainly did foreshadow some aspects of economic organisation under the Third Reich. Rathenau's proposals for the remodelling of capitalism, his conception of a new elite controlling a society based on autonomous corporations suggest that he believed that only a Fascist type of society (though perhaps one closer to the ideas of Salazar than to those of Hitler) could make the world safe for capitalism.

Rathenau was undoubtedly an intellectual because he had general theoretical ideas about the world. Above all, one can see that he was an intellectual in the actual way in which he operated as a capitalist, in the vision of a rationalised and technologically advanced economy which he was trying to realise in his own professional activities. But he was also an intellectual in another sense, in that he wanted above all to be taken seriously as a writer and philosopher and to be accepted as an equal by some of the leading writers of the day – Wedekind, Hauptmann, Dehmel and Stefan Zweig, for example, all of whom he knew. His stormy friendship with Maximilian Harden was important to him because for a time Harden appeared to treat him as a real writer and as a serious contributor to one of the principal intellectual and literary reviews of the early 1900s. Yet, if he is considered just as a writer it would be hard to avoid the verdict of a critic who wrote shortly before Rathenau's death:

These books, in spite of a wide circulation in a period avid for metaphysics, have not exercised the slightest influence. There is not a trace to be found of real effect on the older or younger generation of really front-rank intellectuals. Today they already seem to be in the same class as the poems, architecture and music of crowned heads; works of a superior educated dilettante of somewhat uncertain taste, who has no idea of what has been done before him or around him, without critical awareness of what he owes to others and what is just a new formulation. . . . Compared with his essays in the field of philosophy even a Lotze seems an intellectual giant or an Emerson a creative genius.[44]

They are harsh words but not unjustified. One of Rathenau's tragedies was a misplaced sense of vocation and a sense that he was missing something. In a cruel phrase his friend Lili Deutsch summed up this aspect of his character: 'He never had any real feelings: he just had a longing for feelings'. His acute analytical intellect and his practical and administrative ability did not satisfy him. It is as if he felt that only by rising above the limitations of his Jewish birth and his inner hesitations and anxieties into some purely spiritual realm could he be taken at his own valuation. Instead his writings only made him more enemies and made him even more of an outsider so that he found himself in a false position from which he was never to escape. To the question from which we started, 'Was Rathenau an intellectual or an industrialist?' we must alas return the answer that he was a successful industrialist who thought he was an intellectual.

Notes

1. H. Kessler, *Walther Rathenau: his Life and Work* (London, 1929) remains an indispensable starting-point for any study of Rathenau's career. See also J. Joll, 'Walther Rathenau: Prophet without a Cause' in *Three Intellectuals in Politics* (New York, 1960); P. Berglar, *Walther Rathenau* (Bremen, 1970); D. Felix, *Rathenau and the Weimar Republic* (Baltimore, 1971).

2. See H. Pogge von Strandmann, Introduction to *Walther Rathenau: Tagebuch 1907-1922* (Düsseldorf, 1967); *idem*, 'Rathenau, die Gebrüder Mannesmann und die Vorgeschichte der zweiten Marokkokrise' in I. Geiss and B.-J. Wendt (eds.), *Deutschland in der Weltpolitik des 19. und 20. Jahrhunderts* (Düsseldorf, 1973), pp. 251-70; *idem*, 'Widersprüche im Modernisierungsprozess Deutschlands' in D. Stegmann, B.-J. Wendt and P.-C. Witt (eds.), *Industrielle Gesellschaft und Politisches System* (Bonn, 1978); *idem*, *Unternehmenspolitik und Unternehmensführung* (Düsseldorf-Wien, 1978), pp. 225-40. I am much indebted to Dr Pogge von Strandmann's important research in attempting this reassessment of the relationship between Rathenau's ideas and his business career.

3. A complete edition of their correspondence will appear in 1980 as one of the volumes in the Rathenau Gesamtausgabe, edited by Hans Dieter Hellige and Ernst Schulin. J. Joll, 'Rathenau and Harden: a Footnote to the History of Wilhelmine Germany' in M. Gilbert (ed.), *A Century of Conflict 1850-1950* (London, 1966), was only able to use part of this correspondence.

4. W. Rathenau, *Der Kaiser: eine Betrachtung* (Berlin, 1919), p. 27.

5. E. Ludwig, 'Rathenaus neues Buch', *Der Tag* (Berlin), 6 Jan. 1914; E. Schulin, 'Zu Rathenaus Hauptwerke' in E. Schulin (ed.), *Walther Rathenau. Hauptwerke und Gespräche*, Rathenau Gesamtausgabe, vol. II (Munich and Heidelberg, 1977), p. 538.

6. See H. Pogge von Strandmann, 'Rathenau, die Gebrüder Mannesmann und die Vorgeschichte des Zweiten Marokkokrise' in Geiss and Wendt (eds.), *Deutschland in der Weltpolitik*.

7. D.G. Williamson, 'Walther Rathenau and the KRA August 1914-March 1915', *Zeitschrift für Unternehmensgeschichte*, vol. 23, no. 2 (1978).

8. See G. Feldman, *Army, Industry and Labor in Germany 1914-1918* (Princeton, 1966) and *idem*, 'The Political and Social Foundations of Germany's Economic Mobilisation', *Armed Forces and Society*, vol. III, no. 1 (1976).

9. Walther Rathenau, 'Apologie' in *Kritik der ꞇ̣eifache Revolution* (Berlin,

1919), p. 9; Kessler, *Walther Rathenau*, pp. 265-6.
10. Kessler, *Walther Rathenau*, p. 316.
11. Pogge von Strandmann, *Unternehmenspolitik*, p. 52.
12. W. von Blücher, *Deutschlands Weg nach Rapallo* (Wiesbaden, 1951), p. 156.
13. These three works have been reprinted as vol. II of the Rathenau Gesamtausgabe: Schulin (ed.), *Walther Rathenau*.
14. Schulin in 'Zu Rathenaus Hauptwerke', pp. 508, 535.
15. St(efan) Z(weig), 'Walther Rathenau Kritik der Zeit', *Neue Freie Presse* (Vienna), 12 June 1912 in Schulin, 'Zu Rathenaus Hauptwerke', p. 525.
16. 'Zur Mechanik des Geistes', *Hauptwerke*, pp. 126-7.
17. R. Musil in *Neue Rundschau*, July 1914, ibid., pp. 556 ff.
18. 'Zur Mechanik des Geistes', *Hauptwerke*, pp. 287.
19. Schulin (ed.), *Walther Rathenau*, pp. 562 ff.
20. 'Von kommenden Dingen', *Hauptwerke*, p. 303.
21. Ibid., p. 333.
22. Ibid., p. 372.
23. Ibid., p. 497.
24. Ibid., p. 422.
25. To Fanny Künstler, 19 Aug. 1914 in M. von Eynern (ed.), *Walther Rathenau – ein preussischer Europäer. Briefe* (Berlin, 1958), p. 117.
26. W. Rathenau, *Staat und Vaterland*, 1918, p. 43.
27. 'Von kommenden Dingen', *Hauptwerke*, p. 470.
28. Ibid., p. 496.
29. Pogge von Strandmann, *Unternehmenspolitik*, p. 139.
30. Ibid.
31. Ibid., p. 141.
32. Ibid., p. 145.
33. Ibid.
34. To Ernst Norlind, 1 Apr. 1917 in W. Rathenau, *Briefe* (Dresden, 1926), vol. I, p. 250.
35. Pogge von Strandmann, *Unternehmenspolitik*, p. 60.
36. H. Pogge von Strandmann, 'Widersprüche im Modernisierungsprozess' in Stegmann *et al.* (eds.), *Industrielle Gesellschaft*, p. 236.
37. 'Zur Kritik der Zeit', *Hauptwerke*, p. 61.
38. To Hermann Gottschalk, 7 Dec. 1920 in Rathenau, *Briefe*, vol. II, p. 280.
39. To Dr P.A., Ascension Day 1917, ibid., vol. I, p. 280.
40. 'Von kommenden Dingen', *Hauptwerke*, p. 346.
41. D.G. Williamson, 'Walther Rathenau: Realist, Pedagogue and Prophet, November 1918-May 1921', *European Studies Review*, no. 6 (1976), pp. 99-121.
42. E. Federn-Kohlhaas, *Walther Rathenau* (Dresden, 1927), p. 82.
43. W. Rathenau, 'Deutschlands Rohstoffversorgung'. Lecture to *Deutsche Gesellschaft 1914*, 20 Dec. 1915 in *Gesammelte Schriften*, vol. V (Berlin, 1929), p. 41.
44. K. Singer, *Staat und Wirtschaft seit dem Waffenstillstand* (Jena, 1924), p. 145.

POLES, CZECHOSLOVAKS AND THE 'JEWISH QUESTION', 1914-1921: A COMPARATIVE STUDY

Antony Polonsky and Michael Riff

The effect of the First World War in causing a marked increase in political anti-Semitism in Germany and Austria has long been recognised. Equally, the impact of the massive pogroms which accompanied the civil war in the Ukraine and the attempt to deal with the peculiar past of the Jews in Soviet Russia on Marxist-Leninist lines has been widely documented. Less attention has been devoted to the way in which the war modified and intensified the 'Jewish Problem' in the newly independent states of Eastern Europe. In this chapter we will describe how this 'problem' developed in the very different environments of Poland and Czechoslovakia, both states in which national questions were to be at the very centre of political life throughout the inter-war years.

The position of the Jews in the Polish lands had begun to deteriorate seriously even before 1914. This was most evident in the areas ruled by Russia. The catastrophic crushing of the 1863 uprising led here to widespread disillusionment with the seemingly hopeless pursuit of independence through insurrection. Instead the view was increasingly held that Poles could best improve their situation by concentrating on economic goals which would transform and modernise Polish society. The last part of the nineteenth century was indeed a period of substantial economic growth for the Congress Kingdom, that part of Russian Poland whose autonomy, granted by the Congress of Vienna, was almost entirely abolished after 1863. Industrial production trebled between 1860 and 1870 and increased five times between 1870 and 1900. Warsaw grew to be a metropolis with nearly 650,000 inhabitants, while Lodz became a major textile centre with a population of 350,000.

These developments inevitably affected the position of the Jews. In 1842, Jews had made up 11.1 per cent of the population of the Congress Kingdom. By 1865 this had risen 13.48 per cent and by 1909 to 14.64 per cent. In that year Jews made up nearly a fifth of the population of Warsaw and Lodz. They constituted considerably more than a third of the entire urban population and in many smaller towns were in a clear majority.[1]

Industrialisation broke up the old Polish-Jewish economic symbiosis. Although relations between Poles and Jews before 1863 had often been marked by tension and conflict, the Jews had a clearly defined economic role as intermediaries. With industrialisation, the Russian confiscations and the economic difficulties of agriculture, particularly from the 1880s, many Poles moved to the towns. Russian policy meant that access to the civil service was barred to them, while the Jews were in a strongly entrenched position in many trading and entrepreneurial fields. Yet the immediate result was not a rise in anti-Semitism. The Positivists had favoured Jewish assimilation and their calls for a modernisation of Jewish life and the incorporation of the Jews into the Polish community evoked a corresponding response from the Jewish elite.

From the 1890s the situation began to change. The economic development of the Congress Kingdom and the fact that the legal position of Jews was better than in the Russian Empire led to an influx of Jews from Lithuania and Byelorussia. These 'Litwaks' were widely attacked by both Poles and Jews as an alien element and as agents of 'Russification'. More important, these years saw a revival of Polish nationalism and a rejection of the principal beliefs of Positivism. The main ideologist of this new nationalism was Roman Dmowski. In his view, only vigorous and thrusting nations had the right to survive. The Poles should abandon their sentimental belief in the equality of rights of all nations and pursue a policy of ruthless national egoism. Even at this stage he employed biological language to describe his attitude to the Jews. Only a small percentage of them, he argued, could be 'absorbed' by the Polish nation. The remainder should be compelled to emigrate, since they impeded the formation of a native Polish middle class.[2]

In the initial period of their activity, the National Democrats, as Dmowski's followers came to be known, called for the re-creation of a 'Greater Poland' with frontiers approximating to those of the pre-partition Republic. The revolutionary upheaval of 1905-7 created widespread alarm among the possessing classes in the Congress Kingdom and the National Democrats thus became convinced that they should seek a compromise with the Tsarist authorities. The real dangers, they claimed, were the twin challenges of revolution and German imperialism, and they were prepared to co-operate with the Russian state against these two enemies.

In the reactionary climate which prevailed following the crushing of the revolution of 1905-7, anti-Jewish sentiments were also espoused by a number of other political groups. The journal *Prawda*, which had long supported the Positivist viewpoint, became the organ of 'progressive anti-Semitism'. In its pages, former Liberals and Positivists called for the 'de-judaising' of Polish towns and the end of Jewish assimilation. By 1912, the situation had reached such extremes that a leading conservative review, the *Biblioteka Warszawska*, could write, 'If one sought for a word to define the prevailing attitude of Polish public opinion towards the Jewish problem, that word would be anti-Semitism.'[3]

Matters were brought to a head by the election to the fourth Russian Duma in Warsaw in 1912. In the elections to the earlier Dumas, the Jews, who formed a substantial proportion of the restricted electorate, had not voted as a bloc in order not to antagonise Polish opinion. This had not stopped the Polish deputies from adopting anti-Jewish postures. There were three candidates from Warsaw in the 1912 election. The National Democrats nominated Dmowski, while the historian Jan Kucharzewski represented a group which had split off from the National Democrats, because they were felt to be too willing to collaborate with the Tsarist authorities. The prosperous Jewish voters were originally inclined to vote for Kucharzewski. But he made clear his contempt for them. He even told the Jewish representatives who approached him that he did not want their support and that the Jews should abstain from any participation in Polish politics. As a result, the Jews voted *en bloc* for the socialist candidate, Eugeniusz Jagiełło, who was accordingly elected.

The election was followed by an intensification of anti-Jewish agitation and calls for a boycott of Jewish shops. This spread to the countryside, where it sometimes took violent forms. In May 1913 a mob in Planów, south-west of Lodz, burnt down a Jewish shop, killing seven people. Not without justification did the eminent Polish scholar Professor Baudoin de Courtenay write in 1913: 'The actions which our youth are now being encouraged to undertake amount to denunciation and the commission of open outrages against others. Children brought up in this way are excellent candidates to become bandits and hooligans.'[4]

In the other parts of Poland, the situation was not as acute. Jews had received full civil rights in Galicia (Austrian Poland) in the 1860s, but the backward economic situation of the province meant that the traditional economic role of the Jews had not been seriously modified by 1914. The small Jewish elite was either Germanised or Polonised, while the bulk of the Jewish community was still dominated by religious orthodoxy. One of the principal problems the Jews faced was that since the majority of the community was concentrated in East Galicia, it was inevitably caught in the growing national conflict between Poles and Ukrainians. Some sections of the developing Peasant movement in West Galicia did begin to attack Jewish predominance in small trading around the turn of the century, while in Lvov, groups linked with the National Democrats in the Congress Kingdom also grew in force. But the Polish aristocratic conservatives, who governed the province from the granting of autonomy in the 1860s through to 1914, set themselves firmly against the adoption of anti-Semitic policies.

In Prussian Poland, the 'Jewish problem' had largely disappeared by the outbreak of the war. The early granting of civil rights and the rapid economic development of Germany led to large-scale Jewish emigration, above all to Breslau and Berlin. In 1912 there were only 20,000 Jews in Prussian Poland and they were seen by the Poles as part of the local German minority. Moreover, the need of the Poles to enlist the support of progressive sections of German opinion in their struggle to resist Germanisation meant that the Polish parties, in spite of the dominance of National Democratic sentiments, were loath to espouse openly anti-Jewish policies. At the same time, developments in this area were often alluded to by anti-Semites as the correct way to deal with the Jews.

The war re-opened the Polish question which had lain dormant since 1864. The partitioning powers soon began making plans for the future of Poland and attempted to win over the Poles by promising to satisfy their national aspirations. In August 1914, the Russian Commander-in-Chief issued a manifesto offering the Poles 'autonomy' within the Tsarist Empire. The Austrians favoured the incorporation of Congress Kingdom as the third constituent part of a reorganised Habsburg state. This provoked opposition from the Hungarians and, as Austria's role in the war declined, it was resisted by the Germans, who wanted to reserve for themselves the dominant position in the area.

The war widened the already deep divisions within Polish political life. One group, led by the former socialist Józef Piłsudski, hoped to make use of the conflict to spark off an anti-Russian insurrection. When this failed he was compelled to pursue his goals through co-operation first with the Austrians and then with the Germans. Alliance with the Central Powers was also advocated by the Galician conservatives who hoped that the Congress Kingdom would be united with Galicia and enjoy a similar status. Ranged on the Russian side were the National Democrats and their allies, who looked to the Tsar to satisfy their national demands.

The first two months of the war saw a worsening of the positions of the Jews in the Congress Kingdom and Western Russia. In an attempt to allay suspicions that they were pro-German, a number of leading Jewish figures in Warsaw issued a declaration affirming, with reference

to the Grand Duke Nikolai's manifesto, that 'together with the entire
country, the Jewish group awaits the dawn of new life which has begun
for Poland.'

This did not prevent the National Democratic *Gazeta Poranna* from
replying: 'Is it not clear that the consolidation and economic independence of the Polish group, its independence *vis-à-vis* the Jews, will be one
of the elements of reunified Poland's programme of action.'[5]

The Russian high command did not hesitate to blame their initial
defeats on the Jews, who were also being denounced in the National
Democratic press for spying. The Grand Duke Nikolai, a convinced
anti-Semite, established a special bureau to deal with espionage and
took rigorous action against suspected Jewish spies, over a hundred of
whom were executed. Jewish hostages were taken in those parts of
Galicia captured by the Russians and the anti-Jewish campaign culminated in the notorious order of the Grand Duke expelling several
hundred thousand Jews from the front-line area. At the same time all
Hebrew and Yiddish newspapers were banned.[6]

It is not surprising, therefore, that the Jews enthusiastically welcomed
the Russian defeats in the spring of 1915 and people of Jewish origin
constituted a significant proportion of the officers and soldiers of the
Polish legions set up by Piłsudski to fight alongside the Austrians.[7]
After the Russian withdrawal, the Congress Kingdom was divided into
two unequal parts; the larger northern area with most of the industrial
centres, including Warsaw, was governed by the Germans, while the
smaller southern section was ruled by the Austrians.

It was above all in the German zone that a number of significant
policy innovations were made. Indeed with the occupation of not only
the Congress Kingdom but also the Baltic states and large parts of
Byelorussia and the Ukraine, the Germans controlled the destiny of the
bulk of European Jewry. Palestine, increasingly a focus for Jewish
national aspirations, was ruled by Germany's ally Turkey. After their
initial victories, the Germans made grandiose plans for the reorganisation of Europe under their hegemony and they were anxious to find a
place for the Jews in these schemes. As a result the German Foreign
Office set up a special Department of Jewish Affairs and also encouraged
a group of German-Jewish activists to set up a 'Committee for Eastern
Questions'.[8] The Jewish question was also seen as a means of propa-
gandising the aims of the Central powers and, given the almost complete unwillingness of the British and French to raise this issue for fear
of irritating the Russian government, German efforts met with a certain
amount of approval in neutral circles, above all in the United States.

Yet it should be stressed that the Germans did not have a consistent and clearly thought-out plan for the Jews of Poland. German policy fluctuated constantly and was heavily dependent on changing perceptions of the Polish problem itself and on the different individuals entrusted with its implementation. Indeed by 1917, the difficulties of the war had led to severe economic exactions in the Congress Kingdom which fell heavily on the urban Jews and did much to undermine German popularity in Jewish circles. So too did the arbitrary behaviour of the often anti-Semitic officers and men entrusted with confiscations and the levying of taxes and German demands for compulsory labour service.[9]

German rule, on the other hand, saw a major revival of Jewish political life. Banned Jewish newspapers began to reappear and many new ones were established. When a system of universal primary education was set up in 1915, the German authorities initially laid down that the language of instruction for Jews should be German. This was strongly opposed by the Poles and the Jewish assimilationists who wanted a single-school system with Polish as the language of instruction, and by other Jewish groups (the orthodox, the *folkists* and even the socialist Bund) who wanted Yiddish and, ultimately, the Zionists, who fought for Hebrew. The German authorities yielded to this pressure and a number of individual Jewish organisations were established to foster the development of separate school systems.

Direct political activity also followed. In 1917, a Zionist Union in Poland was set up as well as a party of the religiously orthodox Zionists, the Mizrachi. In addition to pressing for the establishment of a Jewish state in Palestine, the Zionists called for the recognition of the Jews as a distinct national group, whose civil rights would be guaranteed and which would enjoy internal autonomy. Similar demands for cultural autonomy were also put forward by the *folkists*, though they rejected emigration to Palestine as a solution of the Jewish problem.

The domination of Jewish political life by radical elements alarmed the German authorities. With the help of Jewish orthodox circles in Germany, they sponsored the organisation in 1916 of a party of the orthodox, the Aguda, as a counter-weight. At this time, the Germans were contemplating the establishment of religious autonomy for the Jews, which they believed would lead to an improvement of Polish-Jewish relations. The Aguda soon grew to be one of the most powerful Jewish political groupings in Poland, but its German origin led to its being regarded with suspicion both by the Poles and by other Jewish political groups.

Polish-Jewish relations improved after the establishment of German rule. The groups which supported the Central powers, generally referred to as 'Activists', had been in opposition to the National Democrats before the war, and were by and large less anti-Semitic and less willing to indulge in anti-Jewish demagogy. The sudden change in atmosphere was described by a Jewish journalist as follows:

Immediately the National Democratic leaders fled from Warsaw, the Polish capital changed in aspect. As if by the stroke of a magic wand, Warsaw was moved westwards... The masses learnt, to their great astonishment, that the peaceful coexistence of Poles and Jews, far from harming Polish interests, created an agreeable atmosphere of peace and calm. All Poles felt a certain satisfaction, while as for the Jews, they received this change in the situation with enormous enthusiasm.[10]

When elections were arranged for the Warsaw City Council, the more moderate Jewish groups (the Zionists, the Orthodox and the Assimilationists), anxious to avoid a repetition of the events of 1912, reached an agreement with the major Polish political organisations to divide the seats. In the elections the majority of Polish seats was won by 'Activists'. When he took office, the new mayor and large landowner, Prince Zdzisław Lubomirski, declared that it was his intention to aid the entire population 'irrespective of class or religion'.[11]

Yet at the same time an element of tension persisted. Even those Poles best disposed towards the Jews were basically unwilling to accept the idea of an autonomous Jewish group as was being demanded by the *folkists* and Zionists and, in their own way, by the Bundists. These demands were frequently seen by Polish observers as German-inspired. Thus the Conservative newspaper *Czas* wrote on 3 July 1916: 'We are perfectly well aware that our enemies and opponents are exploiting the Jewish question to break up our national unity.'

In November 1916, the Central powers proclaimed an 'independent' Polish state with undefined boundaries. This was at first welcomed both by 'Activist' political circles and by most Jewish groups. At a meeting in Warsaw to celebrate this event, Jewish speakers stressed the liberal principles which had inspired the great Polish humanists and expressed the hope that now that Poland had been freed from Russian influences, it would rediscover its true traditions. Similarly, when a legislature, in the form of the Council of State, was established in January 1917, the leadership of the Jewish community in Warsaw declared its support for this institution.

In the course of 1917, it became clear that the German effort to win over Polish opinion was failing. The essentially fraudulent nature of the 'independence' granted to the Poles in November 1916 was soon apparent, and Piłsudski, after some hesitation, refused to aid the Germans in recruiting Poles to fight on the side of the Central powers and also counselled his followers in the legions against taking an oath of loyalty to the German authorities. As a result, in July 1917 he was arrested and interned in Magdeburg. At the same time the February Revolution in Russia aroused considerable enthusiasm in radical circles, both Polish and Jewish, and further undermined the prestige of the Germans. So too did the detachment of the Chelm district from the future Polish state and its assignment to the Ukraine in the Treaty of Brest-Litovsk in March 1918. By this time, the only support the Germans enjoyed came from conservative groups representing, above all, the large landowners.

The resolution of the Polish question thus came increasingly to hinge on the decisions of the Western allies. After the Russian withdrawal from the Congress Kingdom, Dmowski had moved to Western Europe on a Russian diplomatic passport, but had not been able to obtain much support from the British and French governments before the February Revolution. The collapse of the Tsarist regime strengthened his position and in August 1917 he and his associates established a 'Polish National Committee' in Lausanne. Though for the moment this did not set itself up as a Polish government-in-exile, it asked the Allies to recognise it as an official Polish organisation representing Poland in the Western states of the coalition. In September it was duly recognised by the French government as an intermediary between it and the Polish Army which was being set up in France. The Committee now moved to Paris and in October and December 1917 it received similar recognition from the UK, Italy and the United States.

The fact that a man with so dubious a record as Dmowski seemed likely to play a dominant role in the new Polish state alarmed Jewish leaders in the West and stimulated them to seek a *rapprochement* with the National Democrats. Some Polish circles were also aware of the damage Dmowski's image could do to the Polish cause. As early as the summer of 1915, two progressive Polish politicians linked with the 'Activist' camp, Stanisław Patek and August Zaleski, came to London. Their aim was, above all, to dispel suspicions in the West that the groups they represented were unreservedly pro-German, but they also met Jewish leaders in London and attempted to reassure them.[12]

The action of Patek and Zaleski seems to have led Jewish circles in the UK to believe they could bypass the National Democratic-dominated Polish National Committee in their dealings with the Poles. In 1917, the 'Anglo-Jewish Committee' held several meetings devoted to the Jewish question in Poland and even attempted to set up a conference of Polish and Jewish representatives in a neutral country. In a memorandum to the British government on 26 November 1917, the Committee explained that it could not enter into discussions with the Polish National Committee because of Dmowski's anti-Semitism. This argument was not sympathetically received in British government circles and the conference proposal lapsed.[13]

In these conditions, a direct approach to the National Democrats could not be avoided and it was in the United States that the most important exchanges took place. In January 1918, Woodrow Wilson had committed his government to the re-establishment of an independent Polish state within its ethnographic limits. Since Dmowski and the Polish National Committee were hoping to incorporate into the new Poland large areas in which the majority of the population was Lithuanian, Byelorussian or Ukrainian, any support for their territorial aspirations, even from the Jews, was welcome. The desire for some understanding was reciprocated by important sections of the Jewish leadership in the United States. Already before Dmowski's arrival in America in the summer of 1918, a meeting took place in April attended by Ignacy Paderewski (the Polish pianist, who was a supporter of the Polish National Committee, but who had distanced himself from Dmowski's anti-Semitism) and three representatives of the American Jewish Committee, including its Chairman, Louis Marshall. At this meeting, while admitting that Dmowski was an anti-Semite, Paderewski claimed that the other members of the Polish National Committee were not. If the Jews abandoned what he described as their 'attitude of decided hostility' towards Poland and supported Polish territorial ambitions, Polish-Jewish relations would rapidly improve.[14]

Further Jewish approaches to Paderewski followed, and as a result, in June 1918, he decided that in order to allay Jewish fears, the Polish National Committee should be persuaded to issue a declaration in favour of Jewish equality and civil rights. This initiative did not have very beneficial consequences. The Polish National Committee in Paris drastically modified Paderewski's original draft, so that it could easily be taken as a criticism of the Jewish demand for communal autonomy. It is thus not surprising that Paderewski waited for a month before showing the declaration in its new form to his American-Jewish contacts.

Marshall, the principal Jewish spokesman, told Paderewski that he regarded it as quite inadequate in the light of the tension which had marked Polish-Jewish relations and suggested direct talks with Dmowski in order to break the deadlock.[15] Three meetings accordingly took place in October, two with Marshall and one with Brandeis.[16] These conversations did not prove particularly fruitful. When asked to condemn the anti-Jewish boycott, Dmowski replied that he could not do so as this would undermine his political credibility. He did promise that if the Jews supported Polish territorial aspirations, their position would improve. At the last meeting on 14 October, the Jews called for the appointment of a Jewish representative to the Polish National Committee and again demanded the ending of the boycott. Dmowski now promised the latter, if the Jewish representatives issued a declaration calling on the Jews in Poland 'faithfully to serve Poland and to work and fight for a united and independent Poland'.[17] Paderewski was also present at this meeting and the heated tone of the discussion led him to an uncharacteristic expression of anti-Semitism. The boycott, he claimed, was not the work of Dmowski, but was 'a patriotic protest against a serious and for an oppressed people, inpardonable [*sic*] offence'.[18]

The failure of these talks had important consequences. They greatly strengthened Dmowski's belief in a Jewish world conspiracy directed against Poland. As he wrote later: 'As my American visit came to a close, I was aware of what I had known before my arrival – that at the peace conference the bitterest opponents of our cause would be the Jews.'[19] The Jewish leadership in the West was seriously alarmed at the prospects for Jews in the new Poland. The American-Jewish Committee now sent a delegation to Wilson which submitted to him a memorandum on Polish-Jewish relations. In Jewish circles, the idea of a treaty to protect Jewish rights gained ground and eventually took the form of the Minority Treaty concluded between Poland and the Allied and Associated powers.[20]

The defeat of the Central powers was followed by the rapid collapse of the authorities they had established in Poland. In early November, Piłsudski returned in triumph. He took the offices of Commander-in-Chief and head of state, exercising, as he was later to put it, the powers of a 'dictator'.[21] Though he had, in the past, been linked with the left and his original Cabinet was composed largely of socialists and radical Peasant party politicians, Piłsudski had no intention of introducing advanced social policies for which he felt Poland was too weak and which he believed would compromise the country in the eyes of the victorious coalition. He was also eager to dispel Allied suspicions that he was pro-German. He therefore attempted to create an all-party coalition, which would include his old and bitter opponents, the National Democrats. After two months of political intrigue, this coalition was eventually established on 16 January under the premiership of Ignacy Paderewski.

The setting up of the Paderewski government only papered over the deep divisions which existed within its ranks on what kind of new Poland was to be established. Piłsudski saw in the crisis of the Russian state the opportunity to create a secure territorial basis by detaching the border areas of Lithuania, Byelorussia and the Ukraine and linking them with Poland in a federation. The Poles were to play the dominant role in this federation, but Piłsudski was probably sincere when he claimed that it was his intention to respect the rights of the other national groups. This could hardly be said, however, for some of his allies. The large landowners in Eastern Poland were primarily concerned to safeguard their estates. Dmowski and the National Democrats wanted to establish a unitary national state. The eastern border of this state was to be considerably to the east of the area of solid Polish settlement and the other Slavs and Lithuanians in those areas were to be subject to a vigorous policy of Polonisation.

Neither of these groups was prepared to accept the demands for autonomous status on the part of what was probably now the majority of Polish Jews. Immediately after his return to Poland, Piłsudski had received a delegation from the Jewish political parties, headed by the Zionist Itzchak Grynbaum, which had presented him with a memorandum affirming the 'postive attitude' of the Jewish community towards his government. The Zionists, it claimed, were 'ready to take part in the reconstruction of the Republic and the consolidation of its democratic government as is demanded by the people'. At the same time, it called for the granting of 'national autonomy' to the Jews. Piłsudski promised to consider this memorandum and also undertook to take 'energetic measures' against anti-Semitic excesses.[22] Yet his attitude soon proved a disappointment to the Jews, above all because of his policy of conciliating the Polish right in order to create a government of national unity. Paderewski was even less sympathetic to Jewish demands. On 18 February 1919, he met a delegation of Jewish leaders and assured them that he would do everything he could to ensure equal rights for the Jews. Yet he also declared that he was 'absolutely opposed' to the programme of the autonomists.[23]

Zionist calls for Jewish autonomy were not universally supported by the Jewish community. They aroused opposition, not only from the Aguda, which pursued its traditional policy of conciliating whatever government was in power, and the Bund, which at this stage believed the socialist millennium to be at hand, but also from the *folkists* who saw the Zionists as powerful rivals. Nevertheless, the Zionists did succeed in holding a major conference of Jewish organisations which supported their aims at the end of December 1918. It was at this meeting that a Provisional Jewish National Council was established.[24] This Council participated in the elections for the Constituent Assembly which took place on 26 January. The electoral system worked against Jewish representation, and as a result the Jews, who made up 11 per cent of the population, received only 3 per cent of the seats in the Sejm. Of the eleven Jewish deputies, six represented the Jewish National Council. Three of the other five Jewish deputies were also strong protagonists of the right of Jews to recognition as a national group. The elections thus saw a decisive defeat for the Jewish assimilationists who won only two seats. However, this development was bitterly opposed by all Polish groups, including the socialists. The only concession made to the Jews was the granting in February of autonomy for local religious communes which was rejected by most Jewish parties as an attempt to strengthen the influence of the more politically compliant orthodox groups.

The Jews were soon faced with more serious problems. The years 1919 and 1920 were dominated by the struggle to establish Poland's frontiers, a struggle which had extremely deleterious effects on the position of the Jews. The new state found the burden of establishing and maintaining a large army a heavy one and the forced levies and contributions which made this possible fell heavily on the largely urban Jewish community. The Poles showed little understanding for the desire of Jews in ethnically mixed areas such as East Galicia or Lithuania to maintain a neutral posture in the national conflicts there. At the same time, the fact that Jews constituted a significant proportion of the Communist leadership both in Russia and in Poland and that a small percentage of the Jews had welcomed the Bolshevik Revolution was seized upon as a means of discrediting the post-war revolutionary wave as a primarily Jewish phenomenon.

Not surprisingly, the end of the war was followed by a series of anti-Jewish outrages.[25] These took different forms in the various parts of Poland. The year 1918 had been very difficult in Galicia, with severe food shortages and widespread starvation. Spontaneous popular unrest boiled over and often manifested itself in attacks on Jewish shopkeepers.

In order to defend themselves, the Jews in Krakow were given permission by the Polish Liquidation Commission, which had taken over from the Austrian authorities, to establish their own self-defence organisation which received arms and provisions from the military department of the Liquidation Commission. This policy was soon countermanded by General Roj, the Polish military commander for the Krakow region, and the members of the Jewish militia were ordered to surrender their arms. The Jews were then bitterly attacked in the nationalist press for 'attempting to arm themselves against the Polish state' and a series of violent incidents followed.[26]

In Lvov, the Jews were inevitably caught up in the Polish-Ukrainian conflict and their desire to remain neutral was interpreted by the Poles, though not by the local Ukrainians, as a hostile act. After the capture of Lvov by Polish forces on 22 November 1919, the Polish military command issued a proclamation accusing the Jews of treason. This provoked a wave of anti-Jewish violence in the course of which at least 72 Jews were killed and some 300 wounded. The damage was estimated at 110 million crowns. In addition, measures were taken to deprive Jews of the posts they had held under Austrian rule in schools, the civil service and the railways.[27]

In eastern Poland serious excesses also took place as the ill-disciplined and poorly paid troops of General Dowbór-Muśnicki, strengthened by volunteers from the local population, moved eastwards, driving out Byelorussian and Ukrainian nationalists as well as the Bolsheviks. These incidents are well documented in the unpublished diary of Stanisław Michał Kossakowski, adjutant of the Polish General Commission for the Civil Administration of the Eastern Territories.[28] They were explained in the following way by the socialist daily *Robotnik* on 12 March 1919:

> Clearly a significant factor is the quality of the soldiers making up the Lithuanian-Byelorussian division. They are drawn almost exclusively from the forces established in Russia [after the February revolution] by Gen. Dowbór-Muśnicki and have been seasoned by the marauding adventures of his 1st Corps to play the role of brutal and ruthless troops. The special mission with which they were entrusted in Russia — the crushing of peasants and Jews — has clearly deformed them psychologically.

The worst episode took place in Pińsk, a town with a predominantly Jewish population. It was occupied by Polish troops on 17 March without any fighting. On 5 April a meeting of about 100 people took place in the local Zionist club for the distribution of charity from Jewish institutions in the United States, including *Matzos* for Passover. This meeting was authorised by the local military authorities. Nevertheless, on the orders of the military commander of the town the club was surrounded by troops, and all those present were arrested. That night, 35 people, including women and children, were executed by firing squad. The remainder were only saved as a result of the immediate intercession of representatives of the principal charity involved, the American Joint Committee, with the Polish authorities in Warsaw.[29]

Similar incidents took place after the Poles took Lublin, Lida, Wilno and a number of other towns. They aroused widespread shock and indignation in Western Europe and the United States.[30] Balfour, the British Foreign Secretary, was even provoked to write to Paderewski in June 1919 calling on the Polish authorities to take steps to protect the Jews, to which Paderewski replied that his government had 'taken all the necessary measures referred to by your Excellency to check anti-Jewish movements in Poland'. At the same time he claimed that 'the majority of racial conflicts are due to provocation both from within and without the country.'[31]

Indeed, the general reaction of Polish society was very disappointing to those who hoped that independence would lead to an improvement of Polish-Jewish relations. The anti-Semitic groups consistently denied that any organised anti-Jewish violence had occurred, or claimed, if it had, that it was the fault of the Jews themselves. Attempts to publicise what was taking place were attacked as part of a campaign to blacken the name of Poland and undermine Polish territorial claims. More alarming to the Jews was the attitude of some progressive and left-wing circles. In reply to a protest of the Swedish Social Democrats, Ignacy Daszyński, one of the most prominent members of the Polish Socialist Party (PPS), replied that the pogroms in Galicia were the work of Austrian marauders and that they were 'directed against speculation'. He did concede that unfortunately some innocent people had suffered.[32] In June 1919, he denied that any pogroms had taken place in Poland and declared: 'If somebody falls victim to street battles, in struggles as bitter as those for the possession of Lwów, Lida or Wilno, they cannot be called victims of pogroms.'[33] Yet in all these cases, most Jewish casualties occurred after the fighting was over. An even more hostile attitude towards the Jews was adopted by the principal peasant leader, Wincenty Witos.

These attitudes were not universally shared. In April 1919, the

PPS-dominated Council of Workers' Delegates in Warsaw voted unanimously to condemn the pogroms, which it claimed were being organised by reactionaries.[34] A similar motion was unanimously adopted after the Piński massacre, holding the Army responsible for what had taken place.[35] Similarly, the parliamentary faction of the PPS severely censured the Army for the excesses which had occurred after the capture of Lublin in April 1919. The wave of anti-Jewish incidents was also condemned by the former Austrian-Hungarian Minister of Finance, Leo Biliński, who was to hold high office in post-war Poland, by General Alexander Babiánski and by Professor Baudoin de Courtenay. The eminent Polish writer Andrzei Strug made a public protest against what he called the 'conspiracy of silence' in government circles and in the press concerning the anti-Semitic atrocities.[36]

The signing of the Minorities Treaty on 28 June 1919 between Poland and the Allies led to a further outbreak of anti-Jewish sentiment. The treaty was bitterly resented in Poland as an infringement of Polish sovereignty and as providing a lever for German revisionism. Again the Jews were violently attacked as its main instigators. In fact, Jewish opinion was divided on the Treaty, which was attacked as too provocative by the assimilationists and to a lesser extent by the orthodox and some Jewish economic organisations. Nevertheless, the majority of Jewish parties welcomed its conclusion and hoped that it would give them an increased measure of security.

They also hoped to use their parliamentary representation to alleviate the plight of the Jewish community. The bulk of Jewish deputies, who now numbered thirteen, were linked up with the Free Association of Deputies of Jewish Nationality which comprised the National Jewish Parliamentary Group; they, in turn, were connected with the Jewish National Committee (6 deputies), the Orthodox (2 deputies) and the *folkists* (2 deputies). The assimilationists (2 deputies) and the left Zionist, Dr Ignacy Schipper, remained outside the Association. The fact that no elections were held at this stage in the Polish eastern territories meant that the Jews, along with the seven German deputies, were the only representatives of those national minorities, which were to make up over a third of the population of the Polish state. They were thus the continual target of attacks by the Polish right, particularly when they all attempted to raise the question of anti-Jewish atrocities. Nevertheless, the posing of parliamentary questions, which were immune from press censorship, brought to light many abuses of authority and helped to improve somewhat the situation of the Jews.[37]

However, the Jewish deputies were unable to prevent the passage of a number of laws adversely affecting the position of the Jews. These included a law making Sunday a compulsory day of rest, which was adopted in December 1919.[38] This inevitably damaged the interests of the bulk of Jewish workers, artisans and shopkeepers who, being orthodox, did not work on Saturdays and were now compelled to take a further day off. The law was evaded on a massive scale and created a large amount of bribery as the police took money not to enforce it. Many Jews were also adversely affected by the law on nationality which was passed in January 1920 and which denied the right to Polish nationality to people who had not been inscribed on the register of permanent residents kept by the Russian authorities in the Congress Kingdom. This affected for the most part recent Jewish immigrants from Lithuania and Byelorussia. As non-citizens they were subject to a number of special restrictions in the difficult post-war years. In 1920, for instance, their dwellings were requisitioned and they were expelled from Warsaw and other large cities.[39]

The renewal of conflict with Soviet Russia in the second half of 1919, which culminated in the Polish attempt to dislodge the Ukraine from the Soviet state in April 1920, led to more anti-Jewish outrages. The passage through eastern Poland of the Polish forces, above all the largely National Democratic soldiers of General Haller as well as the allied troops of General Bulak-Balakhovitch and Semyon Petlyura, was accompanied by a series of anti-Jewish atrocities, pillaging and the public humiliation of orthodox Jews who had their beards cut off. The Polish offensive was initially successful and Kiev was taken on 7 May.[40] Polish lines were, however, seriously overextended and the Soviet counter-offensive brought the Red Army to the outskirts of Warsaw. It also saw the creation in Białystok of a Provisional Revolutionary Committee for Poland. This included a number of veteran Jewish communists, such as Feliks Koń and Józef Unszlicht, but the key roles were played by ethnic Poles, Julian Marchlewski, Feliks Dzierzyński and Edward Próchniak.

The threat to Warsaw and the fear of revolution led to heightened anti-Semitism and to attempts to discredit Communism as a Jewish phenomenon. An official Army poster represented Bolshevism as the Devil with obviously Jewish characteristics, sitting on a pile of skulls. In another poster, soldiers of the Red Army were shown waving a blue and white flag with the Star of David.[41] According to a letter of the Polish episcopate to the bishops of the world:

Bolshevism is truly aiming at the conquest of the world. The race which leads it previously subordinated the world to it through gold and the banks. Today, driven by the age-old imperialist drive which flows in its veins, it is undertaking the final conquest of all peoples under its yoke. All the slogans which are used: People, Workers, Freedom and so on are only masks whose aim is to hide the true goal.[42]

In this atmosphere, it is not surprising that the retreat of the Polish troops was accompanied by a series of anti-Jewish outrages. Pogroms took place in Mińsk-Mazowiecki, Siedlce, Luków, Włodawa and Białystok. Alleged spies were executed by court martial on the scantiest evidence. Thus in August 1920, Rabbi Chaim Szapiro of Płock was shot by the Army for allegedly directing the fire of the Bolsheviks on the Poles, only to be exonerated several years later by a Polish court.[43]

At the same time, the national crisis created by the war with Soviet Russia led to an attempt at establishing an improved relationship between Poles and Jews.[44] In December 1919, Paderewski fell from power and was succeeded by Leopold Skulski. Now the dominant figure in the government, Piłsudski began to think of an attack on the Soviets. He was well aware how the maltreatment of the Jews had harmed Poland in the eyes of the West. A few days before the establishment of the Skulski government Alfred Nossig, a German Jew of Polish origin with many connections in Polish official circles, arrived in Warsaw in the hope of playing the role of mediator between the Jews and the Polish government. The preliminary negotiations were difficult and took nearly three months, partly because of differences between the Jewish parties. By March, however, a Jewish Inter-party Committee had been established which agreed that its minimum negotiating position was that the Polish government should take action against pogroms and anti-Jewish agitation; it was also to demand that all administrative and cultural restrictions still in operation against the Jews be lifted and that the question of Sunday rest be settled in a manner satisfactory to the Jews.

The first meeting with Skulski on 31 March 1920 did not go particularly well, although the Prime Minister did agree to take action against anti-Semitic excesses. Contacts continued and the government, after some delay, set up a Council for Jewish Questions. The government of Władysław Grabski, which succeeded that of Skulski on 23 June 1920, was keener to reach an agreement, partly because of Poland's difficult diplomatic position and partly because Grabski, though a

National Democrat, was genuinely interested in promoting a Polish-Jewish *modus vivendi*. On 15 July, the Council for Jewish Questions met for the first time and Grabski spoke on the 'The Jewish problem and the need to find a solution for it'. He also appealed to the various Polish groups to moderate their demagogy and issued orders to the Army and civil authorities aimed at preventing anti-Jewish excesses. At the next two meetings of the Council, Grabski promised to use his influence to curb anti-Semitic outbursts in the press and proposed giving the Council a permanent status attached to the Cabinet.

The grave national crisis caused by the threat to Warsaw led to the fall of Grabski and the establishment, in July 1920, of an all-party government headed by Wincenty Witos, a man not known for his friendly sentiments towards the Jews. The Council met again on 27 July, but the political will to effect change was no longer there. A Jewish delegation was received by the new Minister for Military Affairs, Piłsudski's close confidant General Kazimierz Sosnkowski. He assured them that he had given orders to the Army to stop anti-Jewish excesses, but that he doubted their efficacy since ninety per cent of the officers and men had been brought up in a spirit of 'savage hostility' to the Jews. He further declared that he was 'powerless' in relation to General Haller's troops.[45]

The failure of these talks caused bitter disillusionment in Jewish political circles. Indeed, the period after the relief of Warsaw was not followed by any real improvement in Polish-Jewish relations. At the height of the crisis, a number of volunteer militias had been set up. Jews were encouraged to enlist by the Jewish parliamentary faction and a United Jewish Organisation Committee for National Defence was set up. Several thousand Jews volunteered, but they soon encountered the hostility of the anti-Semitic General Haller, who was named Commander of the volunteer army. Jewish volunteers were kept separate from their divisions and concentrated in special barracks under guard. Some were even sent to penal battalions. After the battle of Warsaw, on the confidential orders of General Sosnkowski, Jewish officers and soldiers were arrested and placed in a concentration camp at Jabłonna near Warsaw, where they were guarded by notoriously anti-Semitic troops from Western Poland.[46]

The final Polish offensive was accompanied by anti-Jewish excesses and the forced evacuation of Jews from the front in the Warsaw region. The non-Polish troops of Petlyura and Bulak-Balakhovitch were particularly brutal. Where some Jews had participated in the organisations set up by the Polish Revolutionary Committee, Jews were held collectively responsible.

Once the worst danger was over, tension did ease somewhat. *Robotnik* published an article attacking the government for interning Jews in Jabłonna and a letter of protest against the government's action was also signed by intellectuals and politicians, including the writers Andrzej Strug and Stefan Zeromski, Professor Baudoin de Courtenay and several leading members of the PPS.[47] On 9 September, the camp at Jabłonna was finally wound up and the soldiers and officers interned there sent back to their regiments. The second convoy from the camp fell victim to a mysterious railway accident near Lublin, as a result of which, according to official figures, about twenty people were killed and scores injured.[48] Jewish sources have claimed that the casualties were even higher.

On 12 October 1920, the preliminaries of peace were signed between Soviet Russia and Poland. The struggle to establish the frontiers of Poland was effectively over (although the future of Upper Silesia had still to be decided) and a measure of peace returned. How far this would lead to an improvement of the position of the Jews would be revealed in the following years. Certainly the events of 1918-20 cast a heavy shadow over Polish-Jewish relations and impeded the establishment of a satisfactory *modus vivendi* with the Jewish community which now numbered over 3 million people, or 10 per cent of the total population.

Although profoundly affected by the course of the First World War, the Jewish Question in the lands which in 1918 became the Czechoslovak state had a history very much of its own. In its modern form, at least in the Bohemian Crownlands (Bohemia, Moravia and Austrian Silesia), it can be traced back to the Revolution of 1848, when the era of *Landespatriotismus* came to an end and national and socio-economic strife began. The strong trend towards Germanisation amongst the Jews and their intermediary role in the nascent capitalist economy of the Habsburg domains, as entrepreneurs, wholesalers, traders, inn-keepers, money-lenders and pedlars, meant that they soon found themselves in the midst of the ensuing struggle between the Czechs and the Germans.

Their dilemma became more poignant in the 1880s with the political and economic emergence of the Czechs and the rise of German as well as Czech anti-Semitism. Even though they may have registered their 'language of daily use' (*Umgangssprache*) as Czech with the census-taker and voted for Czech candidates at election time, the Jews of Bohemia, Moravia and Silesia continued to opt for German culture. Any reversal of the process was made virtually impossible by the intensification of Czech anti-Semitism in the 1890s. German anti-Semitism, on the other hand, because most Jews lived in Czech- rather than German-speaking areas, tended to affect Jewish sentiments only indirectly. For the most part, it did not prevent them from reading German newspapers and books or sending their children to German schools and universities. Put simply, the majority of Jews in the Bohemian Crownlands took their German cultural assimilation (acculturation), even if they spoke fluent Czech, for granted and welcomed the positive advantages it brought them in terms of career opportunities and wider cultural horizons. They could, what is more, continue to exist as culturally assimilated Germans without identifying themselves with German nationalism, whereas to become Czech would not simply have entailed the adoption of the Czech language, but also a whole-hearted commitment to the aims and ideals of the Czech national movement. This would have been a daunting task, even in the best of circumstances.[49]

Even though by 1918 the situation in Slovakia bore some similarity to the one outlined above, it remained significantly different at least until the advent of war. For one thing, under Hungarian rule Slovakia remained both politically and economically underdeveloped. The vast majority of the population continued to be engaged in agriculture under semi-feudal conditions and, thanks to the limited system of suffrage, without the right to vote. A nationally aware Slovak middle class, as such, hardly existed. Consequently, the cultural nationalism of the Slovaks continued to have little scope to develop a political dimension.[50]

While the Hungarian government's liberal policy of Magyarisation ostensibly provided an impetus for Jewish assimilation, the general economic backwardness of the region and the size and compactness of the Jewish community, especially in the north-east, meant that its potential was never fully realised. The life-style of the handful of Magyarised Jewish families who played such a dominant role in the little industrial development that took place in Slovakia remained in stark contrast to that of the majority of their co-religionists. They lived in the villages and the small towns as inn-keepers, petty traders, middle-men and pedlars, steeped in a milieu of religious orthodoxy and tradition. Even so, in the 1910 census over half, or 76,553, of the Jews in Slovakia entered their nationality as Magyar on the basis of mother tongue. Only 4,956 registered themselves as Czech or Slovak, while 58,300 indicated their nationality as German, of whom a high percentage were presumably Yiddish-speakers.[51]

In this situation, it was hardly surprising that for economic, and to a lesser extent for national and religious, reasons popular resentment against the Jews was widespread. Yet, because of the generally under-developed state of Slovak political life, political anti-Semitism as such was ironically slow to gain a foothold.[52] The position of the Jews in Sub-Carpathian Ruthenia, who were to constitute the greatest concentration of Jewish population in the Czechoslovak state (15.4 per cent of the total inhabitants of the province), was in some ways similar to that in north-eastern Slovakia.[53]

While there is no reason to suppose that anti-Jewish feeling on religious and economic grounds did not exist, until the period of Czechoslovak independence it was devoid of a political dimension. The Jewish Question in Sub-Carpathian Ruthenia only started to develop in the 1920s and was as much concerned with the Jews' own adaptation to changing economic circumstances as the problems of anti-Semitism and assimilation.[54] In that sense, the situation was not altogether dissimilar to that in Poland.

The outbreak of war in August 1914 was to influence greatly the development of the Jewish Question throughout Central and Eastern Europe, including what was to become independent Czechoslovakia. In the Bohemian Crownlands the Jews soon found themselves caught up in a wave of patriotic fervour. With few exceptions, the Czechs, while they may have welcomed the war as a probable vehicle for political change, were reluctant to support the Dual Monarchy.[55] Amongst the less assimilated Jews of north-eastern Slovakia the outbreak of war was no doubt viewed in very equivocal terms. Being on the whole strictly observant Jews, they found service in the Imperial Army an anathema; moreover, they lived in close proximity to the fighting. The attitudes of Magyarised Jews, it can be presumed, did not differ substantially from those of their co-religionists in Bohemia, Moravia and Austrian Silesia.

Given the circumstances, it was not surprising that anti-Jewish feeling was again aroused amongst the Czechs. A general feeling existed that in their commitment to the Austro-German cause the Jews were being 'more Popish than the Pope', so much so that Jews were often quite unjustly accused of denouncing Czechs to the authorities for unpatriotic remarks and defeatism.[56] What no doubt irked the Czechs even more than the support given to the war effort by the Jewish neighbours was the breast-beating patriotism generally exhibited by the Jewish-owned press in Austria and Germany. The 'Presse-Juden' were again seen to be at their evil ways.

Even Czech activists who had in the past done their best to combat the rise of anti-Semitism could not restrain their resentment at the strength of Jewish support for the Austrian cause. No less a man than the future President of Czechoslovakia, Thomas Garigue Masaryk, whose outspoken refutation of the blood libel at the time of the Hilsner ritual murder trial some fifteen years earlier had won him the admiration of Jews around the world, expressed such feelings.[57] According to the Prague German writer and Zionist activist Max Brod, when he and Franz Werfel approached Masaryk to gain his support for moves to found an international peace movement, they were rebuffed on the grounds that their time would be better spent restraining the patriotic zeal of their co-religionists. Unfortunately for them, according to Brod, the Czech leader had during their conversation been given the news of yet another Czech patriot being supposedly denounced by a Jew.[58] We also know from R.W. Seton-Watson that Masaryk was so concerned about the attitude of the Jews of Prague that in October 1914 he took up the matter during secret discussions with the Statthalter of Bohemia, Prince Thun. He implored him to 'hold back the Jews and render them less aggressive ['herausfordend'], otherwise there might be a pogrom, which would only be the beginning, and would be infinitely regrettable'.[59]

One of Masaryk's closest collaborators, Jan Herben, the editor of the daily *Čas*, must have had similar thoughts as he witnessed a patriotic procession of Jews pass his office window during the summer of 1914. He wrote in his memoirs, 'I could not breathe as I saw this most warlike of Austrian tribes.'[60]

It was, however, not as if all Jews of Bohemia and Moravia were unanimous in their attitude to the war. In addition to the large number who must have become hostile to it after the prospect of a quick and decisive victory diminished, there were those who were decidedly in the Czech camp. After all, a small but vocal minority of the Jews of the Bohemian Crownlands, even in the face of the mounting Czech anti-Semitism of the 1890s, remained committed to the ideal of Czech-Jewish assimilation.

They continued to hope that if only the Jews would withdraw their support for the German element in Bohemia and Moravia, they would win acceptance amongst the Czechs.[61] Even after the outbreak of war their support for the Czech cause remained unrelenting.

As the war dragged on and the shortages of food, coal and consumer goods became more severe, animosity against Jews in the lands that were to constitute the First Czechoslovak Republic took on an added dimension. As in times past, the words Jew and profiteer became synonymous. Even though there is no reason to suppose that the Czech, Slovak or Ruthenian peasant took any less advantage of the situation than the Jewish trader, it was the Jew who was singled out in the later war years and immediate post-war period as a universal hate figure. Yet, during the war itself, although there were strikes and demonstrations, anti-Jewish unrest did not take place.[62]

Jews, none the less, looked to the future with considerable apprehension. They feared, most of all, the removal of the protective umbrella of Habsburg rule, which in the past had generally shielded them from the worst excesses of anti-Jewish feeling. Jews were, however, not only apprehensive about Slav nationalism and anti-Semitism. From 1916 onwards, with stalemate at the front and increasing hardship at home, German anti-Semitism was again on the upsurge in both Austria and the Reich. Jewish industrialists and financiers as well as petty traders were believed to prosper while 'good' Germans gave their lives at the front and suffered privation at home. Matters were exacerbated by the influx of considerable numbers of Jewish refugees from Galicia (the East), some of whom managed very quickly to establish themselves as successful traders and businessmen. Their exotic appearance and religious orthodoxy inevitably made them a favourite target of Jew-baiting everywhere.[63]

Despite the general air of worry and pessimism, Zionism had not yet emerged as a viable alternative for the majority of Bohemian, Moravian, Slovak and Ruthenian Jews any more than it had elsewhere in Central or East Central Europe. From their midst emerged the nucleus of the Jewish National Council (of Czechoslovakia) founded on 22 October 1918, four days before the Czechoslovak Republic officially came into being,[64] with the self-declared aim of representing the interest of the Jews with the authorities of the new state.[65]

Of perhaps greater significance for the development of the Jewish Question in Czechoslovakia was the 'conversion' of Masaryk to the Zionist position. Although he had already expressed pro-Zionist sympathies as early as 1909,[66] incidentally much to the consternation of the Czech-Jewish Movement who looked to his brand of humanist nationalism holding sway in the Czech camp,[67] it was only after he went into exile in 1915 to work for Czechoslovak independence from abroad that he became a wholehearted supporter of the Zionist cause. Of crucial importance in this regard was the support Masaryk won for the Czechoslovak independence movement in Zionist circles.

It was in the United States, however, where he had already enjoyed the sympathy of the influential and well-to-do Jewish community of

New York for his courageous stand in the Hilsner affair that he met with the greatest success. Masaryk himself was the first to admit the importance of Jewish support in furthering the Czech cause. In his memoir of the Czechoslovak movement for independence from abroad, *Světová revoluce* (*The Making of a State*), he wrote:

> Like everywhere else, the Jews in America supported me. And particularly in America the Hilsner case rewarded me. This time I came together personally with many representatives, both of the orthodox as well as of the Zionist view. Among the Zionists I mention Mr. Brandeis, a member of the Supreme Court and of Bohemian extraction: he was a good friend of President Wilson's and enjoyed his confidence. . . In America the Jews are treated fairly in the press; it was very fortunate for us that this power was not against us.[68]

Masaryk went even further in emphasising the good reputation he enjoyed amongst world Jewry, perhaps to the point of exaggeration. When in conversation with the Czech writer Karel Čapek he noted:

> During the war I saw how useful the Hilsner affair had been to me: the Press of the world is largely managed or financed by Jews [*sic*!] they knew me from the Hilsner case, and repaid me for what I had done for them then by writing favourably about our case – or at least not unfavourably. That helped us a great deal politically.[69]

Masaryk's overestimation of Jewish influence notwithstanding, the support given to the Czechs in Jewish circles, especially in the USA, was of significance, particularly if we bear in mind the difficulties experienced by Masaryk and his colleagues in gaining Allied acceptance for the aim of Czechoslovak independence. What ultimately brought recognition by the Entente powers of the movement for Czechoslovak independence, however, was the decision on the part of the powers themselves to use the Czechoslovak Legions in Russia in the Allied military intervention against the Soviets.[70]

Still, this did not mean that the Czechoslovak National Council, as the representative body of the movement for national independence was called, and later the Czechoslovak government were not sensitive about the effect which their handling of the Jewish Question might have. The rise of anti-Semitism in Central and Eastern Europe generally, and actual anti-Jewish violence on a large scale in Poland, the Ukraine and Romania as well as Zionist claims to a Jewish National Home in Palestine had made Western public and governmental opinion attune to the fate of the Jews. It was not without significance, for example, that Masaryk's reply to the American Zionists, on receiving their congratulations on the occasion of the founding of the Czechoslovak Republic, should have virtually taken on the character of an 'act of State':

> In the name of the National Council and, as I am empowered to say, in the name of our entire people, I thank you most heartily. . . There remains only one just arrangement for us, and that is to guarantee the minorities the same rights in everyday life and in our schools. . . Naturally the same program applies to the Jewish minority. Jews will enjoy the same equal rights as the other citizens of our country.[71]

Masaryk even went so far as to proclaim his attitude towards Zionism:

> In regard to the Zionist movement, I can only express my sympathy for it and the nationalist movement of the Jewish people, in general because it is of great moral value. . . I know that it is not a movement of political chauvinism, but represents the moral rebirth of their people.

In the meantime, at home the authorities were in the process of establishing control over the republic they had proclaimed. The birth of the Czechoslovak Republic on 28 October 1918 was not accompanied by anti-Jewish or for that matter anti-German unrest in Prague.[72] Power passed relatively smoothly into the hands of the National Committee[73] which was intent on preventing a breakdown of law and order, lest it be exploited by the far left. It was no doubt mindful too of the damage that such unrest could have on the new-born Republic's image abroad. Once the Imperial Garrison, consisting mainly of troops of Hungarian and Romanian origin, was withdrawn, patrols of volunteers from the Czech sports and gymnastic association, the Sokol (roughly equivalent to the German Turnverein), as well as students, workers and firemen were organised by the National Committee to maintain public order.[74] As a result, the people of Prague greeted independence with jubilation and little else than the removal of the Imperial Eagle and German inscriptions from official buildings, road signs, uniforms, shopfronts and German cultural installations. Elsewhere in the Bohemian Crownlands the situation remained similarly calm.

In Slovakia, however, the situation was different. Although the new liberal-democratic Hungarian government under Count Michael Karolyi demonstrated itself to be just as unwilling to relinquish non-Magyar territory as the royal government it succeeded on 1, November, not until the Armistice of Belgrade (13 November) did it actively try to assert its control over Slovakia. On 4 November the Prague National Committee sent a small detachment of gendarmes and a four-man 'government' under Vavro Šrobár to proclaim the Czechoslovak Republic, but their efforts proved to little avail. In parts of Slovakia Hungarian authority collapsed and a wave of unrest swept through the region. Soldiers, often armed, struggled home from the fronts; angry peasants attacked the country mansions of the landowners, Hungarian officials, priests and Jews, the symbols and perpetrators in the popular mind of Magyar exploitation and oppression.[75]

The situation remained confused for quite some time, especially since there was no boundary as such between Slovakia and Hungary. Slovak politicians acted at variance with Czechoslovak government policy; one of them even proclaimed a separate 'East Slovak Republic'. Given these conditions, many Jews not surprisingly longed for a return of Magyar rule. Only with the occupation of Slovakia by Czechoslovak troops (mostly Legionnaires newly returned from the Italian front) at the end of December 1918 and the beginning of January 1919 did calm finally return to the region.[76] It was, as we shall see, not to last for very long.

Bearing in mind that events in Poland, the Ukraine and Romania had made Western public and governmental opinion sensitive to the Jewish predicament in Central and Eastern Europe, it is curious that the events in Slovakia did not come to the attention of the world's press, or in any formal way to the Entente governments.[77] More curious still is the lack of attention received both inside and outside Czechoslovakia, when anti-Jewish unrest, beginning with attacks in Prague of an anti-German character on 1 and 2 of December 1918, actually did occur in the Bohemian Crownlands.[78] It seems strange, for example, that not even *The Jewish Chronicle*, the leading Anglo-Jewish weekly, reported the pogrom of 3/4 December at Holešov in Moravia during which two Jews lost their lives and virtually the entire Jewish quarter of the town was gutted.[79]

Strictly speaking, however, it was not as if a complete curtain of silence, from whatever quarter, was hung over the affair. Reports of the excesses eventually appeared in two of the German-language dailies in Prague, *Bohemia* and the *Prager Tagblatt*,[80] as well as the Zionist weekly published in Prague, *Selbstwehr*.[81] It is, nevertheless, significant that on the day the unrest started in Prague (1 December) the Police Commissioner (the Polizei-Direktion), using the appropriate Austrian legislation still in force, ordered the suspension of publication of both *Bohemia* and the *Prager Tagblatt* for eight days. *Bohemia*, according to the police decree, was about to publish material bound to affect adversely the relations between Czechs and Germans, which was deemed contrary to the interests of the Czechoslovak state. In particular, the authorities objected to a leading article on the unrest included in the issue about to be printed.[82]

Although the suspension was lifted by the Czechoslovak government after two days, the affair became a minor *cause célèbre* with a spate of mutually recriminatory articles appearing in the Czech and German dailies of Prague over the next week or so.[83] They reveal that, if it did not take an active part in initiating the suspension, the Jewish National Council tacitly approved of it.[84] This may belie the Committee's policy of regarding too much publicity about anti-Jewish unrest as deleterious to its efforts to establish good relations with the new Czechoslovak government. Equally, the Committee may have feared that reporting the unrest in the German press of Prague would only incite further attacks in the city itself or lead to its spreading to other parts of the new Republic. As far as the Jewish National Committee was concerned, the excesses could not have come at a more inopportune time. In anticipation of Masaryk's return to Czechoslovakia and the coming peace negotiations, it was anxious not to undermine its chances of winning official recognition of the Jews' status as a National Minority. They also hoped to gain governmental support for the Zionist programme generally. The new Czechoslovak government, for its part, was presumably anxious to avoid bad publicity about the treatment of Jews so as not to tarnish its image with the Entente powers (as was happening with Poland). The authorities were, moreover, worried about anti-Jewish violence, fearing that any outbreak of civil disorder could potentially be exploited by the extreme left and the Bolsheviks.

As early as November 1918 Czech leaders were calling for the exercise of calm and restraint *vis-à-vis* the Jews. In mid-November, for instance, the newly appointed Czechoslovak Minister of National Defence, Vaclav Klofáč, who had held openly anti-Semitic views as an aspiring National Socialist politician,[85] at a meeting of supporters of his own National Democratic Party in Prague counselled his fellow countrymen to maintain good relations with the Jews, 'as the latter were on terms of sincere friendship with the Allied Powers and President Wilson'.[86] The new Prime Minister, Karel Kramář, whose attitude towards the Jews had likewise been far from friendly, in referring to the pogroms that had taken place declared that without wanting to take up a philosemitic position, he regarded every Jew who was loyal to the new state in the same way as any other member of the nation: 'We must absolve the test whether we are a nation of culture ['eine Kulturnation'] . It would not be clever politics on our part to seek revenge against those who were against us.'[87] President Masaryk, on the other hand, acceded to his advisers and removed from the speech to the nation he gave on his return from exile (20 December) the passage in which he warned against anti-Semitism.[88]

This was but one indication that the Jewish Question was still very much a sensitive issue in Czechoslovak political life. Many Czechs could simply not forgive the support given by Jews to the Austro-Hungarian war effort; nor could they easily relinquish the resentments they traditionally harboured against Jews. Soon anti-Jewish articles again appeared in *Venkov*, the organ of the Agrarian Party, and *Národni listy*, the daily of the National Democrats. Indicative of the changing mood in Prague was an article by the writer Jaroslav Hilbert which appeared in *Venkov* on 4 December. As in the 1890s, it was the German Jews of Prague who were held responsible for provoking popular unrest: 'Prague German Jewry is for us an incorrigibly hostile element. It lacks, however, the valour and moral courage to engage us in direct, knightly combat.'[89] Earlier in the article, he blamed the Jews of Prague as well for the influx of Jewish refugees from Galicia, whom he referred to as 'the darkest, most materialistic and dirtiest race on which the sun ever shone'.

Nevertheless, for the time being the Jewish National Council seemed satisfied with the policy of the Czechoslovak government towards the Jews. At a meeting with the newly arrived British representative to Prague, Cecil Gosling, on 19 January 1919, a delegation of the Jewish National Council merely expressed its regret for not being represented in the Cabinet, as in the Ukraine (*sic*!), by a Minister for Jewish Affairs.[90] Although the subject of pogrom-like excesses and popular hostility towards the Jews was raised at the meeting, the matter came in for more detailed discussion some days later; significantly, it was in the context of a statement on Jewish national aspirations. The 'only effective measure' of countering anti-Semitism, the representatives of the Jewish National Council argued, would be the recognition of the national rights of the Jews of Czechoslovakia and their direct representation in the National Assembly. Only in this way, they believed, could one hope to correct the 'erroneous impressions' amongst the

Czechs of Jewish support for the German cause.[91] While maintaining that the majority of Czechoslovak Jews were, if not Zionists, 'National Jews',[92] the Jewish National Council did not want to force anyone to declare himself a Jew. Rather it desired that all those professing Jewish nationality be recognised as a nation under Czechoslovak law.[93]

The Jewish National Committee, as indeed the Czechoslovak government, put a good deal of faith in having its aims realised at the Paris Peace Conference. Even before the war ended, the government of the United States, acting on the initiative of the Zionist Organization of America, had announced its support for the conclusion of 'minorities' treaties with the successor states of Eastern Europe. And the Balfour Declaration of November 1917 gave every indication that the British government was sympathetic to the general aims of Zionism. What is more, on the basis of statements by Masaryk and others, the Committee had every hope of winning the acceptance of its programme by the Czechoslovak government.

It therefore came as a great disappointment to the representatives of the Committee at the Conference when the Allies accepted the proposal of the head of the Czechoslovak delegation, Foreign Minister Beneš, that the specifically 'Jewish clauses' of the Polish 'Model Treaty' would be removed from the version to be signed by his country.[94] Neither the Jewish delegates themselves nor the intervention of Nahum Sokolov or the Anglo-Jewish leader Lucien Wolf managed to bring about a reversal of this decision. Not even the threat to mobilise Jewish opinion in the United States in favour of the inclusion of the clauses had any effect, and a last-minute attempt to secure an intervention by Masaryk also failed to materialise.[95]

Beneš remained steadfast in his position that for Czechoslovakia to accept specific provisions for the protection of Jewish rights would put her on a par with Poland and Romania, and this her treatment of the Jews did not warrant. It would, moreover, imply both a general lack of faith in the ability of the Czechoslovak authorities 'to respect certain human rights which are regarded as a matter of course' and a support for Zionism against assimilationism, which the Czechoslovak delegation did not feel it was in a position to do.[96] Equally, Beneš was concerned lest a concession to the Jews would lead to similar demands for specific rights from the national minorities in the Czechoslovak state.[97]

The Allies accepted Beneš' proposals, first of all because they agreed with him that it would not be feasible to turn Czechoslovakia into a Central European Switzerland, with each national group guaranteed some form of political, territorial and cultural autonomy.[98] They moreover sincerely believed that Czechoslovakia, as far as the Jewish Problem was concerned, represented a very different case from Romania, or especially Poland. If the British reports on the subject are an indication, they were in any case convinced that anti-Semitic unrest had not taken place in Czechoslovakia on anywhere near the scale on which it had occurred in Poland or elsewhere and that the Czechoslovak government's policy towards the Jews was above reproach.[99]

While this assessment of the situation was essentially accurate, it did not tell the whole story. Czechoslovakia continued to be plagued by anti-Jewish agitation and excesses until after the peace treaties had been signed, even if they were quite minor by Polish or Ukrainian standards. During the Peace Conference itself there was trouble. On 23 and 24 May 1919 demonstrations in Prague against profiteering and high prices led to the looting of shops in the city centre and the industrial suburbs. Although mostly Jewish-owned businesses were affected, non-Jewish firms, as in the disturbances during December 1918, also came under attack.[100] In order to prevent further violence, shops in Prague organised impromptu sales and with the aid of Legionnaire guards proceeded to sell all their goods at rock-bottom prices.[101] Characteristically, the dailies *Venkov* and *Národní listy* reported the demonstrations so as to deflect popular animosity away from Czech farmers, against whom there was widespread resentment, towards the Jews.[102]

In Slovakia anti-Jewish feeling again flared up with the invasion by the troops of Bela Kun's Hungarian Soviet Republic (1 May-23 June 1919). Slovak patriots accused the Jews of constituting a fifth column, blaming them in particular for the ease with which the Hungarians managed to gain control of Eastern Slovakia and penetrate deep into the central part of the province.[103] Fearful of what might happen, Dr Chaim Weizman, acting on behalf of the Zionist Organization in London, wrote to the Czechoslovak Minister Plenipotentiary on 8 July 1919 to express his concern and remind the Czechoslovak government of the probable negative effect on Western opinion if the authorities failed to keep the situation under control.[104] A reply from the Minister for Slovakia, Šrobár, (dated 14 September 1919) was sent by the Czechoslovak Legation on 3 October, some three weeks after the peace treaties had been signed. Framed in the frankest of terms, it rejected out of hand any allegation that the Czechoslovak government in Slovakia had been remiss in its responsibilities. It had, on the contrary, he maintained, gone out of its way to do just the opposite and explicitly pointed the finger of blame at the Jews themselves.[105] One is inevitably led to wonder whether Šrobár would not have couched his allegations in more careful language or omitted them altogether, had he replied to Dr Weizman before rather than after the treaties had been signed.

Despite the efforts of the Czechoslovak government to the contrary, the atmosphere in the country and for that matter in the region as a whole remained unsettled. The broadly based coalition government formed under Masaryk's aegis which took office on 15 September 1920 faced a myriad of problems, including political extremism from both the left and right. There was the need for economic recovery and reorientation. While it showed itself adept at dealing with the Slovak nationalists as represented by the Catholic People's Party under Hlinka, it was not as successful with either the German or the Czech right. With the return from exile of the German nationalist leader Rudolf Lodgman, tension between his supporters and the right-wing National Democrats, headed by Kramář, increased. In November, incidents between the German population and the Czech military took place in the towns of Cheb (Eger) and Aš (Asch) and, as could be expected, each side accused the other of provoking it.[106]

The situation took a radical turn for the worse with the spread of the unrest to Prague on 16 November after news reached the city of the forced closure of the Czech school in Cheb.[107] The ensuing disturbances soon took on a strong anti-Jewish aspect. Over the next three days rampaging mobs attacked individual Germans and Jews as well as their property. The German Theatre was occupied by members of the Czech National Theatre and the Jewish Town Hall in the old ghetto was ransacked.[108] If we are to believe a report in the Viennese *Neue Freie Presse*, the rioting was so intense that the American Consul in Prague was motivated to allow the American flag to be flown from the Jewish Town Hall in order to protect the Galician refugees being housed there temporarily.[109] Anti-German disturbances took place as well in the Moravian towns of Brno and Prostějov, although it is not clear whether in those instances Jews or Jewish property came to grief.[110]

Even though the disturbances of November 1920 were the last instance of anti-Jewish violence in the First Czechoslovak Republic, anti-Semitism remained a strong political and social undercurrent until the country's demise in 1938/9. Up to the 1930s it erupted, as it were, in the right-wing nationalist press and in Czech and Slovak literature as well as in the form of the occasional anti-Jewish remark, whether it was at the local pub or the National Assembly. It was an anti-Semitism which the Czechoslovak Zionist leader Felix Weltsch quite rightly termed 'tolerable' ('erträglich').[111] It appeared especially so when compared to conditions in the rest of Central and Eastern Europe. The

Jews of Czechoslovakia, for the most part, had neither to suffer a barrage of anti-Semitic propaganda and abuse, as in Germany and Austria, nor face the danger of physical attack, as in Poland or Romania.

Clearly, the Czechoslovak case was different from that of Poland. This was as much the result of demographic and economic factors as of the political experiences of each nation before independence. Czechoslovakia was, in a sense, blessed on all accounts. The size of its Jewish population was not a problem in itself; its economy was at least partially industrialised and its leadership as well as a large proportion of its people were, to a degree, politically experienced. Czechoslovakia was, moreover, fortunate in having political leaders, most notably President Masaryk, who realised the negative consequences, both at home and abroad, of failing to combat, let alone condemn, anti-Semitism.

Certainly the Jewish problem remained acute in Poland throughout the inter-war period, in spite of a number of attempts to improve Polish-Jewish relations, most notably during the non-parliamentary government of Władysław Grabski (1923-5) and in the first years after the *coup* which brought Piłsudski back to power in May 1926. Indeed, from 1935 onwards, anti-Semitism became a central feature of the political platform of the government, seriously weakened as it was by Piłsudski's death. It was seen both as a means for winning over younger adherents of the nationalist right and as a method for resolving Poland's increasingly acute social problems. The majority of the Polish political elite, brought up in conditions of national oppression in Russia and Germany, never understood the importance of those symbolic gestures and practical steps which could have done much to reconcile all the national minorities, and not only the Jews, to the new state. Not without some justification did Beneš refer to Poland as a 'northern Balkans',[112] a phrase which aroused tremendous resentment amongst Poles.

Although in Czechoslovakia a *modus vivendi* in the relations between Jews and non-Jews had been found, a basic change in the pattern of the Jewish predicament did not occur. While the proportion of Jewish children attending Czech primary schools increased considerably, in 1928 there were still far more Jews enrolled in German secondary schools and institutions of higher learning, in spite of the fact that in the censuses of 1921 and 1930 over 46 per cent of the Jews in Bohemia, for example, registered themselves as being of Czech nationality.[113] In Slovakia, where in 1930 over half the Jews professed themselves to be of Jewish nationality, the situation was more complicated. It can, nevertheless, be presumed that a high proportion of the Jewish population there continued to show a preference for Magyar as opposed to Slovak acculturation. Even if large numbers of Jewish children attended Slovak schools, the first language of Slovak Jewry remained Hungarian.[114] To a certain extent, the same was true of the Jews of Sub-Carpathian Ruthenia, except that the majority of families continued to speak Yiddish in the home and amongst other Jews.[115]

Assimilation was undermined in Poland by the weakening of those Polish groups which had previously supported it (most importantly, the Krakow conservatives), growing anti-Semitism and the radicalisation of the Jewish masses. Yet, paradoxically, the inter-war years were also to be accompanied by an intense process of acculturation (the adoption of the Polish language and the weakening of the more extreme forms of Jewish orthodoxy) which could have paved the way in more propitious times for a degree of harmonious coexistence between Poles and Jews.

Another striking feature common to both Poland and Czechoslovakia was the increasingly obvious political bankruptcy of the Jewish assimilationist groups and the domination, if only for a brief period, of Jewish political life by the Zionists. Demands for the recognition of the Jews as a distinct national group were the result of many factors – the Balfour Declaration, the intensification of harassment and anti-Semitism, the development of Jewish cultural life, particularly in Yiddish and in Hebrew, and the impact of the emergence of other national groups, such as the Slovaks and Ruthenes, who had previously seemed doomed to national extinction. They meant that the easy assumptions centred around the belief in emancipation as the panacea in the Jewish Question could no longer be upheld.

Notes

1. For figures on the Jewish population of the Congress Kingdom, see B. Wasiutynski, *Ludność żydowska w Polsce w wiekach XIX i XX* (Warsaw, 1930), pp. 8-9; A. Eisenbach, *Kwestia równouprawnienia Żydów w Królestwie Polskim* (Warsaw, 1972), p. 69; M. Rosenfeld, *Polen und Juden* (Berlin, Vienna, 1917), p. 26. According to the census of 1909, Jews constituted 21.7 per cent of the population of Warsaw and Lodz. In 22 towns in the Congress Kingdom, the Jews made up 50 per cent of the population, in 33 60 per cent, in 21 70 per cent, in 12 80 per cent and in 5 90 per cent.
2. These views were set out in *Myśli nowoczesnego Polaka* (1904), *Niemcy, Rosja i kwestia polska* (1908) and *Upadek myśli konserwatywnej W Polsce* (1914).
3. *Biblioteka Warszawska* (1912), vol. III, p. 391.
4. J. Baudoin de Courtenay, *W kwestii zydowskiej* (Warsaw, 1913), p. 58.
5. This exchange is quoted in L. Schipper, A. Tartakower and A. Hafftka (eds.), *Żydzi w Polsce Odrodzonej* (Warsaw, 1933), vol. 1, pp. 486-7.

6. On these developments see *Die Juden im Kriege*. *Denkschrift des Jüdischen Sozialistischen Arbeiterverbandes Poale-Zion an das Internationale Sozialistische Bureau* (n.p., 1915).

7. See W. Konic, 'Żydzi w legionach (1914-1917)' in Schipper *et al.* (eds.), *Żydzi w Polsce Odrodzonej*.

8. On this see N. Goldmann, *Staatsmann ohne Staat. Autobiographie* (Köln-Berlin, 1970), pp. 77-9.

9. For details on the effect of German exactions, see the anonymous memorandum 'Zur Lage der Jüdischen Bevölkerung in Polen und Litauen. Generalgouvernement Warschau und Ober-Ost. Vertraulicher Bericht vom Juli 1917', which was prepared for the use of the parliamentary faction of the German Social Democrats, cited in P. Korzec, 'Problem żydowski w życiu politycznym Polski 1900-1939' (unpublished), pp. 52-5.

10. *Opinia Żydowska*, 11 Aug. 1915, quoted in Schipper *et al.* (eds.), *Żydzi w Polsce Odrodzonej*, p. 492.

11. Ibid., p. 497.

12. On these contacts, see D. Mowsowicz, 'Poylish-yidishe ferhandlungen in oysland in der ershter velt-milkhome', *Ivo Bleter*, vol. XVI (1940).

13. Ibid., pp. 123-4.

14. W. Stankiewicz and A. Piber (eds.), *Archiwum Polityczne Ignacego Paderewskiego* (Ossolineum, 1973), vol. I, pp. 334-9.

15. For Brandeis' letter to Paderewski, ibid., pp. 487-8.

16. For these meetings, see ibid., pp. 500-2, 506-8, 516; R. Dmowski, *Polityka polska i odbudowanie panstwa* (Warsaw, 1925), pp 396-7; D. Mowsowicz, loc. cit., p. 118; J. Tenenbaum, *La question juive en Pologne* (Paris, 1919), pp. 40-3.

17. Dmowski, *Polityka polska*, p. 397.

18. Stankiewcz and Piber (eds.), *Archiwum*, vol. I, p. 501.

19. Dmowski, *Polityka polska*, p. 397.

20. On this see *Comité des Délégations Juives auprès de la conférence de la Pais: Les droits nationaux des Juifs en Europe orientale. Recueil d'études* (Paris, 1919); N. Feinberg, *La question des minorités à la Conférence de Paix de 1919-1920 et l'action juive en faveur de la protection internationale des minorités* (Paris, 1919); E. Viefhans, *Die Minderheitenfrage und die Entstehung der Minderheitenschutzverträge auf der Pariser Friedenskonferenz 1919* (Würzburg, 1960); P. Korzec, 'Polen und der Minderheitenschutzvertrag (1919-34)', *Jahrbücher für Geschichte Osteuropas*, vol. 22, no. 4 (1975), pp. 515-55.

21. J. Piłsudski, *Pisma zbiorowe* (Warsaw, 1937), vol. VI, p. 28.

22. On this meeting, see L. Halpern, 'Polityka żydowska w sejmie i senacie Rzeczy-pospolitej polskiej 1919-1933', *Sprawy narodowościowe*, vol. I, no. 1 (1933), pp. 29-71.

23. For this conference, see Korzec, 'Problem', p. 126.

24. On this conference, see Halpern, 'Polityka żydowska', pp. 31-2; I. Grynbaum, *Polityka żydowska w ostatnich dziesięcioleciach* (Warsaw, 1930), pp. 14-15.

25. These have given rise to a considerable literature. There is space here only to cite the most important items: *Sir Stuart Samuel, Report on His Mission to Poland* (London, n.d.); Reports by Senator Henry Morgenthau, Professor Homer Jackson and General Jadwin, reprinted in *The Jews in Poland* (Chicago, 1920); I. Cohen, 'My Mission to Poland 1918-19', *Jewish Social Studies*, vol. 2 (1951); L. Chasanovitsch (ed.), *Les pogroms anti-juifs en Galicie et en Pologne en Novembre et Decembre 1918* (Stockholm, 1919); *La situation des Juifs en Pologne. Rapport de la commission d'étude designée par la Conference Socialiste Internationale de Lucerne* (Brussels, Paris, 1920); *Bulletin du Comité des*

Delegations Juives auprès de la Conférence de la Paix (Paris, 1919-25) (altogether 27 issues appeared); S. Kovalsky, *L'anti-semitisme polonais* (Lausanne, 1919). Some aspects of the Western response to these events are discussed in N. Davies, 'Great Britain and the Polish Jews 1918-20', *Journal of Contemporary History*, vol. 8, no. 2 (April 1973), pp. 119-42. The Supreme Allied Council sent a mission to Poland in February 1919 to investigate anti-Jewish excesses. It was headed by two French generals, Joseph Noulens and Henri Albert Niessel. Its report played down anti-Jewish atrocities, largely because its writers seem to have felt that knowledge of these would hamper French plans for intervention against the Bolsheviks. Yet ironically it has been published and cited with approval in present-day Poland in *Najnowsze Dzieje Polski 1918-1939* (Warsaw, 1969) vol. XIV, pp. 196-219.

26. For these events, see Chasanovitsch (ed.), *Les pogroms*, pp. 19-46.

27. J. Bendow (i.e. J. Tenebaum), *Der Lemberger Judenpogrom* (Vienna, Brno, 1919).

28. This is in the archives of the Polish Academy of Sciences in Warsaw. It is cited by Korzec, 'Problem', pp. 154-5.

29. On the Pinsk events, *La Situation des Juifs en Pologne*, pp. 22-33; B. Hoffmann (ed.), *Toyzent yòr Pinsk* (New York, n.d.), pp. 219-30; A. Shohat, 'Parashat Hapogrom Be Pinsk Ba-hamishah be-april 1919', *Gal-Ed* (1973), pp. 135-73. In 1921 a parliamentary commission called for action to be taken against the perpetrators of the massacre and compensation paid to the victims. In the following year, the Polish government did offer to pay compensation, but at the same time those principally responsible for the events (Listowski and Grobicki) were promoted to the rank of general.

30. *La situation des Juifs en Pologne*, p. 22.

31. For the foreign reaction, see Korzec, 'Problem', pp. 110-19; Stankiewicz and Piber (eds.), *Archiwum*, vol. II, pp. 219, 229-30.

32. E. Silberner, *Sozialisten zur Judenfrage* (Berlin, 1962), p. 346.

33. *La Situation des Juifs en Pologne*, pp. 65-6.

34. Chasanovitsch (ed.), *Les pogroms*, p. 96.

35. Korzec, 'Problem', pp. 124-5.

36. Ibid., p. 125.

37. On this see Halpern, 'Polityka żydowska', pp. 29-71.

38. On this see Korzec, 'Problem', pp. 149-53.

39. Ibid., p. 153.

40. Details of these atrocities can be found in the socialist paper *Robotnik* and also in the Jewish press in Poland.

41. These examples are cited in A. Nossig, *Polen und Juden. Die Polnisch-jüdische Verständigung. Zur Regelung der Judenfrage in Polen* (New York, 1920), pp. 45-6.

42. Ibid., p. 45.

43. On this incident see E. Eisenberg (ed.), *Plotsk-Toldot Kehilah* (Tel Aviv, 1967), pp. 193, 399.

44. For these negotiations, see Nossig, *Polen und Juden* and the article by I. Grynbaum in *Encyclopaedia of the Jewish Diaspora* (Jerusalem, 1973), vol. XII, cols. 72-150.

45. Nossig, *Polen und Juden*, pp. 47-57.

46. On the question of Jablonna, see M. Audus, 'Na marginesie wspomnienia Witosa', *Zeszyty Historyczne*, no. 20 (1971), pp. 173-7. An attempt to minimise the importance of this incident was made by the leader of the Polish Socialist Party in exile: Adam Ciołkosz, 'Dzielnica żydowska obozu w Jabłonnie', *Zeszyty Historyczne*, no. 20 (1971), pp. 178-97. His views were attacked by Y. Trunk in *Tsukunft* (May-June 1973), pp. 226-30. Much material on the episode was

provided by the publication in Poland of the minutes of the Council for the Defence of the State (*Rada Obrony Państwa*). For this, see A. Leinwand and J. Molenda (eds.), 'Protakoły Rady Obrony Państwa' in *Zdziejów stosunków polsko-radzieckich. Studia i materiały* (Warsaw, 1965), vol. I, pp. 136-317. Particularly important are the discussions on pp. 258, 259 and 262.

47. Korzec, 'Problem', pp. 165-6.

48. Audus, 'Na marginesie wspomnienia Vitosa', pp. 176-7.

49. For further details see M.A. Riff, 'The Assimilation of the Jews of Bohemia and the Rise of Political Anti-Semitism, 1848', PhD thesis, London, 1974; M.A. Riff, 'Czech Antisemitism and the Jewish Response before 1914', *Wiener Library Bulletin*, nos. 39/40 (1976), pp. 8-20.

50. V.S. Mamatey, 'The Establishment of the Czechoslovak State' in *A History of the Czechoslovak Republic* (Princeton, 1973), pp. 8-10.

51. L. Rothkirchen, 'Slovakia I, 1848-1918' in *The Jews of Czechoslovakia* (Philadelphia, 1968), vol. I, pp. 76-80.

52. *Der Prozess von Tisza-Eszlár* (Vienna, 1883).

53. Census of 15 February 1921 cited in 'Podkarpatská Rus' in *Masarykùv Slovnik Naučný* (1931).

54. A. Sole, 'Subcarpathian Ruthenia: 1918-1938' in *The Jews of Czechoslovakia*, vol. I, p. 133.

55. The Czech writer and former officer in the Czechoslovak Legion in Russia, Rudolf Medek, wrote in his memoirs that with the assassination at Sarajevo he felt that the national independence of the Czechs had been brought one step closer. R. Medek, *Pouť do Československa. Valečné paměti a vzpominky z let 1914-1920* (Prague, 1929), pp. 19-21.

56. C. Stölzl, *Kafkas böses Böhmen* (Munich, 1975), p. 91.

57. B. Černý, *Vražda v Polné* (Prague, 1968); F. Červinka, 'The Hilsner Affair' in: *Yearbook of the Leo Baeck Institute*, vol. XIII (1968); J. Herben, 'Masaryk and Anti-Semitism' in *Masaryk and the Jews* (New York, 1945), pp. 3-24; T.G. Masaryk, *Světová revoluce* (*The Making of a State*) cited in Herben, 'Masaryk and Anti-Semitism', p. 82.

58. Max Brod, *Streitbares Leben* (Berlin, 1969), p. 98.

59. R.W. Seton-Watson, *Masaryk in England* (London, 1943), p. 41.

60. J. Herben, *Kniha vzpominek* (Prague, 1936), p. 457, cited in Stölzl, *Kafkas böses Böhmen*, p. 92.

61. Riff, 'Czech Antisemitism'.

62. L. Otahalová (ed.), *Souhrnná hlašeni presidia pražského mistodržitelstvi o protistátní a protivalečné činnosti a čechách 1915-1918* (Prague, 1957).

63. See W. Jochmann, 'Die Ausbreitung des Antisemitismus' in W.E. Mosse and A. Paucker (eds.), *Deutches Judentum in Krieg und Revolution 1916-1923* (Tübingen, 1971), pp. 409-510.

64. The Czechoslovak Provisional government formed on 14 October, issued a Declaration of Independence in Washington on 18 October. To a large extent, the action of the Provisional government, itself formed in reaction to the attempt by the Socialists to proclaim a republic on 14 October, followed Emperor Charles' Manifesto of 16 October promising a federalisation of the Austrian half of the Empire.

65. A.M. Rabinowicz, 'The Jewish Minority' in *The Jews of Czechoslovakia*, vol. I, pp. 155-7. The Jewish National Council of Czechoslovakia was the first such body to be formed and it was the only one to predate the Armistice. It was followed by the establishment of similar bodies in Vienna, Lemberg, Cracow, Stanislava, Czernowitz and Zagreb. *The Times*, 17 Jan. 1919.

66. F. Weltsch, 'Masaryk and Zionism' in *Masaryk and the Jews*, pp. 78-80.

67. Ibid.

68. Masaryk, *Světová revoluce*, cited in Weltsch, 'Masaryk and Zionism', p. 82.

69. K. Capek, *Conversations with TGM* (London, 1900), p. 189.

70. V. Olivová, *The Doomed Democracy. Czechoslovakia in a Disputed Europe, 1914-1938* (London, 1972), pp. 62 ff.

71. *New York Tribune*, 7 Oct. 1918.

72. Following the looting of Jewish property in the South Bohemian town of Písek on 14 October in the wake of the attempt to proclaim a socialist Czechoslovak Republic, Max Brod warned the Zionist Organization in Copenhagen of the possibility of anti-Jewish excesses accompanying Czechoslovak independence. Letter from M. Brod to L. Herrmann, Zionist Archives, Jerusalem, File L6/ 29/ XXIII, cited in Rabinowicz, 'The Jewish Minority', p. 246; Brod, *Streitbares Leben*, p. 237.

73. F.L. Carsten, *Revolution in Mitteleuropa, 1918-1919* (Cologne, 1973), pp. 41-2; Mamatey, 'Establishment of the Czechoslovak State', pp. 25-7; Olivová, *The Doomed Democracy*, pp. 90-2.

74. *Bohemia*, 29 Oct. 1918; *Neue Freie Presse*, 28 and 29 Oct. 1918.

75. Ludovit Holotík, 'The Jewish Problem in Slovakia', *East European Quarterly*, vol. I (1967), p. 33; Mamatey, 'Establishment of the Czechoslovak State', pp. 30-3; Rothkirchen, 'Slovakia II, 1918-1938' in *The Jews of Czechoslovakia*, p. 86; Letter from V. Srobár to Minister of Foreign Affairs, Prague (for C. Weizman), Zionist Archives, Jerusalem, L8/183, cited in Rabinowicz, 'The Jewish Minority', pp. 225-6.

The situation appears to have been hardly different in purely Magyar villages in Slovakia, let alone in Hungary proper. P.J. Diamant, 'Slowaken und Juden', *Neue Jüdische Monatshefte*, vol. III (25 Dec. 1918), p. 122.

76. Mamatey, 'Establishment of the Czechoslovak State', pp. 30-2.

77. A certain N.S. Rawson reported to the Foreign Office the contents of a letter he received from a Jewish friend in Budapest vaguely purporting anti-Jewish unrest in Slovakia. Although the FO had no means of verifying this information, it took for granted that the Czechoslovak authorities were doing their best to contain the situation. 'Excesses in Hungary', Public Records Office, London, FO 371/3139, File No. 212638.

78. *Bohemia*, 5-7 Dec. 1918; *Neues Wiener Tagblatt*, 2 Dec. 1918; *Prager Tagblatt*, 3-11 Dec. 1918.

Disturbances in which the looting of Jewish property took place were reported from other towns in Bohemia, including Příbram and Kolín. The largely German-speaking town Ústí nad Labem (Aussig) was likewise affected, and as in the disturbances elsewhere non-Jewish property also came under attack. One common thread running through the unrest was the participation of what appear to have been demobilised troops of the former Imperial Army.

79. *Bohemia*, 5 Dec. 1918; *Encyclopedia Judaica* (Jerusalem, 1970), vol. VIII. In this pogrom-like outrage it would appear that a unit of the newly constituted Czechoslovak Army went on the rampage.

80. *Bohemia*, 5-7 Dec. 1918; *Neues Wiener Tagblatt*, 2 Dec. 1918; *Prager Tagblatt*, 3-11 Dec. 1918.

81. *Selbstwehr*, 6 Dec. 1918, cited in Stölzl, *Kafkas böses Böhmen*, p. 97.

82. *Bohemia*, 5 Dec. 1918; *Selbstwehr*, 17 Jan. 1919.

83. *Bohemia*, 5-12 Dec. 1918; *Prager Tagblatt*, 3-11 Dec. 1918.

84. *Bohemia*, 7 Dec. 1918.

85. See Riff, 'Czech Antisemitism', p. 16.

86. *Jewish Chronicle*, 23 Nov. 1918.

87. *Bohemia*, 13 Dec. 1918. Kramář expressed similar sentiments a few days before in a speech to the National Assembly on the necessity of bringing the

situation in Slovakia under control: 'All that is happening against the Jews and
Magyars in Slovakia can do nothing but blemish our good name abroad and
endanger the future of the Czechs and Slovaks'.

88. F. Peroutka, *Budování státu* (Prague, 1936), vol. I, p. 473.
89. Cited in *Bohemia*, 5 Dec. 1918.
90. Letter from C. Gosling to Balfour, 21 Jan. 1919, Public Records Office,
London, FO 371/3540, File No. 16445.
91. Letter from C. Gosling to Lord Curzon, 25 Jan. 1919, ibid., File No.
20976.
92. Ibid.
93. Ibid. Significantly, about a third of the letter concerned itself with
information provided by the Jewish National Committee of Czechoslovakia on
the deteriorating position of the Jews in Poland.
94. J.W. Brügel, *Tschechen und Deutsche* (Munich, 1967), pp. 99-100;
Rabinowicz, 'The Jewish Minority', pp. 169 ff.
95. Letter from the Zionist Organization to Dr Hugo Herrmann, 19 Oct.
1919, Zionist Archives, Jerusalem, File Z 4/ 583, in Rabinowicz, 'The Jewish
Minority', p. 230.
96. Ibid.
97. Brügel, *Tschechen und Deutsche*, pp. 99-100.
98. Ibid.
99. Memorandum from HMG Representative at the Paris Peace Conference
entitled 'The Jews and the War', Public Records Office, London, FO 371/3419;
FO 371/3139 and 3540.
100. *Večerní české slovo*, 22 and 23 May 1919.
101. *Našinec*, 25 May 1919.
102. *Národní listy*, 24 May 1919; *Venkov*, 22 May 1919.
103. Letter from V. Šrobár to Ministry of Foreign Affairs Prague (for C.
Weizman), cited in Rabinowicz, 'The Jewish Minority', pp. 225-6.
104. Letter from C. Weizman to the Minister Plenipotentiary, 8 July 1919,
cited in ibid., pp. 223-4.
105. Cited in ibid., pp. 225-6.
106. Brügel, *Tschechen und Deutsche*, pp. 155-6; Olivová, *Doomed
Democracy*, p. 130.
107. *Lidové noviny*, 17 Nov. 1920; *Neue Freie Presse*, 17 Nov. 1920.
108. *Neue Freie Presse*, 19 Nov. 1920; see also Franz Kafka, *Briefe an Milena*
(Frankfurt, 1952), cited in Stölzl, *Kafkas böses Böhmen*, pp. 99-100.
109. *Neue Freie Presse*, 19 Nov. 1920.
110. *Lidové noviny*, 18 and 19 Nov. 1920. Interestingly, *Lidové noviny*,
published in Brno, made no mention of the anti-Jewish aspect of the unrest in
Prague.
111. F. Weltsch in *Selbstwehr*, 26 Oct. 1928.
112. P. Wandycz, 'The Foreign Policy of Edvard Beneš' in *A History of the
Czechoslovak Republic*, p. 221.
113. Herrman, 'Structure and Development of the Jewish Population of
Bohemia and Moravia, 1754-1953', unpublished manuscript, Table IV.

In addition to those Bohemian Jews who registered themselves as being of
Czech and German nationality in 1921 and 1930, 13.7 and 20.5 per cent,
respectively, declared themselves to be of Jewish nationality. The majority were
people who would have otherwise registered themselves as being of German
nationality, but were either Zionists or felt they could not associate themselves
with the German element in the Czechoslovak state. In paying special regard
to the Jewish case the interests of the Czechoslovak government were served
on at least two counts. First, it was able to weaken the positions of the German

and Magyar minorities and, secondly, it was able to be seen to comply with the spirit of the 'minorities' clauses of the Treaty of Saint-Germain. Yet the registration of Jewish nationality was made possible by executive decree rather than an act of parliament. The Czechoslovak authorities were reluctant to see a special case be made into a legal precedent with far-reaching implications.

114. Rothkirchen, 'Slovakia II', pp. 100-3.
115. Sole, 'Subcarpathian Ruthenia', pp. 137 ff.

5 WAR AND THE APPROPRIATION OF NATURE

George L. Mosse

Why one more analysis of the First World War — the most discussed war in history? War breeds myths about war. Out of the Great War evolved a myth of the war experience which not only exerted a powerful influence on the post-war world, but through its pre-emption of nature as part of the myth hinted at the cataclysm to come. The significance of nature for both soldiers in the field and for the post-war myth is documented in memoirs, letters, films and books about war heroes — so abundantly documented, in fact, that any discussion of the myth must be suggestive rather than comprehensive.

While total war gave rise to social transformations, to the centralisation of power, and to new concessions to the working classes, in the post-war world bourgeois Europe succeeded in recovering its equilibrium and achieving a new stability.[1] Yet the way in which men perceived the world they lived in did not recover from the war experience: for surviving veterans, it was not the reality of the recent war that mattered, but the myth of the war experience as it evolved among wartime volunteers that was important. It was the myth of the war that they came to accept in the post-war world. Bill Gammage, writing about Australian soldiers, suggests a basic reason for widespread acceptance of the myth: while veterans tried to forget the tragedy of the war years as quickly as possible, they sought to remember the security, purpose and companionship of the war.[2] There is good reason why veterans are apt to tell and retell their own war experiences, for the war, however horror-filled, was at the same time the high point of their lives and gave meaning to an otherwise routine existence. Many a popular wartime song celebrated a new-found freedom from the burdens and the tedium of daily life.

Myths and symbols make it possible for men and women to confront the burdens and dangers of life; they are the mediating filters through which all phenomena are perceived. They function both by aggrandising events and by reducing them to the commonplace, by providing justification and a means of coping. Thus the unprecedented experience of the war was lifted into the sacred and was joined to the Christian ideal of death and resurrection. Regiments were blessed in church before marching off to war, while fallen soldiers, sometimes even those who were not Christian, were buried under crosses, the very symbols of meaningful life and heroic death. Walter Flex, one of the most popular German writers during the war, likened the conflict to the last supper: 'the sacrificial death of our people is only a repetition willed by God of the deepest miracle of life, the death of Christ'.[3] Seen from this perspective the First World War was part of the Christian drama symbolised by military cemeteries with their crosses of sacrifice and their chapels of resurrection.

But the war was also trivialised, cut down to size to make it a manageable, integrated part of peoples' lives. Objects of daily life, especially those associated with leisure-time activity, were appropriated, as it were, by the war: drinking mugs appeared as Hindenburg mugs, inkstands as miniature soldiers, while board games, toys, circuses and the theatre reflected military and patriotic themes. The First World War seized on film and photography as new media for elevating war to the sacred and reducing it to the trivial, and made film perhaps the most important transmitter of the war experience in an age that was becoming increasingly oriented to the visual at the expense of the literary. In film as in other media the myth of the war, and the role of nature in the myth, were significant.

I

The war was accompanied by a heightened awareness of nature, and this can tell us much about the impact of the myth of the war experience: how it widened human perceptions to encompass and confront the horrors of war. Nature as an integral part of the myth helped men to transcend the threatening reality of war, to point men's perceptions away from the impersonality of the war of modern technology and massed armies, and towards the pre-industrial ideals of individualism, chivalry and the conquest of space and time. The snowy heights of the Alps and the blue skies over Flanders fields made it possible for an elite of men to possess or appropriate what seems to be immutable in a changing world — a piece of eternity. Moreover, nature could point homeward, to a life of innocence and peace. Nothing is more exemplary of this particular Arcadia — this transcendent function of nature — than the scenes in Walter Flex's *Wanderer Between Two Worlds* (1917) where Flex and his friend Wurche lie in virgin fields behind the trenches; or the scenes of sun-drenched soldiers bathing in a pond behind the front that Paul Fussell found were among the most frequently used images in English war literature. They are images that can be found often in the work of German poets and writers during and after the war.[4]

Soldiers lived close to nature whether in western trenches where they rarely saw the enemy or out on the great eastern plains. This familiarity with nature was well expressed by a soldier in the trench journal *Die Feldgraue* (1916): 'the wood which surrounds the battle lines shares its fate with that of the soldiers waiting to go over the top, and when clouds cover the sun the pines, like the soldiers beneath them, shed tears of unending pain. The wood will be murdered just as the soldier is certain to be killed in leading the attack.'[5] Nature and man symbolise each other's sadness in the face of certain death. But such close identification of man and nature, more often than not, turned thoughts of destruction into the hope of resurrection, and symbols of death and destruction came to be paired with symbols of hope. A German memorial card for fallen soldiers shows, for example, a huge crow sitting next to a destroyed tree while in the background a cross stands haloed by the glowing sun.

This reaching for and identification with nature just as nature was being destroyed — this idealisation of nature at the precise moment when man was murdering the wood — has a long history behind it, for a high esteem for nature accompanied its destruction throughout the industrialisation of Europe. The German Youth Movement of the turn of the century, searching for genuine personal or patriotic values outside of and opposed to bourgeois and industrial society, had attempted to integrate man and nature in its concept of the genuine. Some of the most lyrical passages about nature written during the war, such as those in Flex's stories, fused wartime experience with that of the youth movement. Nature as the genuine, as Arcadia behind the front, and as symbolic of a home front remembered as a collection of valleys, mountains and small towns, suffused wartime images in writing and picture postcards sent to or from the front. A scene in one of Germany's most popular wartime plays, *Der Hias* by Heinrich Gilardone (1917), shows a chorus singing the national anthem against a background of peaceful fields and woods bathed in the light of dawn; a village is in the distance, on the left of the stage there is a factory, while in the centre a hill supports a German oak; the machine is set in the garden.[6] The homeland was never envisaged as Berlin or Frankfurt, the cities from which many writers and artists came; their work reflected, rather, the revolt against industrialism, the search for the eternal forces of nature that had characterised the youth movement to which so many of them had belonged.

Nature symbolised the genuine, sadness and resurrection – but always, at the same time, a piece of eternity that could be personally appropriated and that legitimised wartime sacrifice. That sacrifice was symbolised by the Heroes Woods, the one new type of military cemetery to come out of the First World War. I have written about them elsewhere,[7] but here the link between nature, Christian symbolism and national sacrifice that they exemplified must be emphasised: the dead resting under their crosses within a living wood served to symbolise the cycle of death and resurrection (often a huge cross of sacrifice was placed in such a wood, completing the Christian symbolism). 'Living nature' was to take the place of dead graves. The symbolism of the tree and the wood was specifically German, associated, typically enough, with innocent nature. By creating Heroes Woods, so we are told, the native village truly honoured its fallen.[8] Such a cemetery stood not only for innocence and eternal life but also for historical continuity: the national past as an eternal and immutable force was part of nature, and sometimes sites associated with the ancient German past were sought out. There was tradition behind the concept of woodland gravesites, for the oak had long been the sacred German tree, and during the wars of liberation it had been proposed that German heroes be buried under German oaks; the victory of 1871 had been celebrated by planting so-called 'Emperor's oaks'.

The immediate inspiration for the Heroes Woods was Hans Grässel's *Waldfriedhof* (wood cemetery, 1907), in Munich, from whose curving paths only a wood of tall trees is visible, within which the tombs are hidden. Nature was used to disguise death – not wild and untamed nature, but nature integrated into the orderly appearance of the cemetery. Grässel believed that 'beauty is order', and that the romantic sense which cemeteries often inspire must not be allowed to interfere with that orderly harmony which was to dominate death as it was supposed to dominate life. The dead were to find rest in the same kind of surroundings that brought calm to the restless human spirit. Thus the forest, a national symbol, came to be used to disguise the reality of death. The hero of *Der Hias* wants to be buried in a forest of oaks once victory has been won, and his girlfriend is full of understanding: 'I also know the splendid German wood.' She does not associate this wood with death but with 'the German spring'[9] and in so doing draws on that popular German literary tradition in which the wood is a symbol of resurrection, of spring which follows winter. Spring and resurrection, the forest of oaks, nature as symbolising the nation: such perceptions formed a tradition which made it possible for wartime nature to be viewed as a transcendent reality easily translated into the myth of the war experience.

The Heroes Woods appropriated nature as a living symbol of eternity for those who had made the final sacrifice, but also as a veil that disguised death beneath the beautiful but orderly wood. It is significant, as will become apparent, that in France Éduard Herriot did not call for Heroes Woods, but for 'Jardins Funèbres', and that in England as well pastoral metaphors exemplified the death and resurrection of the fallen. The scarlet poppy had literally bloomed even in the midst of the devastated plains of Flanders, an almost miraculous sign of hope among the wounds of war. The English with their pastoral tradition had an eye for the beauty of this flower, reminiscent both of the red flowers of pastoral elegies and the scarlet of a homoerotic tradition which could serve to symbolise wartime camaraderie.[10] The poppy became England's symbol of wartime sacrifice.

That the Germans could not exalt their young heroes through such a symbol of camaraderie and innocence we shall soon discover. In Germany greater emphasis was placed on historical tradition and rootedness, exemplified not only by the symbolism of the Germanic wood rather than a flower, but also by a controversy over the production of uniform crosses for graves of the fallen: should they be mass-produced, or should they be the work of traditional craftsmen? That a factory had already started to mass-produce such crosses was regarded as blasphemy by those architects most closely involved in the design of military cemeteries.[11] In Britain the uniform headstones were often mass-produced, the inscriptions then hewn by hand. Such opposition to mass-production was opposition to modernity, which was seen as incompatible with the sacred. Though this view had a long history behind it on both the Continent and in England, the pre-industrial nostalgia associated with the myth of the war experience was much stronger in Germany than in England.

Everywhere nature, as opposed to modernity, became associated with the cult of the fallen soldier. The reactionary, backward-looking character of modern nationalism was strengthened through this myth, and the experiences of wartime soldiers with nature were seen, at least in retrospect, as genuine. Again, the association of the genuine with opposition to modernity was particularly strong in Germany. From Hermann Löns to Joseph Magnus Wehner, writers never tired of proclaiming the virtue of the genuine brought to the surface by the war. As Hermann Löns wrote in 1910, 'What is culture, what meaning does civilisation have? A thin veneer underneath which nature courses, waiting until a crack appears and it can burst into the open.'[12] These words were written not in anger but in praise. The war turned the crack into an open floodgate in the eyes of many a German writer. Such praise for the genuine was often coupled with an exaltation of wartime camaraderie — the affinity between men who understand the meaning of sacrifice because they have been reborn, and, as it were, released from the shallowness and hypocrisy of modern bourgeois life.

Mass-manufactured headstones notwithstanding, the fallen in England were associated with the pastoral. The flowers on English graves were intended to recreate an English garden pointing to home and hearth, with English yew introduced here and there because of its association with country churchyards; so Sir Frederic Kenyon, the principal member of the War Graves Commission, tells us. Once again, the cult of the fallen points to the rural scene. Rupert Brooke's poem 'The Soldier', perhaps his most famous, symbolises England through 'her flowers to love/her ways to roam', by her rivers and her sun. Yet a note of realism is introduced into Sir Frederic's report to the War Graves Commission which is absent in German discussions about military cemeteries. The idea of a Heroes Woods, of making a cemetery unrecognisable, is flatly rejected. A cemetery is not a garden.[13] Indeed, British military cemeteries do not disguise death, but transcend it through the Cross of Sacrifice which dominates the graves of the fallen.

There was an attempt in Germany after the war to elevate the lily aster to a flower of remembrance because of its liturgical colour associated with death. But this association was with death in general and not with that of the wartime fallen in particular. And though many individual organisations, like the Red Cross, had their symbolic flowers, the official day of mourning (*Volkstrauertag*) would never have its poppy.[14] The journal of the German War Graves Commission (*Kriegsgräberfürsorge*) went so far as to contrast the 'tragic-heroic' of Germanic cemeteries with the sea of flowers used by the English and asserted that in British, American and French cemeteries we witness a mere dress parade of the dead rather than a celebration of heroic sacrifice.[15] Such a celebration must take place in close association with the surrounding landscape: nature must always participate in reminding the living that those who have died for the fatherland still live.

The cult of the fallen appropriated nature as a symbol of the genuine and of resurrection, with the basic function of nature remaining much the same in German Heroes Woods, English flowered graveyards and French Jardins Funèbres — even where just a soldier's name was carved into a living tree. The fallen do not die and nature disguises the reality of death, as in the Heroes Woods, or, more symbolically, in the poppy blooming among the trenches. Yet this theme of resurrection, however strong in victorious England and France, became the dominating theme in Germany, which had lost the war. While the English dead slept beneath their crosses of resurrection, in countless German memorial volumes the fallen returned to earth to urge the living to revenge defeat or to plead for the restoration of individual dignity in the modern age of mass industrialisation.[16] Always the tragic-heroic is directed against modernity as the enemy of man and of the nation.

Nature as a mask hiding death and destruction, transfiguring the horror of war, was able to flourish once the fighting had ceased. Its use in tidy and orderly military cemeteries or in Heroes Woods was one thing; but on the fields where battle had raged nature achieved transformations on a vaster scale. Some 32 years after the battle of Waterloo Balzac could still find traces of trenches, hills and walls which had played a part in the fighting.[17] But R.H. Mottram, revisiting the Western Front twenty years after the First World War, could only exclaim, 'all semblance gone, irretrievably gone'. The war that seemed a possession 'of those of us who are growing middle-aged' was becoming romanticised through the distance of time.[18] And not only romanticised, but trivialised as well: souvenir stands, carefully preserved trenches that could be visited for a fee, and comfortable hotels in the Salient where hundreds of thousands had died were available to the curious and the tourist. Romanticisation was aided by a tidying-up process in which nature played a key role, for after some debate peasants of the region were allowed to farm again and to reconstitute the landscape that had been devastated by the war. (The disguise was neither permanent nor complete; human bodies continued to be found, and where nature had covered old trenches in the brief years of peace, the Second World War opened new wounds and brought new death.)

Henry Williamson, revisiting the famous Salient in the late 1920s, captured the contrast between past and present:

> Flatness of green fields, clusters of red-tiled, red-brick farms and houses and a dim village-line on the far horizon – that was the Salient today. But then [i.e. during the battle] the few miles were as shapeless as the ingredients of a Christmas pudding being stirred.

Similarly Ypres, once a ruined city, was now 'clean and new and hybrid-English'.[19] To these post-war impressions of a tidied war zone must be added the orderly, well planted and uniform military cemeteries which dotted the region. This was what later pilgrims to the battlefields saw, and many deplored. A writer for the Sidney *Morning Herald* in Australia noted with disapproval that with few exceptions France had hidden her scars beneath blowing grain and nodding poppies.[20] It was this impression of the battlefields that inquisitive tourists must have received, and the pilgrims deplored. By 1927, according to the Saint Barnabas Society which organised many British and Empire tours of the battlefields, the curious outnumbered the pilgrims.[21]

German reactions were similar, yet different. German military cemeteries at the front were often dark and dreary, neglected by the victors until a private German organisation began to look after them. Many young people, so one account of an Eastern Front battle tour in 1926 tells us, were disappointed because they had expected to see shell holes, trenches and devastated forests, whereas time and nature had changed all that. Now the imagination had to be activated in order to be able to 'shudder a hundredfold' when confronting former battle-fields. Initially, on visiting the battlefields, 'we dialogue with the dead'; but in the end rejoicing overcomes lamentation: 'heroism and loyalty – can we be blessed with greater gifts?' The pilgrimage to the battle-field is turned to patriotic ends by the defeated nation as sadness gives place to joy, and the battlefields of the imagination vanish at the sight of fields in harvest. Yet, finally, here the pastoral directs us back to the spirit of war, and the dead spring to life.[22]

English writers considering the now masked fields of battle deplored the change as a deeply personal loss (shortly after 1927 the Saint Barnabas Society discontinued its cheap pilgrimages), while Germans were urged to overcome the change through patriotic fantasy, and the personal experience was absorbed by the national community. Walter Flex expressed this perspective by detaching the Heroes Woods from its function as a resting place for the fallen: all Germany becomes one Heroes Wood.[23] For all that, nature served to mask the horror of war, and Hans Grässel's phrase 'beauty is order'[24] received renewed validity. The combination of order and beauty, so obvious in the reconstructed Flanders plains and on the Eastern Front, served to draw the sting from the reality of the war experience, to tame it into acceptable dimensions. This new landscape was a vital part of the myth of the war experience; it meant that remembrance could be combined with overcoming.

If nature served to mediate between the reality of the war and its acceptance, this occurred not in isolation, but hand in hand with Christianity and the process of trivialisation. Nature was also used to appropriate a piece of eternity, to mask the scars of war in Heroes

Woods and on the Flanders plain, and to create a meaningful link between fighting and dying on the one hand and the cosmic rhythms of nature on the other. Such mediations fuelled the myth of the war experience, the remembrance of the glory and the camaraderie, and the sense of purpose that infused an ordinary life suddenly filled with greater meaning. Always, this appropriation of nature was directed away from modernity and towards a definition of the genuine which was to become an integral part of the myth of the war experience.

II

Who, then, benefited by this myth? Undoubtedly many veterans who now found it easier to deal with and to recapture their past, but above all the nation: if a piece of eternity was appropriated by the identification of nature with war, the nation was spiritualised; if the war was masked by the myth, it was the nation and its war experience, present and future, which would benefit from the masking process. But in the myth of the war experience the mediation of nature also led towards domination by man. While man was part of the immutable rhythm of the universe which gave meaning to his sacrifice, he was also destined to dominate nature, reasserting his individuality even within mass war and mass society.

The symbols of man's domination and individuality suffuse the myth of the war. Mountains figured in the war as 'sacred mountains' (the Kyffhäuser, for example) symbolising the nation but also exemplifying will power, simplicity and innocence; they implied the revitalisation of the moral fibre of the volk. Mountains had not always served this function. Once they had been strong symbols of individual liberty, particularly in the eighteenth and nineteenth centuries, and they had also come to stand for national liberation — it was this aspect of mountain magic which became predominant during the war. By the time the war had ended mountain climbing was at times identified with a certain inner experience and moral comportment that reflected the strength of the nation.

German Alpine clubs advocated such ideas as a justification for mountain climbing. If Ernst Jünger wrote a book called *War as Inner Experience* (1922), by 1936 the German Alpine Club, repeating a pre-war slogan, wrote of 'mountaineering as inner experience'.[25] Even as late as 1950 mountain climbing was said to be a matter of morality and comportment (*Gesinnung und Haltung*). Mountaineering, ever since the nineteenth century, had promoted an idealised man devoted at one and the same time to the nation and to a decent and virtuous life. Louis Trenker, who through his books and films in Germany after the war became the symbol of the mountaineer, wrote in his memoirs that mean and shabby people as a rule do not climb mountains.[26]

The mystique of the mountains came to the fore on the Alpine Front, in Austria and Italy. But after the war, and in defeat, the mountain glory spread to Germany as well. Long before the war, Italy, naturally enough, had treated its Alpine troops as a military elite, and the mountains as 'fonte purissima di spiritualità'. Typically enough, shortly after the war the Club Alpino Italiano issued an 'Alpine-patriotic declaration' which linked mountaineering and national greatness'.[27] Much the same linkage took place in Austria. Looking back at the war, the leader of the Austrian Alpine Club recalled how the memory of snow-white Alpine summits had given him hope in his dugout; for him the snowy mountains symbolised an elitism which lifted the individual above the masses and their materialism. Those who conquer the mountain must be the guardian of its innocence, preserve the temple from becoming a department store where everything is for sale.[28] The 'high altars made out of silver', the snowy heights, symbolise both genuine religious experience and the nation: they are a piece of eternity which makes time stand still, and those who conquer the mountain receive in return the gift of timelessness.

Herbert Cysarz, destined to become a celebrated right-wing literary critic and historian, wrote on behalf of the German Alpine Association that man was in search of myth, and that mountains, like the Volk, seek meaning in the conquest of eternal spaces where hypocrisy, weakness and ugliness have no place. When Cysarz contemplated the war graves in the mountains he visualised the fallen circulating through the air, magnificent and free, resurrected from what he called the garbage of urban streets. Here anti-modernism, once again, has free reign: the longing for immediate access to the sacred, to the wide and open spaces of the cosmos, runs deep and strong. Mountains, Cysarz tells us, leave earthly culture far behind. Time stands still.[29] We return to the genuine, to the appropriation of a piece of eternity through nature, and also to individual and national purification through conquest and domination. The idealised man moves to the fore: patriotic, hard, simple and beautiful.

That post-war Germans would associate this type of man with the film star Louis Trenker is no accident. The immediate post-war years in Germany saw a veritable wave of so-called mountain films, a counterpoint to defeat and to social, political and economic disorientation. Such films presented a healthy and happy world without the wounds of war; they praised 'the beauty of untouched nature'. Reviewing *In Storm and Ice* (1921), one of the most famous of the mountain films, a Berlin newspaper told its readers that mountains and glaciers, 'the victorious splendour of untouched nature', make present-day reality, with all of life's burdens, puny and unimportant.[30] These films were often called 'chaste', conjuring up an innocence lacking on earth. The myth of the mountain as Arcadia did not point to flowering fields behind the front, but to an innocence that implied hardness, domination and conquest among individuals and nations.

Dr Adolf Fank, the first to make such mountain films, 'discovered' Germany's Louis Trenker and Leni Riefenstahl. While Trenker soon began to make films on his own, Riefenstahl acquired great influence over Fank's films, in which human beauty and strength were paired. Riefenstahl was to follow this example in her Nazi documentaries, such as 'Power of the Will', and even in her recent book about the African Ebos. 'Beauty, strength and fate' were identical, she wrote in 1933, surveying her contribution to mountain films. Indeed, she continued, the 'wildly romantic' green valleys, the magic of the still and cold mountain lakes, the utter loneliness and the eternal struggle to conquer the peaks are the building blocks of a vital, fiery and beautiful life.[31] Romanticism and victory, struggle and domination: these ideas were easily transferred from the films of Fank, which had no overt political orientation, to Riefenstahl's nationalist commitment during the Nazi period. Eternity, the quiet of the mountains as symbolic of domination over time, was always present in her work; the appropriation of eternity was opposed to the restless life on earth. 'What excites us at home', Leni Riefenstahl wrote, 'is beyond comprehension on the mountain. Here other values reign; there is no telephone, radio, post, railway or motorcar. And most revealingly: Time, and with it our genuine life, is returned to us.'[32] Louis Trenker, who shared her ideals, put it in an identical way: 'humans come and go, but mountains remain.'[33] Indeed, when Trenker described the war in the Alps, the quiet of the mountains and the people who live in their valleys contrast with the noise of the fighting. Such silence was said to be symbolic of man at peace with himself, so different from the nervousness of man in the city.[34] The mountain folk, the heroes of Trenker's books and films, are men of few words, loyal, honest and strong: those who live in the 'fortress of the Alps' approximate the German ideal type. The peasant stock of Lieutenant Wurche in Flex's *Wanderer Between Two Worlds* produced the same ideal; both stood outside the restlessness and the temptations of industrial civilisation and thus exemplified the eternal roots of the nation.

For Trenker, the mountain people fought a mountain war against the invader: 'man against man'. This war was not one of material, but of individual combat not devoid of chivalry; both the soldiers of the Tyrol who fought in the Austrian Army and the Italian Alpini are made to show respect for each other. In this respect the mountain war is linked to the war in the air, for there too, as we shall see, the concept of chivalry was used to exemplify an ideal of traditional, pre-industrial warfare that made the war and its technology easier to accept. Unlike the wartime aviators, however, those who fought the war in the mountains did not always become a political elite; there was no thought that the brave Tyroleans would rule men and nations. There were too many of them, after all, and their quiet persistence was different from the daring of pilots, though both represented a healthy world and both appropriated something of the eternal which served as a shield against modernity.

Trenker's own political position was ambivalent. His devotion to the Tyrolean struggle for national liberation against Italian and French oppression (as he saw it) led first to the film *The Rebel* (1931) and then to *The Fire Devil* (1940), in which the parallels between the popular revolt against Napoleon and the dictatorship of the Third Reich were implied. This film cost Trenker the support of Adolf Hitler, who had once been one of his most ardent admirers. The Führer was content to see the Tyroleans revolt against the Italians in *The Rebel*, but feared any glorification of popular revolt.[35]

Trenker then attempted to get back into the Führer's favour. His novel *Hauptmann Ladurner* (1940), which glorified a group of war veterans who sought to destroy a supposedly corrupt Weimar Republic, was published by the National Socialist publishing house. Trenker's contradictory attitudes toward National Socialism mirror the symbolism of mountaineering, in which both human freedom and national roots are exemplified. But in the end the pre-industrial imagery of mountain glory, the kind of people who lived in mountain valleys and climbed their heights, restricted the ideal of freedom. The First World War strengthened this mountain mystique, using it to transcend the reality of modern warfare. Clearly, the myth of the mountain stood for stability in the midst of change, for individual worth opposed to the materialism of the masses, and for those virtues which had always been praised by nationalism: hardness, struggle, honesty and loyalty.

The 'sacred mountain' symbolised the nation, and after the war no particular mountain needed to be identified; the entire snow-capped Alps would serve.

After the war, Louis Trenker wrote before the Nazi period, youth found in the mountains what it could no longer find in peacetime, pacifist and philistine Germany: battle in the midst of constant danger, struggle in close proximity to death, heroic deeds and hard-fought victories.[36] The Conquest of the Mountain as a substitute for war — that was the final consequence of the mountain magic which held so many Germans enthralled in a hostile and restless post-war world.

In the mountains as on the plains nature covered the wounds of war. Trenker, in perhaps his most famous novel and film called *Mountains in Flames* (1931), tells us how the wounds carved into the mountains by war were healing. But unlike those who thought themselves deprived by the tidying up of the battlefields of Flanders and the Eastern plains, veterans of the mountain war found this process irrelevant. The mountains remained a powerful symbol for the meaningfulness of the war between nations, for a war that men could grasp and understand. Symbols, after all, must be concrete and touchable before men can realise the thought those symbols express. Mountains, rather than the masses of men and tanks on the battlefields, fulfilled this symbolic function.

III

To the conquest of mountains as part of the myth of the war experience must be added the conquest of the skies. The aeroplane was in its infancy during the war, though one poll taken as early as 1909 revealed that French youth admired pilots above all other professional men.[37] From the very beginning of aviation the pilot was perceived differently from others, such as engine drivers, who also controlled a product of modern technology. After all, the adventure of flying, the conquest of speed and space, the loneliness of the pilot, had all the makings of myth, and the conquest of the sky, where the Gods lived and from which they descended to earth, had always held a vital place in human mythology. More than any other modern technology, the development of aviation was accompanied by a distinguishing elitism, later to become political; it was an elite personified by the 'heroes of the sky' of the First World War and by Saint-Exupéry and Charles Lindberg between the wars. Yet the aeroplane in a special way also exemplified the fear of modern technology, the loss of myth which so many writers and artists lamented towards the end of the nineteenth century. The mystique that grew up around aviation, with modern pilots looked upon as an elite guarding the people and the nation against the inroads of a soulless and impersonal modernity, restored myth to modern technology.

Max Nordau in 1892 had largely blamed railway travel for a degeneration of nerves which made men restless and gave them a distorted vision of the universe. The constant need to adapt to new circumstances, the new speed of time, threatened to destroy clear thought and clean living, the bourgeois order under which, so Nordau believed, political and scientific progress had been achieved.[38] The aeroplane was obviously a greater danger than the railway, for it enabled man to conquer hidden spaces and to challenge the gods. Yet aviation did not demythologise the world; on the contrary, it extended the myths about nature, nation and the so-called natural elites who were their guardians. The heroes of the air, we are told, are like the mythical heroes of the Edda.[39] There was no risk that the new machine would shed its pilot and rush into uncharted space, for myth-making man was still in control.

The aeroplane first became a symbol of national salvation in France rather than in Germany. After all, had not Gambetta left Paris during the Prussian siege in a balloon? And was it not natural to transfer the idea that 'la République monte au ciel' from the balloon to the aeroplane? In French children's literature before the war the aeroplane symbolised national security and *revanche* against Germany.[40] Though Germany was also fascinated by flying, and aviation, like mountaineering, became a national mystique, preoccupation with the fleet made the aeroplane a secondary concern. Most Germans looked upon flying as adventure or sport.

Nevertheless, the pilot soon came to symbolise a new elite almost everywhere. When H.G. Wells heard in 1909 that Blériot had crossed the Channel, he declared that this fact spelled the end of natural democracy. From now on those who had demonstrated their knowledge, nerve and courage must lead.[41] Long before the First World War the pilot came to be surrounded by an aura of mystery; to control an aeroplane was considered not so much a technical feat as a moral accomplishment.

It was often said, not only in Germany, that the struggle of the plane against the hazards of nature was not dependent upon technical superiority but upon the moral qualities of the man in the cockpit, the 'new man' symbolic of all that was best in the nation. Foot soldiers,

Stephen Graham wrote three years after the war's end, did not see in the aeroplane a mere mechanical contrivance but a new human victory over matter.[42] Those who won this victory were the 'knights of the sky', for the moral qualities of the wartime pilot were associated with the popular image of medieval chivalry. The fact that the pilot was alone in the sky, high above the battle raging below, facilitated the linkage between aviation and the hand-to-hand combat of chivalry.[43]

Such knights of the sky were not only loyal, honest and hard like mountaineers, but to a greater degree than the mountain-warriors they respected the enemy. Oswald Boelcke, one of the most famous wartime flying aces, was not alone in dropping wreaths behind enemy lines by parachute in order to salute a brave opponent killed in combat. English and French aviators honoured their German opponents in similar fashion. Moreover, when an enemy pilot was shot down and captured he would often enjoy the hospitality of the local air squadron before becoming a prisoner.[44] Many years later, the National Socialist flying corps asserted proudly that Boelcke would never attack those who were defenseless.[45]

Through such chivalric imagery modern war was assimilated, integrated into the longing for a happier and healthier world where the sword and individual combat would take the place of the machine-gun and the tank. Among pilots in the battle of the skies individualism and chivalry survived both in myth and in reality. This individualism implicit in flying forced aviators to assume an introspective relationship to themselves, as Eric Leed has rightly remarked.[46] Yet the sky signified more than a seat of observation high above the battle: it symbolised also conquering the sky — a piece of eternity, which in turn pointed back to the pre-industrial age, to innocence and Arcadia. Through the war in the air a more courteous age of warfare was invoked in order to mask the might and the horror of modern war.[47]

If pilots symbolised the fight against modernity, they also exemplified the same spirit of comradeship and enthusiasm of youth that pervaded the myth of the volunteers who rushed to the colours in 1914. Pilots, it was asserted in Germany during the war, though hard-bitten, were still boys at heart. They formed a unique wartime camaraderie.[48] All pilots everywhere had the rank of officer, all volunteered and none was conscripted; moreover, the volunteers chosen for the air corps usually had distinguished themselves first in the ground war. Typically enough, in France and Italy a good number of pilots came from the elite Alpine corps. Here then was an elite among the armed forces founded on fact: imbued with the spirit of volunteers, proven in combat and virtually equal in rank, pilots indeed formed a youthful, brave and enthusiastic comradeship.

These qualities were at once joined by myth to those virtues besieged in the modern world. If evil men did not usually climb mountains, the virtuous — those who were courageous, honest, loyal and chaste, ready to sacrifice their lives for a higher cause — ruled the skies. Outward appearance was a sign of inward virtue. Boelcke's biographer emphasises that his eyes were blue like steel, testifying to his honesty and determination.[49] These, then, were the clean-cut young men whose chivalry included contempt for the masses, for all that was degenerate and weak; they symbolised a Germanic order of chivalry.

In addition to the images of chivalry, the image of hunting was frequently used to describe the war in the air. The memoirs of Germany's most famous air ace, Manfred von Richthofen, constantly likened the front to a 'hunting ground' and himself to a hunter. Indeed, Richthofen had been a passionate hunter in peacetime and was apt to take time off from the hunt in the sky to hunt pheasants on earth. The hunting image linked the battle in the sky to the most aristocratic of sports: what had amused an older elite in times of peace was carried on by a new elite in time of war. Richthofen was careful, however, to distinguish his 'joy in war' from other sports; though chivalry prevailed, this was nevertheless a hunt whose purpose was to kill a human enemy.[50]

The English, rather than the Germans, carried the metaphor of sport into the air war. The ideal of fair play was much more ingrained in England than in Germany, especially among the public-school boys from whose ranks almost all pilots came. Likening the air war to a hunt pointed to the horse and rider rather than to the pilot and plane. Technology was once more transcended, and through this transcendence the war was easier to confront and to bear.

The air war was a test of chivalry and courage in which flying aces of all nations displayed the daring of the hunter to set an example for the 'ant-like masses'. The literature of aviation during and after the war was filled with claims that the 'captains of the skies' threw off all nervousness and the rush of time. Here we are back with the symbolism of the mountaineer, whose appropriation of eternity included silence, stability, camaraderie and self-sacrifice. Antoine de Saint-Exupéry, who transmitted the mystique of flying from the First through the Second World Wars, contended that the pilot must be judged at the 'echelle cosmique', that just as the peasant reads the signs of nature, so the aviator receives within himself the three 'elemental divinities', — mountains, sea and thunder. The pilot appropriates a piece of eternity.

Saint-Exupéry's *Wind, Sand and Stars* (1939) summarised the myths of flying: death without fear, the enthusiasm of youth, performance of duty and camaraderie. Though he professed himself a democrat, in reality Saint-Exupéry emphasised the metaphysical dimension of pre-industrial virtues, attacked the acquisition of material goods, and implicitly exalted an elitism which was no different from that of the wartime pilots.[51] The immense popularity of this book was a result of the hunger for both myth and national leadership. The life and thought of Charles Lindberg provide almost a textbook example of how the mystique of aviation could be turned to political ends. His list of 65 moral qualities[52] was a summary of bourgeois virtue as well as of the spirit of adventure and chivalry, and the moral qualities he exemplified as an aviator became identified with the virtues of the American nation which the elite sought to protect against the immigrant horde knocking at the gate. The mystique of flying was turned against parliamentary governments on behalf of an elite which, in the American case, represented the Anglo-Saxon against all other races. Mussolini summarised the myth of the aviator when he asserted that flying was the property of a spiritual aristocracy.[53] Evil men do not climb mountains; nor, it could be added, do they conquer the skies.

All of these perceptions of nature – of verdant fields and a tidy landscape, of rugged mountains, of blue skies – helped to make war more acceptable, disguised it by masking death and destruction. Nature provided silence and rest and eternal values in the midst of the restless movement of war and thus transcended victory or defeat. But nature also symbolised action: adventure, conquest, domination and eventual victory – and in so doing further disguised the reality of war by advancing meaningful and purposeful goals, far from the maddening crowd of the urbanised, industrialised world. In Germany this symbolism helped make the loss of the war irrelevant; the vital continuity of mountains and skies remained, and with it man's longing to express his virtue and manliness through conquest and domination.

Mountain myth and mountain glory had roots deep in the past, and by the time of the First World War mountain climbing had become a popular sport while the pilot, as we have noted, had become the object of admiration in the decade before the war. Nature could fulfil its symbolic function in the war because such a tradition existed in all nations. The war, however, gave these myths new relevance and a new political dimension; for the war tied nature more closely to nationalism than ever before, and to a political elitism which was easily annexed by the European political right.

That flying eventually played a major role in the identity of Fascism was no accident. Here the daring that appealed to youth, the hardness, courage and virtue attributed to the aviator, could be fittingly combined with the commonplace bourgeois virtues Fascism praised. The activism of the aviator was no threat to the respectabilities the Nazis and the Italian Fascists worked so hard to maintain. Small wonder, then, that flying held so large a place in both Fascist myth and Fascist actuality. Although Mussolini learned to fly, and Hitler had good and practical reasons for using aeroplanes in political campaigning (Chancellor Brüning, he thought, controlled the radio), Fascism nevertheless turned necessity into myth. Thus the story entitled 'A Stormy Flight' appeared in almost all primers of the Third Reich. During a campaign flight in bad weather Hitler's plane performed a 'whirling dance'. The Führer alone is serene, in control, convinced of his historical mission and of protection from all danger by Providence; he is the favourite of a Providence that dominates all threatening elements.[54] The status of Hermann Goering in the movement was at least partly based on his membership in the famed Richthofen squadron during the war. In Italy the eminence of Italo Balbo in the Fascist movement predated his exploits in the air, but the group flights he led across the Atlantic and the Mediterranean, intended to demonstrate the superiority of the Fascist elite, certainly helped to make him a hero. Fascinated by modern technology, Fascism none the less sought to transcend it, to use it to mask reality much as nature was used to mask modern war.

However diverse the uses of nature we have discussed, the myths of nature pointed to the past, not to the future. Men by and large associate eternity and immutability with images of bygone days, with an innocence long lost. During the Second World War Marc Augier, a French volunteer in the SS forced to flee to the Austrian Alps, summed up this continuing nostalgia: 'I stood outside sin, the sin of the urbanite. I had returned to the source.'[55] Such backward-looking myths were relatively harmless in the victorious nations, but they served to reinforce Fascism in Italy and to legitimise volkish ideas in Germany.

When nostalgia was combined with the quest for domination, innocence represented no harmless Arcadia. The very evening of that day on which Flex and Wurche had delighted in the sun-drenched pool and the virgin fields behind the front, Wurche examines his sword: 'This is beautiful, my friend, is it not?'[56] For example, Christmas, even in wartime, was supposed both to suggest peace, and to point out the justification for war. For all their praise of virtue and silence, Trenker and Riefenstahl linked such inwardness and respectabilities to the quest for domination; endowed with the same virtues, the aviator conquered the sky and became a hunter of men: the appropriation of eternity was accomplished through the death of the enemy. Surely this use of eternity and virtue points ahead to the radical right between the wars, which believed that eternity could only be appropriated and virtue preserved by destroying the political enemy or exterminating the inferior race.

These perceptions of nature's relationship to war fulfilled an important function: they built a bridge from its horror to its acceptance, from the fright actually felt by most soldiers to the enthusiasm attributed to the volunteers. But we shall never know precisely for whom this myth functioned in wartime, for resignation and fatalistic acceptance seem to have been common to the vast majority of soldiers, and the myths of nature became part of the war experience after and not during the war. (Typically enough, almost all sources used in this paper date from between the two world wars.) After the war, these perceptions of nature could also serve to reconcile the urge to forget the horror with the greater longing to remember the glory. The cult of the aviator, the mountain films and novels, all these and more fed a myth destined to be manipulated towards political ends.

The perceptions of nature we have discussed were part of that myth, but many other ideals such as the cult of the fallen soldier, the glorification of virility and manliness and the longing for camaraderie also fed into this myth. Moreover, we have by no means exhausted the contributions of nature to the myth. Animals played a part. A wartime Easter postcard from Germany shows a bunny looking out from a wood upon verdant fields and a long line of soldiers at arms in a trench; the Easter bunny, the landscape without wounds, the tidy and pretty soldiers – all link war and peace, all link the hope brought by Easter and spring with soldiers at war.

War and peace were joined through nature. Victorious nations were able to emphasise the peaceful Arcadia rather than the necessity of war. But such an Easter greeting from Germany was not a portent for peace; it pointed to a Utopia to be realised once the myth of the war experience had fulfilled its promise. Here the First pointed to the Second World War.

Notes

1. C.S. Maier, *Recasting Bourgeois Europe* (Princeton, 1975), p. 42.
2. B. Gammage, *The Broken Years; Australian Soldiers in the Great War* (Harmondsworth, 1975), p. 270.
3. W. Flex, *Vom grossen Abendmahl: Verse und Gedanken aus dem Feld* (Munich, n.d.), p. 43.
4. P. Fussell, *The Great War and Modern Memory* (Oxford, 1975), p. 303.
5. H.O. Rehlke, 'Der gemordete Wald' in *Die Feldgraue Illustrierte, Kriegszeitschrift der 50. J.-D.* (June 1916), p. 12.
6. H. Gilardone, *Der Hias* (Berlin-München, 1917), p. 85.
7. George L. Mosse, 'National Cemeteries and National Revival: the Cult of the Fallen Soldiers in Germany', *Journal of Contemporary History*, no. 1 (January 1979), pp. 12-15. All references to war cemeteries, unless explicitly footnoted, are based on this source.
8. Stephan Ankenbrand (ed.), *Heldenhaine, Heldenbäume* (Munich, 1918), p. 54.
9. Gillardone, *Der Hias*, p. 33.
10. Fussell, *The Great War*, pp. 243 ff.
11. Mosse, 'National Cemeteries', p. 12.
12. Quoted in G.L. Mosse, *Crisis of German Ideology* (London, 1966), p. 26.
13. Sir F. Kenyon, *War Graves: How the Cemeteries Abroad will be Designed* (London, 1918), pp. 7, 13.
14. *Kriegsgräberfürsorge*, no. 3 (March 1930), p. 42.
15. *Kriegsgräberfürsorge*, no. 10 (October 1932), pp. 146-7.
16. Mosse, 'National Cemeteries', p. 5.
17. H. Balzac, *Les Misérables* (Paris, 1967), Book 2, Chapter XVI.
18. R.H. Mottram, *Journey to the Western Front. Twenty Years After* (London, 1936), pp. 1, 44.
19. H. Williamson, *The Wet Flanders Plain* (London, 1929), pp. 33, 59.
20. *Morning Herald*, Sidney, 25 Nov. 1927, n.p., Clipping Collection, Australian War Memorial, Canberra.
21. *Menin Gate Pilgrimage* (St Barnabas, 1927), p. 3.
22. *Kriegsgräberfürsorge*, no. 3 (March 1926), p. 42.
23. W. Klose, 'Soldatentod', *Wirkendes Wort* (1957-8), p. 35.
24. Mosse, 'National Cemeteries', p. 13.
25. *Der Bergsteiger, Deutscher Alpenverein* (October 1938-September 1939), p. 583.
26. L. Trenker, *Alles Gut Gegangen* (Hamburg, 1959), p. 77.
27. S. Prada, *Alpinismo Romantico* (Bologna, 1972), pp. 8, 94.
28. O.E. Meyer, *Tat und Traum: Ein Buch Alpinen Erlebens* (Munich, n.d.), pp. 206-7.
29. H. Cysarz, *Berge über uns* (Munich, 1935), pp. 53, 79, *passim*.
30. *Der Deutsche Film*, no. 41, 14 Oct. 1921, p. 4; *Film und Presse*, nos. 33-4 (1921), p. 311.
31. L. Riefenstahl, *Kampf in Schnee und Eis* (Leipzig, 1933), p. 25.
32. Ibid., p. 113.
33. L. Trenker, *Berge in Flammen* (Berlin, 1931), p. 267.
34. L. Trenker, *Kampf in den Bergen. Das unvergängliche Denkmal an der Alpenfront* (Berlin, 1931), *passim*.
35. L. Trenker, *Im Kampf um Gipfel und Gletscher* (Berlin, 1942), p. 55 (Trenker-Feldpost-Ausgabe of Helden der Berge).
36. Trenker, *Berge in Flammen*, p. 267.

37. M. Christadler, *Kriegserziehung im Jugendbuch* (Frankfurt, 1978), p. 193.
38. M. Nordau, *Degeneration* (New York, 1968), pp. 39, 41.
39. P. Supf, *Das Buch der Deutschen Fluggeschichte* (Stuttgart, 1958), vol. 2, p. 339.
40. Christadler, *Kriegserziehung*, p. 191.
41. H.G. Wells, 'The War in the Air and other War Forebodings', *Works* (New York, 1926), vol. XX, p. 23.
42. S. Graham, *The Challenge of the Dead* (London, 1921), p. 121.
43. E. Schäffer, *Pour Le Mérite: Flieger im Feuer* (Berlin, 1931), p. 19.
44. For a description of such customs, B.A. Molter, *Knights of the Air* (New York and London, 1918); for Germany, E. Schäffer, 'Die letzten Ritter: Ein Vorwort', in Schäffer, *Pour Le Mérit*.
45. *Flieger am Feind* (Gütersloh, 1934), pp. 40-1.
46. E.J. Leed, *No Man's Land* (Cambridge, 1979), p. 137.
47. M.E. Kahnert, *Jagdstaffel 356* (London, n.d.), p. 39.
48. Ibid., p. 13.
49. J. Werner, *Boelcke* (Leipzig, 1932), p. 10.
50. M. von Richthofen, *Der rote Kampfflieger* (Berlin, 1917), *passim*.
51. A. de Saint-Exupéry, 'Terre des Hommes', *Oeuvres* (Paris, 1959), pp. 169-70; for more about the mystique of flying between the wars, see G.L. Mosse, 'Faschismus und Avant-Garde' in R. Grimm and J. Hermand (eds.), *Faschismus und Avant-Garde* (Königstein-Taunus, 1980).
52. L. Mosley, *Lindbergh* (New York, 1977), p. 93.
53. Quoted in R. Italiander, *Italo Balbo* (Munich, 1942), p. 137.
54. Reprinted in G.L. Mosse, *Nazi Culture* (London, 1966), pp. 191-3.
55. Quoted in R. Bentmann and M. Müller, *Die Villa als Herrschafts-Architektur* (Frankfurt, 1971), p. 136.
56. W. Flex, *Der Wanderer Zwischen beiden Welten* (Munich, n.d.), p. 47.

6 RAPALLO – STRATEGY IN PREVENTIVE DIPLOMACY: NEW SOURCES AND NEW INTERPRETATIONS

Hartmut Pogge von Strandmann

The world's first economic summit took place in Genoa between 10 April and 19 May 1922. Its aim was twofold: to re-integrate Soviet Russia as a fully recognised partner into the world economy and to revitalise Europe economically. The two countries in greatest need of reconstruction were Soviet Russia and Germany, with the Russian government wanting to rebuild its industry and expand it with the help of Western capital and technology. Although Germany was Russia's traditional trading partner, she was not in a position to resume trade links with the Soviet state on a large scale. So the stage appeared to be set for an agreement between the Allies and the Russians, given the right conditions. However, the Russian leaders were suspicious of any multilateral arrangement in case this should lead to political dependency upon the Western powers. The German government joined the Genoa Conference with different expectations. The entire problem of reparation payments to the Allies had been banned from the agenda of the Conference by the insistence of the French government, so the Germans hoped to introduce the subject into the discussion by indirect means. Then, seven days after the opening of the Conference, the Germans and the Russians concluded a spectacular separate agreement at Rapallo which greatly shocked the rest of the world. Ever since, Rapallo has been in the eyes of the West the threatening reminder of the possibility of further separate agreements between Germany and Russia. For the Russians Rapallo has become a model for bilateral agreements based on the principle of 'peaceful coexistence'. For those Germans who approved of the agreement it represented a move towards revision of the Versailles Peace Treaty and the re-establishment of Germany as a Great Power.

Although the contents of the agreement itself were fairly innocuous, the German-Russian action has from the outset been shrouded in myth. Only gradually over the last sixty years has the story come out. So far historians and politicians alike have given German intentions in signing the agreement the benefit of the doubt; they have accepted the incident as a German defensive measure and have found it quite legitimate that

123

Germany should have wished to safeguard her own interests. In this article after examining the following questions: why did the Germans and the Russians conclude their agreement during the Conference, how was it possible to reach an agreement so quickly, who were the initiators of the agreement, and finally did any of the other statesmen either know or approve of the separate agreement beforehand? – a different interpretation is put forward. The German action was not after all a defensive measure, but one that was used in a preventive way, to demonstrate to the Allied powers that Germany regarded relations with Soviet Russia as her domain. The Allies should neither negotiate nor come to any arrangement with Russia over Germany's head.

The October Revolution in Russia and the peace treaty of Brest-Litovsk led many German industrialists for whom Imperial Russia had been one of the greatest economic opportunities before 1914 to hope that they would figure prominently in the industrial reconstruction of the new Russia. While some, notably in the steel sector, based their expectations on German military and political domination, representatives of the electro-technical industry believed in the force of economic penetration. Their plans depended upon a growth economy which would develop a strong demand for electrical goods. The steel industrialists, on the other hand, regarded Russia as a secure source of raw materials; almost as a colony. So both industrial camps were aiming at German predominance, despite the different political goals and the different forms this predominance was to take. However, nothing came of the German plans as defeat and revolution severed all links industry had developed with Soviet Russia.[1]

It was the electro-technical firms Siemens and the AEG (Allgemeine Elektrizitäts-Gesellschaft), both willing and flexible enough to accept an independent Russia, who took the lead in spring 1919 in trying to continue the policy which German industry had been forced to abandon in the autumn of 1918.[2] Walther Rathenau, President of the AEG, even offered himself as a mediator between Germany and Russia because he was convinced that it would not be difficult to meet Russia's 'sincere wish' for an understanding with Germany.[3] The fact that Soviet Russia was governed by an anti-capitalist ideology did not seem to worry industrialists. Despite their contributions to anti-Communist campaigns at home they were not very concerned with the possible effects of Soviet propaganda. They had after all survived the revolution in Germany unscathed. Their wish to exploit the Russian market and to prevent American and British industrialists from becoming Russia's main supplier of industrial goods gradually led to the establishment of more contacts and more negotiations with the Russian side, especially as more and more industrialists became convinced that Communism would last. However, dealings with Soviet Russia were at that time regarded as highly risky as the Soviet state was an unknown business partner. Therefore nothing tangible was to be arranged without the consent of the German government, and the government followed a cautious line in order not to upset the Allies.[4] Nevertheless, when Germany refused the Western request for a blockade of Russia in the autumn of 1919 it became clear that Germany wanted to renew trade with Soviet Russia independently of the West, unless the West was willing to change its attitude. The lifting of the blockade in early 1920 was therefore greeted in Germany with mixed feelings.[5] Yet it allowed the German government to let Britain take the first steps in establishing links with Russia, a policy which did not satisfy a number of German industrialists who brought pressure on the government to speed up moves to establish economic relations. The leaders in the campaign for economic links were Rathenau and his colleague at the AEG, Felix Deutsch.[6] They directed a lengthy memorandum against government policy, in which they expressed their belief 'that political and economic co-operation with our Eastern neighbour should be the aim of German policy', but realised that the timing of such co-operation was more in dispute than the aim itself. However, they were convinced that the present policy of wait-and-see should not be maintained any longer. They argued that the Peace Treaty of Versailles had not formally deprived Germany of her sovereignty and that she was entitled to conclude treaties with Eastern countries. Secondly, they attempted to demonstrate that the Entente powers would not in fact be able to outdo German industry in the short term by being the first to recognise Russia, although this might happen eventually if Germany hesitated too long. Thirdly, they made it clear that the widespread fear of revolution and Communist propaganda was unwarranted. To them it was a domestic problem which bore no relation to the reality of the German economic situation. They added that the lack of success of Soviet propaganda in Germany could hardly be related to the absence of full diplomatic relations between the two countries. Finally, they maintained that as the German government became stronger, it would become increasingly able to deal with any revolutionary threat, and therefore the chances of a Communist revolution in Germany would not be enhanced by the establishment of diplomatic links with Soviet Russia. They also rejected the proposal that they should wait for the Soviet regime to collapse. To their minds this was a dangerous and misleading suggestion, since most indications were that the regime would survive after the White Russian forces had been defeated. And the fact that the Allies were seeking official contacts with Russia appeared to demonstrate that they shared this view.

Rathenau and Deutsch then went on to point out the advantages of closer relations with Russia. They stated that Germany and Russia would form a natural community of interests; that the link with Russia would provide a modest amount of international independence and freedom for Germany and that their common fate as defeated powers would create a strong bond between them. They emphasised Russia's potential as an economic power and consequently the necessity of becoming involved at an early stage in any reconstruction of the economy. They believed that Germany should have a role as mediator between Russia and the Western powers and they alleged that business circles in the United States expected Germany to step in and assume its historical role. Finally, they suggested that a fact-finding mission be sent to Russia. This last suggestion was picked up by the government right away, but the Kapp Putsch and the Russo-Polish war delayed the mission for another year. As Rathenau had previously insisted that a political solution must precede anything else, the arguments in favour of developing industrial contacts were very much played down in the document. In this way he managed to avoid the impression that he was advocating a policy merely on behalf of the AEG.

There were other ideas in the memorandum which anticipated arguments used later to justify the signing of the Treaty of Rapallo. Rathenau was intent on achieving an economic and political *rapprochement* with Russia which would cement the economic partnership.[7] Rathenau's and Deutsch's pressure scored a further success when the agreement for the exchange of prisoners of war was signed on 19 April 1920. From then onwards both industry and government appeared to be pursuing a 'stop-go' policy in a regular twelve-monthly cycle to improve German-Soviet relations until the signing of the Treaty of Rapallo in April 1922.

The agreement of April 1920 was followed by the first spectacular Russian order for 100 steam engines from Germany.[8] In early 1921 this order was followed by a second one for 600 steam engines. The moment Russia had proved to be a reliable trade partner after paying for the first order of steam engines in gold in Stockholm, the Anglo-Russian Trade Agreement was signed on 16 March 1921, to be followed a few weeks later by a German agreement in which the Soviet government was recognised *de facto* but not *de jure*. After that everything pointed to a new agreement, but the German government, of which Rathenau had become a member as Minister for Reconstruction, moved very cautiously. It was caught in a dilemma. On the one hand, the industrialists wanted to control the economic penetration of Russia, but they lacked the necessary capital. So they were forced to look for international backing. But international participation was not easy to come by given the German intention to monopolise exports to Russia. The alternative was to attract foreign governments to encourage the spending of foreign capital in Russia together with Germany and thereby to reduce Germany's reparation debts. To carry out this plan the German side needed Russian as well as Allied consent and support. Rathenau tried to achieve both aims, but was well aware that this might prove to be too difficult and perhaps even unrealistic. Nevertheless from a tactical point of view it was worth pursuing. As Germany and the Allies were bound together by the issue of reparations, it appeared advantageous to give the impression in Russia of the existence of a united capitalist bloc. This in turn could be used as a threat to make Soviet Russia more willing to reach a separate German-Russian agreement. In any case Rathenau knew that Germany would benefit from either a German-Russian agreement or the Russian acceptance of the plan for an international consortium, unless German industry was outflanked by its Allied counterparts. This latter possibility was, however, not regarded as a real danger.

Meanwhile in September 1921 military negotiations between Germany and Russia were renewed. To speed up the process of obtaining some Western aid, the Russians proposed on 28 October 1921 a conference for the economic reconstruction of Europe and declared their readiness to accept certain pre-war debts, given three main conditions – i.e. the granting of low-interest loans, peace and full recognition. Thus by the end of 1921 the prospects for more intensive contacts with Russia did not look at all bad.[9] In order not to lose its advantageous position with regard to Russia, German industry was prepared to go a step further and enter into more formalised arrangements.[10] Thus in Berlin the German Chancellor and Foreign Minister, Joseph Wirth, started negotiations with the Russian representative, Nicolai Krestinski, on 12 December 1921, but a few days had to pass before the official in the German Foreign Office, Ago von Maltzan, who had returned to the Russian desk, was able to issue an invitation to Karl Radek to come to Berlin for further talks, with the aim of preparing either an economic or a political agreement or both.[11]

Radek's visit was withheld from the press. The British Ambassador

Lord D'Abernon was, however, informed about it. He reported to Lloyd George that it was Radek's aim to establish full diplomatic relations with Berlin. He also conveyed to London Radek's opinion that 'if it [the agreement] is delayed until after [the conference of] Genoa it no longer has [any] value for us'.[12]

The negotiations in Berlin took a considerable time, since neither party was in a hurry to reach an agreement; both sides seemed to be playing diplomatic games. They overplayed their hands: the Germans hoped to gain an advantage by insisting on the plan for an international consortium and the Russians tried to threaten the German government by referring to Article 116 of the Versailles Peace Treaty which allowed Russia to receive a share of the reparation payments. Radek negotiated at length with Wirth, Rathenau, Deutsch, Hugo Stinnes and Maltzan. He also met Hans von Seeckt and was involved in finalising a provisional agreement with the aircraft producers Junkers.[13] The negotiations for military co-operation went side by side with the political and industrial ones, although they seldom overlapped. When it became clear that Radek was attempting to achieve an economic or a political agreement before Genoa so that there would be no possibility of an international common front against Russia, the Germans began to delay matters. The German and Russian delegations were playing in counterpoint. Whenever it seemed that an economic agreement might not materialise, Maltzan and Rathenau began to negotiate for a political one and whenever this ran into obstacles Rathenau, Deutsch and Stinnes reverted to the possibility of an economic agreement.

During these negotiations industry and government acted in unison, a fact which was underlined by Rathenau's appointment as Foreign Minister one day after a crucial meeting with Radek.[14] The negotiations carried on until the middle of February, when Stinnes's rejection of a joint venture brought Radek's four-week mission to an end. As the industrial agreement had not materialised he had to return to Moscow empty-handed. Yet a political agreement had been drafted which Radek was able to take with him; its five points corresponded to the first five articles of the Rapallo Agreement. However, Rathenau had no intention of finalising it before the opening of the Genoa Conference.

The German industrialists had further meetings with members of the government to sort out the possibilities of an industrial agreement with Russia, but it is likely that the problem of reparations prevented any further development of an export credit guarantee which Rathenau had suggested earlier in January. It took four years for this scheme to come into operation, but when it did, it boosted German exports to Soviet

Russia considerably.[15]

A few days after Radek had left Berlin, Rathenau explained his policy to the Foreign Relations Committee of the Reichstag.[16] He was quite open about his intentions and emphasised that the door for further negotiations with Russia had not been closed despite Radek's departure. He hoped they would eventually be concluded satisfactorily. He agreed to the Committee's request that he co-operate with the Soviet delegation in Genoa, but made it clear that Germany could not focus her attention exclusively on Russia.

Over the next few weeks Rathenau's option of joining a consortium or going it alone with Russia had to be measured against his reparations policy and any Allied plans for Russia. His plans are now clear in three instances. First, in February Rathenau requested that he come to London to discuss, among other things, draft articles for a possible agreement with Russia.[17] When this request was turned down by Lloyd George, the Krupp director Otto Wiedfeldt was sent to London instead.[18] He had a long talk with the Prime Minister in which he asked for British capital to help either in the multilateral or unilateral efforts of reconstruction in Russia. He told the Prime Minister that the Russians preferred to deal with Germany rather than Britain and hinted that it might be of benefit to Britain to give assistance to German business with Russia. When Wiedfeldt expressed Rathenau's doubts about the efficiency of a consortium Lloyd George replied, 'Let it develop itself and do not kill it right away.' Wiedfeldt doubted that English business-men expected much from the consortium but he could see that it might be useful in establishing an economic framework for more general negotiations with former business owners in Russia. Lloyd George went along with this approach since he was able to envisage British-German co-operation along these lines. When Wiedfeldt voiced his doubts that English firms would be inclined to invest large sums in Russia, Lloyd George replied, 'This will change after Genoa. When the Soviet Government is recognised and when the Bank of England says: Now the way is open; then English banks and businessmen will gladly do it.'

Wiedfeldt reported to Rathenau on 9 March.[19] Three aspects were of particular value to Rathenau. Although the Prime Minister did not want to abandon the consortium plans right away, he was far less enthusiastic about them than previously. Instead he expressed the British determina-tion to do business in Russia either alone or together with Germany. And finally it became clear that Britain would like to recognise Russia at Genoa. With regard to Rathenau's special concern, namely to maintain an understanding with Lloyd George and to stay in contact with him during the Conference at Genoa, the Prime Minister had merely stated that there would be enough time for discussions. Just before the German delegation left for Genoa, Rathenau wrote to Lloyd George denouncing the recent note of the Reparations Commission and then asking whether he could see him in Genoa.[20] Both requests might explain Rathenau's dogged efforts to contact the Prime Minister at the Conference.

Rathenau's determination to keep in touch with the British during the weeks preceding the Conference at Genoa also led to an unofficial meeting at the Board of Trade on 10 March between leading civil servants Ernst von Simson, Carl Bergmann and Albert von Dufour and Sir Sidney Chapman, plus two other officials on the British side.[21] The obvious aim was to work out a common line for the Conference, but both sides kept their options open.

The second issue to affect Rathenau's thinking at that time was the note of the Reparations Commission with its demand for 60 thousand million marks in new taxes. Wirth and Rathenau rejected this demand and handed over their reply on the opening day of the Genoa Conference in order to avoid any disruption. Wirth explained Rathenau's and his position to the Cabinet beforehand and made it clear why 'a good relationship with Russia ... can reduce western political pressure'.[22] He also pointed out that 'our policy must become [more] active.' Within the context of his remarks, Wirth's demand also referred to the desire for a more active policy towards Russia, and indicated that he was more willing than ever before to conclude an agreement with Russia.

The third issue was the conference of Allied experts in London between 20 and 28 March 1922. They prepared a memorandum in which conditions were laid down as to how foreign labour and capital should be used for the reconstruction of Russia. The final memorandum contained some danger signals for Germany. It affirmed Russia's right to claim reparations under Article 116 of the Versailles Peace Treaty. It also made it clear that the equal status of the potential participants in the consortium was in doubt. Moreover there was no longer any serious plan for a common front of all capitalist states towards Russia. All in all, it looked as if Lloyd George was seeking a bargain with Russia and as if France were not interested in one at all.[23]

All this together assumed alarming proportions for Rathenau, and he pointed out to the Cabinet that 'a recognition of the Soviet Government by France and Britain would not be especially comfortable for us'.[24]

The Foreign Minister further stated that the Russian question had become very political:

> How far we want to go in supporting Russia depends on the terms she makes. . . She could join the Versailles Treaty. We could come to an agreement with her about this, but we would have to avoid this leading to a conflict with the Western powers.

This was a revealing statement for all those who understood the situation. It showed that Rathenau was left with three options: to conclude the Russo-German agreement before Genoa, at the Conference or afterwards. The Russians wished to sign beforehand, and it was for this purpose that their delegation passed through Berlin on its way to Genoa. A slightly-modified draft of a political agreement was worked out, but Rathenau successfully delayed any further negotiations.

Were there any signs that the German delegation intended to conclude the agreement at the Conference? So far no direct evidence has come to light, but discussions in the Cabinet indicated that Wirth and Rathenau were prepared to sign. Wirth asked his colleagues

> whether we should become more active right from the beginning of the conference; in particular whether we should tackle the Russian problem first and then turn to the middle-European one; I am in favour of some action, from a domestic point of view as well.[25]

Another indication that a signing at the Conference had been seen as a possibility is to be found in Maltzan's letter to Under-Secretary Haniel, in which he was very sceptical, although he did not rule out the possibility: 'We will not come to a written settlement of our [Russo-German] relationship while we are here.'[26]

Of course, it would have been possible to sign an agreement after the Conference was over. But this would only have made sense if Germany's special relationship with Russia had not been undermined by a British or French agreement. The chance for an agreement between the Allies and the Russians appeared remote as the Allies wanted to use the London Memorandum of March as the basis for any agreement. The German delegation welcomed the Memorandum as it confirmed their earlier assessment that a quick understanding between the Allies and Russia would be impossible.[27] The industrial adviser, Bücher, wrote from Nervi:

To my mind the Russians are not able to accept it and I do not consider that there is any tactical risk of falling between two stools provided we proceed correctly. Personally I am even a bit relieved by the contents [of the Memorandum] for if the entente had made acceptable proposals to Russia, then our position towards Russia could easily have been ruined.[28]

What the German delegation did not know was that Lloyd George and the French Foreign Minister, Barthou, had made it clear to the Russians that they did not feel bound by the proposals since they represented the private opinion of the experts. This meant that there was still room for bargaining.

So after the opening of the Conference and the handing over of the Memorandum to the Russians at a meeting of a special subcommittee, Lloyd George and the Italian Foreign Minister, Schanzer, arranged a private meeting with Barthou at the British residence, the Villa d'Alberti.[29] On that occasion the Western statesmen tried to reach an agreement on how to proceed in the special committee over the question of debts, the restoration of foreign private property, compensation and the Russian claim for the damages which had occurred during the wars of intervention. While they were airing their views, Barthou began to realise the purpose of this meeting and asked Lloyd George 'if it was proposed to talk with the Russians privately', and agreed to this when it was confirmed. Schanzer was then requested to arrange the meeting with the Russians for the next day (14 April) because, as Barthou put it, 'you go to bed with them.'[30] None of the politicians disagreed when Lloyd George insisted that the Germans should be excluded from this meeting. This should not come as a surprise if Lloyd George's train of thought in February and March is taken into account. But could there have been another reason? The Prime Minister presumably knew something of the German-Russian negotiations and the subsequent draft agreement, which stipulated the mutual renunciation of all debts. As the Germans might have suggested the same remedy for the Allies, this would have put the latter in a position which Lloyd George was anxious to avoid.

Maltzan noted in his two memoranda, which were written shortly after the Treaty of Rapallo was signed and which were to defend the German action, that the Allies had invited the Russians for unofficial talks on 13 April, and also that the first round of these talks had already taken place on the same day.[31] Maltzan, eager to make a good case for the German action, twisted the facts. And it should be mentioned here that Maltzan's accounts, which have formed the basis of the historiography about Rapallo for the last fifty years or so, seem to be often incorrect. It was on the next day, 14 April, that Lloyd George tried to reach an agreement with the Russians at his villa.[32] However, an impasse was soon reached because of Western insistence on the separation of private and public debts, and Lloyd George's refusal to pay compensation for the interventionist wars. Eventually the meeting broke up without an agreement having been reached, although two more meetings were arranged for Saturday, 15 April. The press communiqué agreed to by all participants was handed out to eager journalists:

> Representatives of the British, French, Italian and Belgian delegations met under the presidency of Mr. Lloyd George at a semi-official meeting to examine, with the Russian delegates, the consequences of the report of the London experts. Two conversations were devoted to this technical examination which will be continued tomorrow with the assistance of experts nominated by each delegation.

According to Maltzan's account, the negotiations with the Russians led to a discussion of Article 116, although there is no trace of this in the British documents. In fact Germany was not mentioned at all. As it is improbable that Maltzan was misinformed, it has to be assumed that he fabricated rumours to suit his case. Maltzan further distorted the facts when he referred to the visit of Amadeo Giannini, an Italian official, on Friday at 10.00 or 11.00 p.m. It emerges from the British records that Schanzer had sent someone with Lloyd George's consent to see the German delegation; this person was obviously Giannini. Maltzan recorded that the talks with the Russians had gone well.[33] This was not the case! But as Giannini had not been present at the talks on that day, he could only have passed on what he had been told. In Maltzan's first and short account Giannini only mentioned some of the items which had been discussed. His mission was only semi-official and therefore it was unlikely that he asked the Germans what they thought about the London Memorandum. When the German delegation met Lloyd George after the Treaty of Rapallo had been signed Maltzan repeated 'that Dr. Giannini had intimated that they [the Allies] had arrived at an arrangement with the Russians in regard to pre-war debts'.[34] Lloyd George denied this and made it clear that 'there must have been some misunderstanding, and perhaps Dr. Giannini had referred to the Cannes resolutions' of January. It looks as if the Germans used an unclear message by Giannini as a pretext to cover up their action. Lloyd George was probably right when he expressed his surprise 'that a great country like Germany should act on a report like that'. Two interpretations of Giannini's visit are possible. *Either* it was a genuine attempt to tell the Germans what had happened at the Villa d'Alberti, from which it follows that if the report had been clear and simple it would have been difficult for the Germans to misinterpret it. A similar mission had been undertaken to the Japanese by a British official, without the Japanese feeling the need to sign an immediate agreement with the Russians. It is, however, possible that Giannini's report was unclear and thus lent itself to misunderstandings and misinterpretations which might have been welcomed by the Germans. *Or* Schanzer had used Giannini to induce the Germans to resume their negotiations with the Russians in the knowledge that the Allies would not reach an agreement with the Soviets. This possibility can no longer be ruled out, as Schanzer did put up some sort of defence when the Germans were attacked by the French after Rapallo. Furthermore, after the Conference was over Schanzer told the Italian parliament that the Italian delegation had not harboured any resentment towards the German-Russian Treaty but thought it advisable that the other European states should follow suit.[35] As he probably knew that the Germans wanted to sign an agreement with the Russians, Schanzer may have given the German initiative the green light. Lloyd George had agreed to send Giannini and therefore might have known more about the mission than he was later willing to admit. His motivation would certainly have been less pro-German and more anti-French.[36] Until Maltzan's report about Giannini's visit is confirmed by another independent source it can only be used with caution. The British documents, on the other hand, invalidate to some extent Maltzan's two other accounts. Rathenau's letter to Lloyd George of 18 April throws some light on the German tactics. He wrote about his talk with Giannini:

> During a long conversation I pointed out the difficulty of our situation, but from what he said I could not gather the least hope that the cares which were troubling us and which are known to your Gentlemen would be taken into consideration.[37]

Thus the fact that Article 116 had not been mentioned in the negotiations at the Villa d'Alberti was not greeted with relief by the German delegation. Instead it was used by them to create an atmosphere of uncertainty. This served as a tactical ploy to justify the resumption of negotiations with Soviet Russia on Saturday, 15 April, and the signing of an agreement on Sunday, 16 April.

All sources seem to agree that Rathenau instructed Maltzan, after Giannini's visit, to approach the Russians in order to continue discussions which had begun in Berlin before the opening of the Conference. Maltzan met Joffe and Rakovski on Saturday morning. They apparently gave him precise information about the negotiations with the Allies and according to Maltzan told him that these had gone relatively well despite a number of difficulties. When Maltzan raised the question of an agreement, the Russians responded favourably and stated that they still valued co-operation with Germany very highly; they were far from making an agreement with the Allies. Obviously they needed to discuss Maltzan's *démarche* with Chicherin before they returned to him that night. It is difficult to know when they met Chicherin, but probably some time before 4.30 p.m. when the Russian Minister, being late, joined the talks at the Villa d'Alberti.

The meeting of the experts at the Villa d'Alberti had broken up before Chicherin arrived because the Russian side had refused to accept the war debts and the Western experts were unwilling to admit the Russian counter-claims resulting from the wars of intervention. When the Western experts reported the deadlock to the chief negotiators, Lloyd George announced that, although there was now little chance of an agreement, he was still in favour of 'allowing them [the Russians] every opportunity for consideration, and, if necessary, an adjournment to permit them to telegraph to Moscow'.[38] A new initiative by Schanzer was rejected by Barthou. Stubbornness on the part of the French and Russians, who must have realised that an agreement with the Germans was within their grasp, led to the end of the meeting without any result. Lloyd George's earlier suggestion of further communications between Chicherin and Moscow was accepted by the latter; thus there remained a faint possibility of renewed negotiations.

That was all that was achieved on the Saturday afternoon and evening. Maltzan, however, tells a different story. He quoted rumours from sources which were purported to be sound, that the Allies and the Russians had reached an agreement. Apparently the Germans became despondent and according to Maltzan sat around lethargically on their verandah. Even in Maltzan's own terms this story sounds unlikely and smacks of self-justification with regard to their later action. It is striking that the Germans did not attempt to obtain an official statement, since it is most unlikely that the participant powers would have withheld one if an agreement had actually been reached. And it would have been very foolish to have acted on the basis of rumours. It is also noteworthy that Maltzan did not list rumours which gave a contrary indication because they might have undermined a line of reasoning which did not justify the signing of the treaty. Obviously this was, as has been stated before, the aim of the two later written, but well known, accounts.

Recently a new source about the event on Saturday night has come to light.[39] One of those 'rumour-mongers' of Saturday night, Max Reiner, the correspondent of the *Vossische Zeitung*, wrote to Rathenau's biographer, Count Kessler, in 1929, telling the following story. Earlier that evening (15 April) he had warned Rathenau of a pending agreement between the Russians and the Allies which might be signed that evening. Later that night he was alone with Maltzan who informed him of Rathenau's instruction to drive to Rapallo the next morning to prepare the agreement with the Russians. Moreover Maltzan showed a letter to him which Joffe is supposed to have written to Maltzan letting the latter know that the negotiations in the Villa d'Alberti had broken down.

Let us assume that Reiner remembered correctly and that his story was true, apart from the warning to Rathenau. Then Rathenau might have merely been confirming his instruction to Maltzan of the previous night to go ahead, establish contacts with the Russians and possibly drive to Rapallo. As Rathenau and Maltzan must have known that the negotiations in the Villa d'Alberti had broken down, the question remains open as to why there was such a hurry. This point will be discussed later.

Joffe's letter poses different problems. Joffe had not taken part personally in any of the negotiations either on Friday or on Saturday. If he had waited on Saturday outside the Villa d'Alberti until the negotiations were over, it would have been difficult for him to drive over to Genoa, find Maltzan, hand over his letter and then return to Rapallo in time to make the famous phone call on Sunday morning at 1.15 a.m. So it is more likely that he sent Maltzan a personal message. In that case the message cannot have been particularly secret. Anyway its contents were certainly neither new nor startling. The press was told at about 7.30 p.m. on Saturday, as had been agreed by the Allies, 'that the discussions were continuing, but that the Russian delegation required a few days more in which to examine the Allied proposals, and that in the meantime no meeting would be held'.[40] This did not sound like an imminent agreement between the Allies and the Russians. Obviously this news was available to the German side and it can be safely assumed that they had received it. Rathenau confirmed this when he cabled Haniel the next day 'that any delay was impossible because resumption of negotiations between Russia and the Entente could be expected for tomorrow'. This meant that Rathenau was aware that nothing had been concluded on the fifteenth.

Perhaps Reiner was the only journalist who had somehow missed the statement to the press and therefore was a suitably impressionable victim for Maltzan. There was hardly any point in showing Joffe's note to Rathenau as he must have already seen it.

So let us return to the question as to why the Germans hurried to sign a treaty with the Russians on Sunday? The evidence suggests that most people knew that the Allies had not reached any agreement with the Russians. As the existing deadlock might result in a official breakdown and perhaps even in a collapse of the Conference the Germans had to act fast if they wanted to stage their *coup* before it was too late to create a special effect. As long as none of the leading statesmen had told the Germans of the failure of the negotiations between the Allies and the Russians, the Germans were able to use the threat of an agreement to which they were not a partner in a preventive fashion, that is to say to sign with the Russians before the others might do it. Thus Maltzan's defensive accounts have to be put on their head. Given that the Germans were willing to cause an éclat they had to act for fear of losing a suitable pretext. The fact that Germany dressed up her agreement with Russia as a preventive move shows that in the last resort neither Rathenau nor Wirth really believed in an international consortium for developing Russia. They put German industry first and exploited the separate dealings of the Allies to defend the German action.

So far no evidence has emerged which casts doubts on Maltzan's account of Sunday, 16 April: one hour after midnight a member of the Russian delegation rang the Germans and invited them over to Rapallo for further negotiations.[41] Ernst Schulin has reminded us that this telephone call was probably in response to an earlier one by Maltzan who under the instruction of Rathenau contacted the Russians about 11.30 p.m. on Saturday night 'in order to arrange formally [what had been informally arranged in the morning] a meeting for the next day'.[42] Then the Germans waited for the Russians to call back – this eventually happened at 1.15 a.m. The Germans decided to go to Rapallo. Rathenau, according to Maltzan's later stories, was virtually forced by him into going ahead with the German-Russian agreement, although he did not explain why Rathenau should have been so reluctant.[43] It looks as if Rathenau had instructed Maltzan twice to resume contacts with the Russians, on Friday and Saturday evening, and had also asked him to send an urgent telegram to Deutsch asking him to come to Genoa.[44] This was surely not done in order to have talks with the Russians, but in order to finalise the arrangements begun in Berlin. Rathenau must have been very ready to sign given that he had worked for this ever since 1919. Maltzan's claim seems to be unfounded and reveals more about his vanity than about Rathenau. In any case the truth of Maltzan's story must be doubted. It is of course possible that Rathenau was sceptical of the appropriateness of the action at this precise moment and of the reasons to be given. After all, the justification for the German action was built on very shaky grounds.

More was at stake for Rathenau, as he wrote to Koch-Weser later:

> Meanwhile an imponderable aspect of the following facts cannot be ignored: first the treaty was made at a time when the Russians felt deserted by the world, made their feeling plain, and to a certain extent demanded moral support for their people who were deserted by the world. Politics know no gratitude, but do recognise certain germane realities which are not forgotten and which form the beginning of a pattern of relationships which in the end could become a net of common interests.[45]

So on 16 April Rathenau, Simson, Maltzan and Gaus went to Rapallo and signed the original Berlin proposal, updated by the Russians. Germany renounced all claims to compensation on condition that the Russian government would equally not accept claims by third states. In a secret exchange of letters two clauses were added in which Germany was granted an equal position to any third state if Russia were to pay compensation. Germany was not to participate in any venture of the consortium without consulting Russia beforehand, and was to continue to act independently from the consortium.

The news of the Treaty acted like a bombshell. The Allies criticised Germany for her action and went even so far as to ask her to renounce it. To meet the criticism abroad and at home Maltzan prepared his two accounts to defend the German action. Under-Secretary Haniel gave the British Ambassador 'virtually all our available material in order to convince him that the signing of the treaty had not been prepared to create a pre-arranged sensational effect. His comment was: "I am afraid your delegation got stampeded." '[46] Either then or a bit later D'Abernon obtained a copy of Maltzan's short account.[47] This was also passed on to the magazine *Der Ostexpress* and probably to a few other people.

Kessler's story is based on Maltzan's longer account. When he wrote his biography of Rathenau, he asked Under-Secretary Schubert whether he could use Maltzan's account for his book.[48] Schubert agreed and probably discussed with Kessler how to make use of the document. Kessler's version was then read by Gaus, the legal expert in the German Foreign Office who had been present at Rapallo. A few days later Kessler went to see Gaus, who made no objection, but asked Dircksen, the then Ambassador in Moscow, for his opinion. He also asked Kessler to discuss it again with Schubert.[49] It was then arranged with Dircksen that Maltzan should not be quoted literally and that the third person singular should be used instead of Maltzan's 'I'.[50] In addition Kessler's version was censured by the Foreign Office. One reason why the Wilhelmstrasse did not mind Kessler's use of Maltzan's account is surely that it was defensive and tried to justify the German action. Therefore Kessler suggested to Gaus that even a censored publication might be politically useful.

Lloyd George's inaction during the days of 14, 15 and 16 April raises other questions. He was aware of the constant contacts between the German and Russian delegations, he knew about the possibility of a German-Russian agreement and was informed about the Germans' activities on 15 April. So, since he made no approaches to the Germans until he invited them to tea on the Sunday afternoon that Rathenau was to sign the agreement, is it possible to conclude that he had no serious objections to the agreement?

At a meeting after the Rapallo Treaty had been signed Lloyd George pointed out that

> although at the time he had no idea that the Russo-German arrangement was in prospect, he had remarked to Signor Schanzer that he thought such an arrangement was conceivable, and that it would be a great danger to Europe if the Russians and Germans came together. . . When observing this he had absolutely no idea that it was imminent. This move was however so obvious a one to anyone responsible for the destinies of Germany.[51]

Barthou then asked Schanzer whether he had been aware of the latest German-Russian move when he had arranged this gathering. Schanzer denied this, but stressed that 'this accord between Germany and Russia which it was easy to foresee, but which could not be prevented, would acquire a greater power if no agreement were reached by the conference with Russia'. Barthou now threatened to break up the Conference, but

Lloyd George and Schanzer pleaded for moderation. Barthou then teased the Prime Minister by saying that he was sorry that Lloyd George had had to use the word 'anger' so often in his remarks. When Lloyd George 'said that he was angry', Barthou retorted 'that he was very cool for an angry man', to which the Prime Minister replied: 'The more angry he was, the cooler he became.' It was obvious that Barthou suspected that Schanzer and Lloyd George knew more than they were willing to admit and were trying to induce him to keep the Conference open.[52] The discussion about what steps to take was deferred. At a social occasion that evening the Prime Minister told Julius Hirsch, the Permanent Under-Secretary in the German Ministry of Economics: 'The thing would not matter if you had concluded it three weeks beforehand or three weeks after Genoa.' Hirsch asked, 'So you hold, Prime Minister, the material bearing far less relevant than the timing?' 'Naturally,' Lloyd George replied.[53]

How much the British and Italians really knew is difficult to assess, but since the British had broken the Russian code and were informed of the talks between the Russians and the Germans, it seems reasonable to assume that they had an idea of what was going on.[54] Because of Barthou's suspicion, Lloyd George had to adopt a tough line against the Germans when the note of protest was drawn up on 18 April, although Schanzer did succeed in moderating this somewhat. Nevertheless, Germany was to be excluded from further negotiations between the Allies and the Russian delegation.

Just before the first meeting between Lloyd George, Wirth and Rathenau after Rapallo, Sir Edward Grigg passed on an unofficial message sent by the German Chancellor's adviser, Moritz Bonn. Apparently Wirth wanted to come to a settlement with Lloyd George

> but cannot withdraw the treaty unless the Russians agree to a joint withdrawal. He says the Russians will not do this at present, but believes they will do it on a hint from you. . . [Lloyd George]. It is quite evident that Dr. Wirth feels he cannot in loyalty to a colleague throw over Dr. Rathenau, is seeking a way out, and would prefer this to withdrawing from the First Commission.[55]

This was a somewhat devious method of communication and an attempt to preserve good relations with the Prime Minister whilst putting the blame for the agreement on to Rathenau. The latter might have consented to Wirth's initiative, although this is doubtful. So at the meeting with Wirth, Rathenau, Maltzan and Dufour, Lloyd George tried to press the Germans to withdraw the Treaty, but Rathenau refused and repeated the by now well known arguments.[56] The Prime Minister would not have any of this, accused Rathenau of not having communicated through the proper channels and alleged that Maltzan had not talked about the Russian-German negotiations when meeting anyone connected with the British delegation. Although the British accusation rings true, Wirth defended the German action by referring to Giannini's visit, whereupon Maltzan mentioned similar messages he is supposed to have received from members of the Little Entente on Saturday. No agreement was reached, but, due to Schanzer's mediation and Lloyd George's insistence on closing the matter, any disruption of the Conference was avoided, especially once the French delegation had been brought into line.

Once the initial upset had passed, the Rapallo Agreement had little effect on the Conference and compelled neither the French and Belgians nor the Russians to make any substantial concessions. It was the Allied insistence on the Soviet recognition of Tsarist debts which prevented any real progress being made. So Lloyd George removed this issue from the agenda of the Conference, and arranged for it to be discussed at a special conference at The Hague in July 1922. However the German-Russian Agreement set a precedent which may not have been entirely unwelcome to the British Prime Minister, who realised that a similar agreement would have to be arranged if British trade with Russia was to expand. When Dufour of the German Foreign Office asked him in the middle of May whether he therefore found Rapallo quite useful after all, Lloyd George answered after a pause, with a crafty smile: 'Well, it nearly overthrew the applecart.'[57]

The Russians regarded Rapallo as a 'moral victory'. They had prevented the emergence of a capitalist front and demonstrated that France and Britain were impotent to impose their conditions on Russia. Germany and Russia tried to regain their international manoeuvrability, Germany against France and Russia against a potential Western bloc. For Germany Rapallo was an important step towards revisionism while Russia wanted to demonstrate its intention to practise coexistence based on bilateral agreements with capitalist states.

Although these questions were important, the Treaty of Rapallo has been interpreted too often merely from a diplomatic point of view, but such a view has tended to overlook the aim of the agreement and the role of the industrialists in preparing it.[58] It was to emphasise the importance of the industrial aspect of the anticipated agreement that the German delegation included two prominent representatives of industrial associations, Bücher and von Raumer, who were joined later by Deutsch. Although the economic agreement was concluded late in 1925, Rathenau and Chicherin agreed that the Treaty was the framework for the development of economic relations.[59] However, in the situation of 1922 it was easier to agree upon a political formula for later economic co-operation than on an economic agreement itself. This was particularly so as Rathenau hoped that a political agreement would not in the long run forestall the later use of British or even French capital for trading with Russia. Lloyd George's grand design had been shattered before Genoa by the anti-Russians in his Cabinet, by French obstinacy and by Russian unwillingness to accept Tsarist debts. After Rapallo it was extremely difficult for him to salvage anything from the Conference. Rathenau, who was always attracted by grand designs, had left his options open until he realised that an agreement between the Allies and the Russians was out of the question. At that moment he was enough of an opportunist to go ahead, conclude a separate agreement with the Russians and create the éclat. Lord Curzon summed up Rapallo a year later in a lengthy memorandum. It should have prevented the growth of any myths about the German strategy in preventive diplomacy. To him

> the Treaty of Rapallo was a useful instrument for the purpose it was ostensibly designed to serve. It dealt on bold and simple lines with the tangle of claims and counterclaims arising from the war. But the governments not parties to it were not concerned with its intrinsic merits. It was rightly regarded by them as a gesture of defiance, as a gratuitous insult directed by Germany against the Powers, with whom she should have been in collaboration. A great deal of heat was inevitably generated, but there is no evidence to show that the treaty had any permanent results other than those expressly contemplated by it.[60]

'Preventive diplomacy' may have created the éclat that the German government wished for, but it also provided Poincaré with a welcome pretext to harden his attitude towards Germany. Lloyd George's statement that 'if there had been no Rapallo there would have been no Ruhr' does not take sufficient account of Poincaré's policies or of the pressures being imposed upon him by the National Bloc in France.[61]

In contrast to a number of previous studies on Rapallo which are based on Maltzan's accounts, these sources are regarded in this chapter as biased and unreliable. Even Maltzan's later story of the 'pyjama party' has to be doubted. Rathenau's position was far more determined than has hitherto been assumed. Maltzan obviously exploited the early death of his Foreign Minister to boost his image as 'father of Rapallo'. To justify the preventive diplomacy, namely the signing of the agreement, the German side fabricated a rumour which many historians have taken to be a fact. They believed that an agreement between the Allies and the Russians was imminent. Consequently they had no difficulty in explaining the speed with which the separate agreement had to be concluded. However, the German delegation knew better. Once the negotiations between the Allies and the Russians had ended in deadlock the German delegation rapidly lost its pretext for causing an éclat with which the German government, who after all stood for the policies of fulfilment, wanted to demonstrate its political strength. As soon as it looked as if the Allies might ask the Germans to join them, Rathenau quickly signed the agreement which had been prepared in Berlin. And finally the possibility can no longer be excluded that Lloyd George and Schanzer knew of the German intentions, although most historians do not share this view. They had no wish to prevent the Germans from signing, because they could then blame the French for the failure to reach an agreement with the Russians.

Notes

1. See for German-Russian economic relations: G. Rosenfeld, *Sowjetrussland und Deutschland 1917-1922* (Berlin, 1960); W. Baumgart, *Deutsche Ostpolitik 1918. Von Brest-Litowsk bis zum Ende des Ersten Weltkrieges* (München, 1966); H.G. Linke, *Deutsch-sowjetische Beziehungen bis Rapallo* (Köln, 1970); P. Borowsky, *Deutsche Ukrainepolitik 1918 unter besonderer Berücksichtigung der Wirtschaftsbeziehungen* (Lübeck and Hamburg, 1970); H. Pogge von Strandmann, 'Grossindustrie und Rapallopolitik. Deutsch-sowjetische Handelsbeziehungen in der Weimarer Republik', *Historische Zeitschrift*, 222 (1976); W. Zürrer, *Kaukasien 1918-1921. Der Kampf der Grossmächte um die Landbrücke zwischen Schwarzem und Kaspischem Meer* (Düsseldorf, 1978); W. Beitel and J. Nötzold, *Deutsch-sowjetische Wirtschaftsbeziehungen in der Zeit der Weimarer Republik* (Baden, 1979).

See for Rapallo – apart from the above-mentioned titles: T. Schieder, 'Die Entstehungsgeschichte des Rapallo-Vertrages', *Historische Zeitschrift*, 204 (1967); E. Laubach, *Die Politik der Kabinette Wirth 1921/22* (Lübeck and Hamburg, 1968); H. Graml, 'Die Rapallo-Politik im Urteil der westdeutschen Forschung', *Vierteljahrshefte für Zeitgeschichte*, 18 (1970); A. Anderle (ed.), *Rapallo und die friedliche Koexistenz* (Berlin, 1963); R. Bournazel, *Rapallo: naissance d'un mythe. La politique de la peur dans la France du Bloc National* (Paris, 1974); E. Laubach, 'Maltzans Aufzeichnungen über die letzten Vorgänge vor dem Abschluss des Rapallo-Vertrages', *Jahrbücher für Geschichte Osteuropas*, 22

(1975); F. Conte, 'Lloyd George et le traité de Rapallo', *Revue d'histoire moderne et contemporaine*, 23 (1976); R. Himmer, 'Rathenau, Russia, and Rapallo', *Central European History* (1976); E. Schulin, 'Noch etwas zur Entstehung des Rapallo-Vertrages' in H. v. Hentig and A. Nitschke (eds.), *Was die Wirklichkeit lehrt. Golo Mann zum 70. Geburtstag* (Frankfurt, 1979). See for the latest English publication on Russian foreign policy T.J. Uldricks, *Diplomacy and Ideology. The Origins of Soviet Foreign Relations 1917-1930* (London and Beverly Hills, 1979). See for a strict adherence to the primacy of politics, W. Baumgart, 'Deutsch Ostpolitik 1918-1926' in A. Fischer, G. Moltmann and K. Schwabe, *Russia-Germany-America*, Festschrift für F. Epstein (Wiesbaden, 1978).

2. Rosenfeld, *Sowjetrussland*, p. 245; Linke, *Beziehungen*, pp. 45-64.

3. Foreign Office Library, Nachlass Brockdorff-Rantzau, Toepffer to Rantzau, 3 May 1919.

4. Linke, *Beziehungen*, p. 83 f.

5. Ibid., pp. 89 and 92 f; M.L. Goldbach, *Karl Radek und die deutsch-sowjetischen Beziehungen 1918-1923* (Bonn, 1973), p. 49.

6. *Deutsch-Sowjetische Beziehungen von den Verhandlungen in Brest-Litowsk bis zum Abschluss des Rapallovertrages* (Berlin, 1971), vol. ii, pp. 182-92. See also Bundesarchiv Koblenz, R 43 I/1129 and Politisches Archiv Bonn (hereafter PA Bonn), Deutschland 131, vol. 65; Rosenfeld, *Sowjetrussland*, pp. 259 ff; Linke, *Beziehungen*, p. 94.

7. W. Rathenau, *Briefe*, 4th edn (Dresden, 1927), vol. ii, p. 229 f., Rathenau to Hoffmann, 10 Mar. 1920.

8. Pogge von Strandmann, 'Grossindustrie', pp. 284-9.

9. Rosenfeld, *Sowjetrussland*, pp. 346-54; Linke, *Beziehungen*, pp. 142, 165, 172 ff.

10. Rosenfeld, *Sowjetrussland*, p. 351; Linke, *Beziehungen*, p. 192; Achtamzjan, *Sovietsko-Germanskie diplomaticestrie othosenija v 1922-1932 godach* (Moscow, 1974), pp. 30-8.

11. Rosenfeld, *Sowjetrussland*, pp. 167 and 175; Goldbach, *Karl Radek*, p. 107 f.; I.K. Kobljakov holds the view that the initiative for the new round of negotiations came from Moscow: I.K. Kobljakov, 'Neue Materialien über den Rapallo-Vertrag', p. 161 f. in Anderle (ed.), *Rapallo*.

12. HLRO (House of Lords Records), Lloyd George Papers, F/54/2, D'Abernon to Jones, 20 Jan. 1922.

13. See for the military co-operation between the Weimar Republic and Soviet Russia F.L. Carsten, *Reichswehr und Politik 1918-1933*, 2nd edn (Köln and Berlin, 1965), pp. 76-81, 141-57.

14. Linke, *Beziehungen*, pp. 175-89; Pogge von Strandmann, 'Grossindustrie', pp. 291 ff.; Himmer, 'Rathenau', pp. 170-4.

15. Pogge von Strandmann, 'Grossindustrie', pp. 320-5; Beitel und Nötzold, *Wirtschaftbeziehungen*, pp. 65-71.

16. *Deutsch-Sowjetische Beziehungen*, vol. ii, pp. 520-4, 21 Feb. 1922.

17. PRO, Cab. 31/11. See also the unofficial meeting between Chapman and German representatives, ibid., 10 Mar. 1922.

18. Krupp Archiv, WA IV 1418, 1 March 1922; Pogge von Strandmann, 'Grossindustrie', p. 295 f.

19. PA Bonn, Büro Reichsminister, Akten betr. Genua, i. Wiedfeldt to Rathenau, 4 March 1922, in which he agreed to see Rathenau on 9 March.

20. Ibid., 2 Apr. 1922. Rathenau's letter is in English.

21. Ibid., 10 Mar. 1922, PRO, Cab. 31/11, 10 Mar. 1922.

22. I. Schulze-Bidlingmaier (ed.), *Die Kabinette Wirth I und II* (Boppard, 1973), p. 646, meeting with the Länder Prime Ministers, 27 Mar. 1922.

23. D. Felix, *Walther Rathenau and the Weimar Republic* (Baltimore and London, 1971), p. 139.

24. Schulze-Bidlingmaier (ed.), *Die Kabinette*, pp. 675 and 681.

25. Ibid., pp. 677 f. and 685.

26. Linke, *Beziehungen*, p. 200.

27. PA Bonn, Büro Reichsminister, Akten betr. Genua, i, Wiedenfeld's telgram from Moscow, 10 Mar. 1922.

28. Historisches Archiv/Gutehoffnungshütte 30019320, vi b, Bücher, 12 Apr. 1922.

29. PRO, Cab. 31/11, meeting, 13 Apr. 1922.

30. Ibid., second meeting, 13 Apr. 1922.

31. Laubach, 'Maltzans Aufzeichnungen'. It is now well known that Lord D'Abernon used the shorter and Count Kessler the longer version of Maltzan's doubtful accounts. In the English translation of Kessler's biography it is made clear that Lord D'Abernon has used Maltzan's account. As both versions are in some respects identical it was not difficult to guess that Kessler's story was also based on an account by Maltzan. C.H. Kessler, *Walther Rathenau. His Life and Work* (London, 1929), p. 342.

32. PRO, Cab. 31/11.

33. *Deutsch-Sowjetische Beziehungen*, vol. ii, pp. 595-8, Oscar Müller to Ebert, 18 Apr. 1922; Rosenfeld, *Sowjetrussland*, pp. 286 ff.; Laubach, 'Maltzans Aufzeichnungen', p. 557.

34. PRO, Cab. 31/11, meeting between Lloyd George and the German delegation, 19 Apr. 1922.

35. A. Giannini, *Les Documents de la Conférence de Gênes* (Rome, 1922), p. 253, 7 June 1922.

36. Francis Conte holds the view that Lloyd George's tactics were aimed at pushing the Germans into the hands of the Russians so that he could join any German-Russian agreement later. As the Prime Minister was tied by a Cabinet resolution that he should not do anything without France it would not have been easy for him to have arranged an agreement with Russia on his own. Conte then quotes Yan Roudzoutak, whose report about Genoa was published in *Istoricheski Arkhiv* and who believed that Lloyd George wanted to push France, by threatening a separate German-Russian bloc, into taking a more flexible line. Conte overlooks the fact that the negotiations with Russia, which had been going on for several months, were resumed because the German delegation was able to misinterpret deliberately Giannini's visit and the Allied talks with the Russians in the Villa d'Alberti. Conte, 'Lloyd George', pp. 58-64.

37. HLRO, Lloyd George Papers, F/53/3, Rathenau to Lloyd George, 18 Apr. 1922. The official letter of complaint about the separate agreement with the Russians was sent to the German delegation on the same day as Rathenau's letter to the Prime Minister. The German answer of 20 April was unacceptable to Barthou. The Allies then protested against the German excuses for concluding the agreement with the Russians. PRO, Cab. 31/11, Meetings of 21 and 22 April 1922. The letter of protest was dated 21 April 1922.

38. Ibid., 15 Apr. 1922.

39. Schulin, 'Noch etwas', pp. 184-7.

40. PRO, Cab. 31/11, 15 Apr. 1922.

41. According to Maltzan it was Joffe and according to Ljubimov it was Sabinin who made the telephone call. N.N. Ljubimov, 'Die Konferenz zu Genua und der Rapallo-Vertrag' in Anderle (ed.), *Rapallo*, p. 288 f.

42. Schulin, 'Noch etwas', p. 194.

43. The so-called pyjama party was first reported by Lord D'Abernon to whom Maltzan had told the story in 1926. Kessler did not make use of that

particular story in his biography. Only in the English edition does he incorporate this story. As the story makes Maltzan the architect of Rapallo, it has to be questioned, especially as Maltzan does not say why Rathenau should have been reluctant to sign the treaty. Laubach and Himmer equally question Maltzan's story. Laubach, 'Maltzan', pp. 573 ff.; Himmer, 'Rathenau', p. 180. Maltzan's story, together with his two accounts, have helped to create the myth that Rathenau had little to do with Rapallo. This myth was strengthened by the German Foreign Office at the time, as it wanted to dissociate itself for various reasons from Rathenau. The official history of the Weimar Republic during its first ten years of existence refers only to Maltzan in connection with Rapallo and not to Rathenau at all. *Zehn Jahre deutsche Geschichte* (Berlin, 1928), p. 108 f.

44. Linke, *Beziehungen*, p. 277.

45. Ibid., p. 211, Rathenau to Koch-Weser, 9 May 1922.

46. PA Bonn, Abt. IV, Russland, Politik, 2 b, i, Haniel to Rathenau, 25 Apr. 1922.

47. PRO, FO 371/8188.

48. PA Bonn, Abt. IV, Russland, 2 b, iv, Kessler to Gaus, 8 May 1928.

49. H. Graf Kessler, *Tagebuch 1918-1933* (Frankfurt, 1961), p. 561 f.

50. PA Bonn, Abt. IV, Russland, 2 b, iv, Dircksen's note, 29 May 1928.

51. PRO, Cab. 31/11, 17 Apr. 1922.

52. See for the differences between Barthou and Poincaré, Bournazel, *Rapallo*, pp. 169-87. The author also states that the documents in the French Foreign Ministry do not contain much on Genoa and Rapallo.

53. Laubach, 'Maltzans Aufzeichnungen', p. 211; Linke, *Beziehungen*, p. 212.

54. S. Roskill, *Hankey. Man of Secrets* (London, 1970-4), vol. ii, p. 272; Churchill College Cambridge, Hankey Papers, Hankey to Chamberlain, 18 Apr. 1922.

55. PRO, Cab. 31/11, Sir Edward Grigg to Lloyd George, 19 Apr. 1922; Churchill College Cambridge, Hankey Papers, Hankey to Chamberlain, 20 Apr. 1922; M. Bonn, *So Macht man Geschichte* (München, 1953), p. 264 f.

56. PRO, Cab. 31/11, Meeting on 19 Apr. 1922. See also footnote 37.

57. PA Bonn, Handakten Simson, Dufour's report, 16 May 1922; English in the original.

58. The mutual renunciation of claims had been suggested by the industrialists for whom it was not unusual in business operations.

59. PA Bonn, Büro Reichsminister, IV, 6 June 1922.

60. W.N. Meddlicott, D. Dakin and M.E. Lambert (eds.), *Documents on British Foreign Policy 1919-1939* (London, 1974), vol. XIX, p. XI. The memorandum was circulated among members of the Cabinet on 9 April 1923.

61. Kessler, *Tagebuch*, p. 606.

7 THE 'BALTIC PROBLEM' IN WEIMAR'S *OSTPOLITIK*, 1923-1932

John W. Hiden

Historians of the Weimar Republic's foreign policy have not tired of examining Berlin's *Ostpolitik*, but interest has been largely concentrated on the great powers, whilst the newly independent states in East Europe tend to be treated as pawns in a game conducted by giants. This is curious, because the very existence of those small states has invariably been regarded as inseparable from the collapse and temporary eclipse of two of the big powers, Germany and Russia, and this is particularly true of the Baltic republics. Because this contradiction has not been resolved, not enough weight has been given to the fact that the Baltic countries were also the outcome of native aspirations. Although small and weak, the Baltic states had some opportunity to manoeuvre and even to exploit great power rivalry. Thus the interaction between Baltic policies and those of the larger European powers also played its part in the origins of the Second World War. A great deal more has to be known about the so-called smaller powers after the First World War before full justice can be done to this interlocking of the international system, and what follows is a mere contribution towards this larger aim.

Generally speaking, the officials of the Auswärtige Amt used the term *Randstaatenpolitik*, or border states policy, in connection with the efforts of the small East European states to form alliances between themselves after the First World War, but the files in the Bonn archive and on microfilm in London which bear the rubric *Randstaatenpolitik* focus mainly on Poland and the three Baltic states, Latvia, Estonia and Lithuania. It was no accident that German discussions of border states problems were intensified and indeed systematised from 1923 onwards. On 1 November 1923 the signature of an Estonian-Latvian defence agreement marked a distinct phase in the evolution of the various schemes which had been explored since 1919 to bring about a Baltic bloc. In conjunction with Lithuania's seizure of Memel on 10 January 1923, and Poland's success in securing Allied recognition of the border between Poland and Russia on 15 March 1923, the Estonian-Latvian alliance produced a potentially still more alarming and certainly unwelcome situation for German strategists and policy-makers in East Europe.[1] German fears were not lessened by the fact that these developments coincided with the Weimar Republic's own domestic and economic crisis in 1923. The year 1923 was thus a turning point in more than one respect.

Schemes for a Baltic bloc had far more than merely regional significance because they always threatened to become part of the 'barrier' which the Allied politicians sought to build between Germany and Russia immediately after the war, and which was most energetically pursued by France in conjunction with its major East European ally, Poland. The enormous domestic pressure within Germany to revise its Versailles borders with Poland in this respect dovetailed with German interests in curtailing Poland's influence in the Baltic states and reinforced the determination to prevent such a barrier at all costs. This in itself compelled the Weimar Republic to expend effort and energy to cultivate good relations with Latvia, Lithuania and Estonia after the First World War. Nor did the British government conceal its own considerable interest in Baltic affairs in the immediate post-war years. The British followed an economic policy comparable to Germany's in seeking to develop an economic presence in Latvia and Estonia as jumping-off areas for the unknown markets of Bolshevik Russia, but they shared France's interest in retaining the Baltic states as part of a political barrier against Bolshevism.[2] Above all, they exploited their better political standing in the Baltic capitals to counter Germany's developing economic rivalry in East Europe. The Allied blockade of Russia in 1919 created near-impossible conditions for German merchants seeking to resume or open business contacts with the new Baltic republics[3] and, in view of the traditional role played by the Baltic Germans of Latvia and Estonia in East-West commerce, somewhat less than idealistic motives can be seen to have informed the British Premier Lloyd George's espousal of land reform in the Baltic states: 'The sooner the peasants got on the land the better... The German landowners had been a curse to the country and had been used by the German Government as an alien garrison.'[4]

The scale and extent of this early post-war rivalry between private British and German business interests reflected the desperate needs of the new Baltic states. The Russian hinterland had been lost and, because they were saddled with largely agrarian economic structures, the Baltic states were heavily dependent on outside aid, particularly in the form of credit and machines. Politicians like the Latvian Foreign Minister Zigfrids Meierovics deliberately sought to exploit the rivalry between German and British economic interests early in 1921 and the expectation of cashing in on great power competition to penetrate

Russia's markets reached a climax in the Baltic countries prior to the World Economic Conference at Genoa. Baltic leaders faced the problem, however, both of attracting foreign aid and at the same time of trying to control its impact, which of course was a matter of some controversy amongst the diverse political and economic interest groups within the Baltic states. In Estonia in the first half of 1921, and in Latvia from April 1921 under Finance Minister Ringold Kalnings, complex packages of domestic legislation greatly complicated the process of making trade treaties with foreign powers.[5]

The difficulties faced by outside economic interests in negotiating a firm foothold in the border states were increased by the efforts of the Baltic countries to underpin their nascent regional alliances with wider economic and customs agreements. Germany's own experiences in preparing the abortive trade agreement with Latvia in March 1922 provided eloquent testimony to the problems involved. Notwithstanding these setbacks, private German business interests were clearly beating the British at their own game by 1922. As a British businessman complained after a visit to the trade fair in Tallin in spring 1922: 'Germany is doing all the business.'[6] But this can only partly be explained by the Weimar Republic's historical and geographical advantages. Britain's poorer overall performance had much to do with the superior official backing and encouragement of private German interests, for as both British and German officials had argued from the outset, active government encouragement would be crucial in gaining a commercial foothold in the Baltic states.[7] For many countries, such an active policy was hindered because of the general scepticism in Europe about the ability of the small Baltic states to survive for long before being reincorporated in Russia. But as Crohn-Wolfgang of the German Economics Ministry argued when attacking such a passive stance: 'At any rate, the border states are there at the moment and therefore we have a duty to work politically and economically with and in them.'[8]

The relatively greater effort expended by Germany's political and economic advisers and officials was directly related to its defeat in the First World War and the necessity, after the peace settlement had been made, of embracing a range of alternative methods to buttress its long-term plans for revival and for revision of the Versailles Treaty. As General Groener had written in May 1919: 'To conduct a foreign policy one needs power, an army, a fleet and money; all of which we no longer have.'[9] And the former Foreign Minister Friedrich Rosen approved of the reorganisation of the German Foreign Office under the Schuler reforms of 1920 because they also benefited the interests of foreign trade, 'for economics alone were decisive and foreign policy as such pointless'.[10] Gustav Stresemann was later to argue more constructively in *Die Zeit* on 15 May 1923:

> Now that we no longer have our army there are only two sources of German power. One is our united national will and feeling. The second is the German economy... Our economy is the most powerful source of German potential today ... in the last resort every German government must cooperate with the German economy.[11]

The wider importance of such economic ties for foreign policy, as implied in the above quotations, was firmly recognised in the Auswärtiges Amt from the outset.

Indeed the negotiations for temporary trade agreements with all three Baltic countries in 1921 and 1922 had shown a growing inclination on the part of Germany's negotiators to combine the attempt to build an 'economic bridge' to Russia, as Walter Simons had put it early in 1921,[12] with steps to disrupt the regional alliance schemes between Poland and the Baltic states. This conjunction became more marked after the changes in the leadership of the Eastern Department of the Auswärtige Amt in the autumn of 1922 allowed for more effective collaboration with the Reich Ministry of Economics, which had made a constant effort to satisfy the enormous pressure coming from German industry for more active trade with the East.[13] And it was no accident that in March 1922, at a time when the Baltic alliance projects had assumed a more concrete form in the shape of the so-called Warsaw Accord between Poland, Latvia, Estonia and Finland, the head of the Eastern Department, Ago von Maltzan, forcefully stressed the relationship between the day-to-day detail of what was often tedious bargaining with the Baltic governments to settle outstanding differences, and the broader political configuration.[14] Referring to the impact of France's alliance projects on the German-Baltic negotiations, Maltzan advised tactical concentration on Estonia as a more promising target for early agreement in view of the shorter wartime occupation by German forces, in order to put pressure in turn on Latvia and Lithuania to settle their differences with Germany. In fact Lithuania's conflict with Poland over Vilno and Kovno's anxiety to offset its own action in Memel in 1923 by an agreement with Germany over trade problems slightly changed the order of procedure, but the principle remained the same. When Crull opened the discussion in the Auswärtige Amt on 5 February 1923 on the resumption of talks with Estonia he pointed to the necessity, after the agreement shortly to be reached with Lithuania, 'to continue to break open a path through the ring of border states round Russia and to settle differences with Latvia and Estonia'.[15] When the German-Lithuanian temporary trade agreement was signed in May, Maltzan wrote with relief to Germany's new Ambassador to Russia, Brockdorff-Rantzau: 'So one progresses, step by step.'[16] A month later the temporary trade agreement was signed with Estonia, on 27 June 1923.

In effect, then, the turning point in the border states problems in 1923 corresponded roughly with a breakthrough in Germany's trade treaty policies which was clearly not purely fortuitous, but although Germany's trade treaty policies in the 1920s were a central feature of German foreign policy they have attracted relatively little attention. As ever, attention seems to have been concentrated on the economic policy of the Third Reich in East Europe at the expense of what was happening in the 1920s.[17] The attempt made by German officials and economic interest groups in the 1920s to expand Germany's foreign trade through a series of most-favoured-nation treaties with other powers was in itself fraught with difficulties. Not the least of these was the obligation of Germany under the Treaty of Versailles not to make special concessions to single powers without these automatically becoming operative for the Allies. There was also the unresolved question of Germany's customs charges in general. Both factors made the conclusion of permanent as opposed to temporary trade treaties impossible before 1925, which has caused some historians to argue that this year marked the starting-point of trade policies being used for political objectives in East Europe, the German customs war with Poland being the most dramatic example.[18] However, even temporary trade agreements offered German governments opportunities 'actively' to complement their political action to isolate Poland well before 1925, as well as economic gains.

In the first place the 1925 German-Polish trade war was in effect anticipated by the German response to the so-called 'Baltic clause'. This clause was a feature of the network of regional commercial agreements between the border states in the 1920s, whereby in all agreements with third states the Baltic countries reserved the right to make special concessions to each other, particularly in respect of customs duties, over and above those offered under general most-favoured-nation terms.[19] The Auswärtige Amt and Germany's economic experts from the Reich Ministry of Economics found little objection to this, as had been made clear from the earlier negotiations with Latvia in March 1922, but all attempts were resisted by Berlin to make it accept a clause extending such special concessions to Poland as a 'neighbour state', which of course was a target for Warsaw's trade policies. The political nature of Germany's objections was underlined by the fact that the spokesmen for the Reich Ministry of Economics did not regard a customs union as such between the border states as any particular hindrance to German *economic* interests, because it could provide an additional element of stability in the Baltic region.[20] Secondly, temporary trade agreements, such as that concluded with Estonia in 1923, could provide at least an interim guarantee of somewhat fairer treatment for Reich Germans active in or about to become active in the economic life of the Baltic republics. In short, some properly organised legal back-up could be provided for the private German business interests which had so successfully penetrated the Baltic market by 1922, by means of a concerted approach to the detailed restrictions imposed by Baltic domestic legislation.

Like Germany's economic potential, German minorities abroad were regarded by the Weimar Republic's policy makers as a vital foreign policy 'resource' in a time of scarcity. Behind the effort to prop up the German element in Latvia and Estonia (which in this respect at least formed a distinct problem from Lithuania) lay the wider network for the support and care of the *Auslandsdeutsche*.[21] This goal demanded a strategy of encouraging co-operation between German minorities and their host countries in the post-war conditions, when the Weimar Republic suffered the twin disadvantages of more or less violent anti-German feelings and scarce financial resources to provide aid for Germans abroad. In terms of Baltic affairs Berlin was obliged to draw a distinction between Reich Germans and Germans of Latvian or Estonian citizenship (Baltic Germans) in order to demonstrate that it was not meddling in internal Baltic affairs nor continuing its wartime policy of supporting the Baltic Germans.[22] In fact the success of this tactic was bound to depend in large measure on the Baltic Germans themselves, who had for so long enjoyed political, economic and social supremacy in Estonia and Latvia. The policy of positive collaboration practised and preached above all by Paul Schiemann in Latvia was the most dramatic reversal of pre-war Baltic German aims and attitudes. It generated a great deal of conflict with *émigré* Baltic Germans and was acutely painful, but whilst issues of considerable interest are involved here it is enough for our present purposes to stress that the official Baltic German line after 1918 complemented Germany's own Baltic policies because it ensured that substantial German minorities would remain in Estonia and Latvia, to play a role in commerce and industry among other things and thus in Germany's trade policies. Moreover, the fact that Germany bargained so stubbornly over the settlement of differences with Estonia and Latvia can only really be explained by its concern for the German element as a *whole*.[23]

This was illustrated by Germany's defence of the relatively few Reich German landowners affected by the Latvian and Estonian agrarian legislation. In Latvia 42 Reich Germans were affected by Latvia's Agrarian Law of 16 September 1920, and by February 1921 the settlement of this issue had become a *sine qua non* for the assumption of more intensive economic relations between Germany and Latvia. When on 30 April 1924 the Latvian legislature finally crushed hopes of governmental compensation for dispossessed landowners by a slim majority of 15, the question of compensation for foreign landowners was left to be settled between Latvia and the governments concerned. This issue then rapidly became linked with the other major problem holding up the German-Latvian negotiations for a trade agreement, namely the question of German war damages to Latvia.[24] In Estonia some 130 Germans were affected by the Estonian Agrarian Law of 10 September 1919, although most of these had become German citizens after the passage of the law. This was an important point, for when the Estonian government informed the other powers that foreign holdings would not be excluded from any future compensation law, the date for determining citizenship was given as 12 July 1917.[25] Germany's attempts to secure most-favoured-nation treatment for its citizens in Estonia were backpedalled in order to make sure of the provisional Estonian-German trade agreement of 27 June 1923 and, as in Latvia, the whole matter soon became linked with the ultimate fate of a full-scale trade treaty. During the Reichstag debate on the ratification of the 1923 agreement with Estonia the German right-wing deputies Graf Reventlow, Professor Freytag-Loringhoven and Professor Hoetzsch persuaded the politicians to make further progress towards a German-Estonian economic agreement dependent on full most-favoured-nation treatment of Reich German landowners in Estonia.[26]

The complexity of such problems and the way in which they were integrated with other aims of Weimar *Ostpolitik* bears testimony to the extent of the front on which the various industrial, political and departmental interests in Germany were forced to operate under the conditions imposed by Versailles and by Germany's damaged standing in East Europe after the First World War. Moreover, the enforced strategy of long and painstaking day-to-day negotiations to rebuild German influence in East Europe of necessity also reflected the complex patterns woven by the domestic and international policies of the governments and interest groups in the Baltic countries. The greater willingness of the farmers' parties in Estonia and Latvia to sanction fair compensation for agrarian damages than the left-wing parties, the commercial and industrial pressures in the Baltic states towards autarchy, the obsessive concern of Baltic politicians about each minute development in regional alliance projects, all of these were closely monitored and endlessly discussed between the Auswär-tiges Amt and the German representatives in the border states.[27] The head of the key Eastern Department of the German Foreign Office after 1921, Ago von Maltzan, was precisely suited to his role in this respect.

Maltzan's constant effort to observe and point out political prior-ities during the protracted trade treaty negotiations with the Baltic states is quite evident from his correspondence with Brockdorff-Rantzau. Even the choice of personnel was made on carefully argued grounds. When promoted to State Secretary in Cuno's government from November 1922, Maltzan had Eric Wallroth brought back from the Riga Embassy and, as he assured the Count in a private letter to Moscow on 22 December 1922: 'I have only taken this step in the firm conviction that, as ever, I can, in any event, continue to help our Eastern policy... I beg of you not to regard this as desertion.'[28] In fact Wallroth had been in Riga since 1921 during the crucial period prior to the World Economic Conference and he retained the leader-ship of the Eastern Department of the Auswärtige Amt until 1928. His personal stature and commitment and interest in Baltic problems mirrored that of Germany's other representatives in the Baltic states. Unlike the other powers Berlin maintained posts in all three countries on the specific grounds of their greater interest to Germany. Wallroth's successor in Riga was Adolf Koester who, like his predecessor, was an essential figure in the long process of countering anti-German senti-ments in the Baltic countries after the war. Indeed, Koester's distinc-tion as a man of letters, the fact that he had been Foreign Minister in Hermann Mueller's first Cabinet in 1920 and Minister of the Interior from October 1921 to November 1922 in Wirth's second Cabinet, made an enormous impression on Latvian governments and gave Koester considerable influence over those governments as well as over other foreign diplomats in Riga. The fact that Koester fell foul of the more Nationalist-inclined Reich German colony in Riga and was subject to attacks in the Nationalist press at home[29] did not prevent him from enjoying the confidence and close co-operation of Gustav Stresemann after 1923. In Reval, Otto von Hentig, who took up his post in summer 1921, firmly believed that 'on the contrary, influence is only possible via constant effort from a favourable position.'[30] He replaced Dr Henkel, of whom the philosopher Hermann Keyserling had written to Maltzan in July 1920: 'Unobstrusive, generally acknowledged everywhere, he seems to me none the less the right man for the present situation. Germany can only slip into Estonia today through the keyhole, as it were.'[31] Hentig was succeeded by Wedding in 1923, whom Maltzan described to Rantzau as 'an older man, knowledgeable on Russian and Scandinavian affairs'.[32] Here was a continuity of a less dramatic but more constructive kind.

The interest of these personalities in promoting German-Baltic understanding in the 1920s and their role in the various negotiations had to be reconciled with the far larger issues of German-Russian relations. This point was underlined at the first ever joint conference of German ambassadors in the Baltic states, which took place in Riga between 28 and 29 November 1923 to consider the events culminating in the Estonian-Latvian alliance of 1 November. Wedding and Koester were joined by Olshausen from Lithuania and Thermann from the Auswärtige Amt. The discussion concentrated on the political issues after considering the currrent economic negotiations. According to Thermann's account the Estonian-Latvian alliance was 'just the beginning of a larger border states bloc such as has been pursued for a long time on the basis of a common defence against Russia'.[33] Finland was still seen as undecided and wavering between Scandinavia on the one hand, Poland and the Baltic states on the other. Of the remaining powers England was represented as following a purely commercial policy whilst America's combined diplomatic and trade mission in Riga was mainly to transmit information on Russia's economic situation. Russian policy was felt increasingly to be making a distinction between Lithuania on the one hand and Estonia and Latvia on the other. This was a logical distinction in view of the hostility between Poland and Lithuania over Vilno which had dogged the Baltic alliance projects since 1920. Inevitably, most attention was given to Poland and France, particularly in Koester's account, which provided a historical sketch of the regional alliance projects.[34] All agreed, in Thermann's words, that 'the main aim of German policy in the border states is to prevent an alliance which groups these states under Polish leadership against Russia.' Notwithstanding Germany's own concern about the seizure of Memel earlier that year, the German ambassadors continued to stress Lithuania's importance to Germany in view of their shared conflict with Poland. Koester observed:

> We have an exceptionally strong interest in the border states, who are excellent buyers of our goods. In the border states we have an economic outpost for exploiting the Russian market. Politically, we have the greatest interest in the Baltic states keeping out of any alliance with Poland.

Koester also urged that, at least regarding a Baltic bloc under Poland's aegis, 'German and Russian interests coincide perfectly.' In many respects these sentiments echoed those of Seeckt, who had also been reflecting on events in 1923 in the border states and who had argued in a letter to Stresemann that 'the interests of Germany and Russia in the border states run parallel.'[35] But the political experts were far from sharing the General's apparent indifference to the Baltic states as such, not least because of their appreciation of economic and minority issues and because of their consideration of the whole nexus of European relations. Moreover Germany's trade treaty policy makes it difficult to accept those scholars who have talked of a common German-Russian political line on Baltic problems in the 1920s.[36] This approach overlooks the way in which the Treaty of Rapallo signed between Germany and Russia on 16 April 1922 was exploited by the German economic negotiators to try to *consolidate* their own economic relations with the Baltic countries. And whilst the resumption of direct relations between Germany and Russia robbed the notion of the Baltic states as a stepping stone to Russia of some of its force, the pressure coming from industrial circles in Germany for closer economic ties with the East continued.[37] The Auswärtige Amt and the Reich Ministry of Economics, not to mention the host of official and semi-official organisations working in the field of the *Auslandsdeutsche* thus continued to press for agreements with the Baltic states in 1923.

Of course such temporary treaties as those signed between Germany and Lithuania and Estonia in 1923 had an essential part to play in the wider effort to build up economic relations with Russia in accordance with the Rapallo promises. This was highlighted by the fact that the temporary German-Estonian and German-Lithuanian treaties of 1923 provided an overture as it were to the wearisome struggle from the summer of 1923 to hammer out an economic agreement with Russia.

The fitful progress of the latter exchanges underlined the continuing importance of independent and democratically governed border states to those German firms and companies interested in trade with Russia who had their depots in the Baltic states.[38] The effort expended on the German side on behalf of the German element as a whole in Latvia and Estonia reinforced this interest. Those who have wanted to see a threat as such to the Baltic states in the 'Rapallo relationship' have consistently underestimated or ignored the logic of Germany's trade treaty policies. The multiple interests behind these need to be kept in mind when considering what German-Russian efforts were made after Rapallo to develop a more co-ordinated approach to *Randstaaten-politik*. Whilst such co-operation was certainly envisaged at Rapallo,[39] the fact that it did not automatically materialise will surprise no scholar who gives due weight to the uneven development of German-Russian relations prior to Rapallo. As Wipert von Blücher wrote as late as November 1924 in his memorandum on the 'Baltic Problem', although the Rapallo Treaty had become an important factor in relations in the Baltic area:

The difference in the internal politics of both countries [Germany and Russia] will of course make a closer relationship difficult. Moreover, the foreign policy sympathies and interests of both countries cannot automatically be reduced to identical political tactics in the Baltic area.[40]

Blücher had also argued when discussing Franco-Polish interests in the Baltic that:

The one essential factor which is already showing itself in view of the present situation is that the Baltic problem, because of the present allocation of its shores and the way in which this came about, is closely linked with the Versailles Treaty and the Eastern question.

This was of course confirmed when in 1924 and 1925 the domestic balance in Germany, Britain and France made more wide-ranging co-operation over European security a feasible proposition at the very time when Russia's own problems were intensified by the death of Lenin and the struggle for control among his successors. Stresemann inevitably maintained a strong interest in the ties between Germany and the Baltic states during his term at the Foreign Office between 1923 and 1929, because of his own commitment to German trade policies and because of his own revisionist tactics. The key element in Stresemann's strategy after 1924 was the distinction he sought to preserve between Germany's eastern and western borders. The latter were to be subject to a treaty of guarantee eventually provided by the Locarno agreements of October 1925 on the Franco-German and Belgian-German borders, whilst in the East, by contrast, the German-Polish and German-Czech borders were to be subject to treaties of arbitration which, on the German model, specifically did not exclude territorial revision at some more suitable later date.[41] It followed, as State Secretary von Schubert informed the German Embassy at Tallin on 3 April 1925, that although

> sharp criticism has given way to more reasoned judgements, we none the less continue to have a considerable interest in strengthening the argument that such treaties are a suitable means for securing peaceful relations between countries... For this reason I would value it if negotiations with Estonia were to be concluded as soon as possible.[42]

On 17 April 1925, Wallroth also re-opened the idea of a German-Latvian arbitration treaty in a talk with the Latvian Ambassador to Berlin, Voits, an idea first raised by Rathenau just after the Genoa Conference in 1922.[43]

The importance to the Weimar Republic's overall *Ostpolitik* of even the small Baltic countries during its negotiations with the Western powers was emphasised by an interesting episode sparked off by a long memorandum from Adolf Koester, 'Concerning Current Political Trends in the Border States'.[44] This graphically described the obstacles being placed in the way of Germany's efforts to consolidate its economic and political influence in the Baltic countries by Russia's continuing refusal to clarify its own relations with its smaller neighbours. Koester rightly argued that Poland's 'redoubled' efforts 'here in the north' were also related to Polish fears about Germany's security action and France's recognition of Soviet Russia late in 1924. Although he recognised that there was no immediate prospect of a Polish-controlled Baltic bloc, Koester argued for Germany and Russia to give some guarantee to the three Baltic states without Poland. Since Germany had already been discussing arbitration treaties with Estonia and Latvia for some time, it would cost Germany 'virtually nothing to sign guarantee treaties with these states.

> I cannot judge from here whether Russia is ready . . . to conclude guarantee treaties with the three northern border states, which would mean Russia finally abandoning these countries but would also secure for all time Russia's right flank in the event of a military clash with the West. . . In any case I believe that we should do everything to bring Russia to this step.

The German Foreign Office reaction to this idea[45] confirmed that the two major advantages of such a course of action would be that of co-operating with Russia and secondly 'that of relieving our Eastern front' by splitting the Baltic states from Poland. No objections were raised about the talks actually beginning immediately, although the matter could clearly not be resolved until the Locarno negotiations were safely out of the way. The most serious difficulty concerned the formula for a guarantee which would not prejudice German claims to Memel.

Although the project was ultimately stillborn, not least because of German reservations about guaranteeing any territorial frontiers in East Europe in view of its conflict with Poland, it provides a good example of the need to examine events in the wings as well as the larger events at the centre of the stage. Stresemann fully accepted Koester's point about the value of using Baltic problems to offset the bleak relations which had set in between Berlin and Moscow during Germany's talks with the West. Secondly, Stresemann continued to give a more positive twist to Germany's Baltic policies by more openly encouraging the idea of Baltic co-operation with Germany and Russia. In June 1925 hints were dropped to the Latvians and Estonians that Germany would be seeking to persuade Russia to guarantee the border states[46] and in the summer of 1925, German promises to adopt a more accommodating attitude in the economic talks due to resume with Latvia in the autumn were specifically linked with requests that Latvia clarify its relations with Russia and steer clear of any Polish-led combination.[47] It is quite apparent, however, that Stresemann's Baltic policy was certainly not seen simply in terms of German-Russian collaboration. Russian policy towards the border states had persistently refused to treat with them *en bloc*, preferring the road of separate agreements. Germany would therefore have inevitably been the main beneficiary of any such Russian guarantees, which promised to buttress the Weimar Republic's economic policies by providing greater security in the Baltic region. In effect Germany's progress in improving its standing in the Baltic states ran counter to Soviet desires to keep issues fluid there. In addition, since the loyalties of the Baltic leaders were still largely with the Western powers, Germany's imminent success in resolving its relationship with France and Britain was certain to bring a further improvement of German-Baltic understanding.

It is not surprising therefore that Baltic leaders were kept fully informed of the implications of Germany's arbitration treaties with Poland, and of the expectation of change in the German-Polish frontiers in the distant future which underlay the agreements eventually reached at Locarno.[48] Yet although arbitration treaties were central to the Weimar Republic's revisionist policy towards Poland and Czechoslovakia, such treaties were not just an adjunct to revisionism as they have so often been seen. When set in the context of German-Baltic relations as a whole during the 1920s they can also be seen to have been an integral feature of an ongoing German attempt to stabilise relations with the Baltic countries. The offer of arbitration treaties to Estonia and Latvia in 1925 served other long-standing interests too. The Auswärtige Amt reminded the Reich Ministry of Finance that: 'There is virtually no doubt that a treaty of arbitration would confirm Estonia's duty to pay fair compensation' for the Reich Germans affected by the agrarian legislation.[49] Indeed, the German negotiations with the Baltic states reached an important stage in this matter precisely at this time. In Estonia, German efforts to persuade the Reich German landowners to form a special organisation to facilitate a more co-ordinated approach to the question of fair compensation culminated in June 1925 in the formation of the Verband der in Estland enteigneten Reichsdeutschen Gutsbesitzer.[50] In the case of Latvia, efforts were being made, in conjunction with the Schutzstelle für Reichsdeutschen Besitz in den Randstaaten, to reach agreement on a rate of compensation which would be financed by money saved as a result of a German-Latvian deal on their respective claims for war damages, thus neatly and finally removing the two most serious obstacles to the conclusion of an economic agreement. In July 1925 the German-Latvian negotiators at last agreed definitely to resume discussions for a trade treaty in the autumn, using the text of the abortive 1922 agreement as the basis for talks in order to save time. On 10 August Latvia duly played its part in Germany's wider and narrower strategy, so to speak, by signing an arbitration treaty with Berlin.

Stresemann's foreign policy therefore opened up perspectives which would have been difficult to imagine in 1923, not least because the implications of the Locarno agreements made the idea of a Baltic bloc seem increasingly anachronistic. The 'policy of the Warsaw Accord' had had more relevance in 1922, when there were real fears of German-Russian co-operation against the Allied powers. By 1925 there was sufficient evidence to show that, in spite of serious opposition, key sectors in German politics and society were behind the attempt to integrate Germany's policies towards East and West, which certainly made the notion of a 'barrier' in East Europe a somewhat blunt and inappropriate response to the resurgence of German political and economic power. Such considerations coincided with and reinforced the disillusionment of key Baltic leaders about the prospects of a Baltic league, not the least important being the Latvian Foreign Minister, Meierovics. Like others in 1925, he was sensible to the ultimate aversion of both Britain and France to providing any physical defence for the Baltic states. His doubts on this point were reinforced both by the unhelpful Allied response to the abortive Soviet-inspired *coup* in Reval in December 1924, and by Meierovics' own urgent tour of Western capitals in 1925.[51] His conscious change of policy emphasis in the summer of 1925, in favour of accommodation with Germany and against the Warsaw Accord,[52] was by no means endorsed by all the Latvian parties, let alone some of the Estonian leaders, like Kaarel Pusta, but it ideally complemented German Baltic policies at a key moment in the security pact talks. To contemporaries Meierovics' death in a car accident only weeks before the last of the regular conferences of Baltic Foreign Ministers in September 1925 seemed like the end of an era.

After Locarno even the *Latvijas Westnesis*, the organ of the Democratic Centre and hitherto against any orientation of Latvia's foreign policy towards Germany, voiced its disillusionment with the Baltic bloc and with Poland. 'We must therefore regulate our relations with those great powers . . .who are important to us, and that means Germany and Russia.'[53] Growing attacks on Pusta at this time were also seen as symptomatic of the disillusionment with the Baltic bloc in Estonia. As to Lithuania, reports were flowing in to Berlin by November 1925 that the Lithuanian leaders tended to think almost wholly in terms of closer relations with Germany.[54] The improvement in Germany's prospects in the border states was reflected in Stresemann's own memorandum of 24 February 1926, on the prospects for an 'Eastern Locarno'.[55] The German Foreign Minister insisted that the policy of the Warsaw Accord was doomed, particularly in view of the more pronounced opposition of Finland and Lithuania. He was even more scathing about an idea being discussed in the border states that Sweden could be persuaded to join Finland, Poland and Russia in a guarantee pact which would ultimately be extended to the Baltic states. Such a prospect was made still more remote by Russia's persistent revival of the idea of signing separate treaties of non-aggression with the border states in 1926.

In such a context the German-Soviet Non-Aggression Treaty of April 1926 again functioned less as a direct threat than as a model which could be exploited to persuade the border states to reach similar agreements with Russia, thus incidentally relieving Germany of the embarrassment of being asked to guarantee the Baltic states. But this time, in contrast to the period after Rapallo, even contemporary Baltic politicians were more intrigued than alarmed. 'There was little sign in the press', Koester reported from Riga, 'of the uproar that arose a few years ago when the two large neighbours seemed to be getting too intimate with one another.' Koester rightly argued that this was because the border states, in dealing with Russian overtures for non-aggression treaties in 1926, had to solve a problem comparable to that which Germany had apparently already resolved. Namely, a formula had to be found which 'combined the maximum of neutrality towards Russia with full loyalty to the League of Nations'.[56]

True, the shared German-Russian hostility towards Poland found expression in German-Russian exchanges prior to the signature of the Russian-Lithuanian non-aggression treaty of 28 September 1926. However, it was only at this late juncture that there appeared in more tangible form that mutual goodwill between Germany and Russia in handling border states' problems which had first been mooted at the time of the Rapallo Treaty. The Auswärtige Amt reinforced Lithuanian overtures to Russia whilst at the same time ensuring that the Russians dropped any mention of Memel in the text of their treaty with Lithuania.[57] Under the circumstances the Soviet-Lithuanian agreement was yet another nail in the coffin of regional alliance projects and the rightist-Nationalist *coups* in Poland in May 1926, and in Lithuania in December 1926, provided a virtual guarantee of the continuation of the quarrels between Warsaw and Kovno. German spokesmen also encouraged the Latvian-Russian exchanges for a non-aggression pact which, though abortive, provided an essential context for the later Latvian-Russian trade treaty of 2 June 1927. The arrival of the Social Democrat Feliks Cielens at the Latvian Foreign Office, which made the policy of *rapprochement* with Russia possible in the first place, appeared to complete the favourable prospects for a belated degree of German-Russian co-ordination over border states policy.[58] Yet those who have looked forward to 1939 to find a clue to what was happening between Germany and Russia over border states' problems in the 1920s again fail to do justice to the differences between the achievements of Germany and Russia in East Europe during the earlier period or to the premisses of the Weimar Republic's policies in the East.

This point is most easily demonstrated by contrasting the impact of the Soviet-Latvian trade agreement of 1927 with the German-Latvian trade treaty of 28 June 1926. Whereas the former did not produce any great upswing in Soviet-Latvian commerce and offended Latvia's unofficial, if somewhat reticent, protector, Great Britain, in view of Anglo-Soviet discord in 1926/7, the German-Latvian agreement was a key factor in *Randstaatenpolitik*. It was not the mere aside to Germany's anti-Polish policy in the border states that it has become in some diplomatic studies,[59] but represented a climax of seven years' concerted effort by German Foreign Office and Economics Ministry officials to underpin a policy of constructive participation in the political and economic development of the Baltic states. Its successful conclusion was possible not simply because of Baltic politicians' despair at the absence of a positive Franco-British commitment to defend the small states, but because of Germany's apparent success in relating its contacts with Russia to its relations with the Western powers at Locarno and after. This European context played a crucial part in defusing the anti-German feelings and distrust in the Baltic states which had helped to spin the negotiations out for so long in the first place. The German-Latvian treaty at least removed the more serious sources of dispute by providing a linked solution to the two most intractable problems of war damages and compensation for dispossessed Reich German landowners. The 6 million marks which the German government had earmarked to settle Latvia's claims for war damages (originally put at 30 million!) went towards compensating the Reich German landowners in question. Technically, the Latvian government compensated the landowners, but in fact payment was ultimately made from Berlin in accordance with a series of agreements between the German government and the Schutzstelle für Reichsdeutschen Besitz in den Randstaaten.[60]

The treaty provided a more secure basis for the long-term activity of private German business in Latvia and helped to bring to an end the chain of petty discriminations which German businessmen had had to endure in Latvia after 1918.[61] The Latvian Economics Ministry's own journal registered the treaty as a turning point[62] and the welcome given to the agreement in large sections of the Latvian press contrasted markedly with the violence of the later reaction in Latvian business and political circles to the Soviet-Latvian economic agreement.[63] Between 1924 and 1927 Germany contributed an average of 46 per cent of vitally important manufactured goods to Latvia. Moreover Germany continued to be the chief consumer of Latvian dairy products, particularly butter. By the end of the 1920s some 80 per cent of Latvia's butter went to Germany. German capital, some 15 per cent of all foreign capital in Latvia by 1927, was distributed throughout trading concerns, banks and industries, particularly the textile, ceramic, wood and metal industries, with all this entailed for the support of German minorities in general. Such was the situation during the great slump of 1929 that when the Darmstadt National Bank collapsed, the crisis sharpened in Latvia leading to economic collapse, providing somewhat painful proof of the relative weight of German influence.[64] By contrast the Latvian-Soviet treaty provided a dead end, offering nothing like the levels for transit trade originally expected from the agreement.[65]

Nor could Germany's economic weight in Estonia be denied by 1926,[66] although three more years were to pass before Berlin could conclude a trade treaty. After 3 March 1926, when the Estonian law on compensation became known, which was regarded as inadequate by the German landowners, the German government intensified its pressure to make the conclusion of the trade treaty dependent on prior satisfaction for the Reich German landowners. Meanwhile attempts were made by the Auswärtige Amt and the Reich Ministry of Finance, in conjunction with the chairman of the Verband der in Estland enteigneten Reichsdeutschen, Baron Lerchenfeld, temporarily to alleviate the distress of Reich German landowners in Estonia by providing loans in anticipation of Estonian compensation.[67] The announcement by the Estonian government in autumn 1928 that it intended to introduce a scale of double tariffs for those countries with whom it had not yet signed a trade treaty changed matters dramatically. By this time most of the Reich Germans in Estonia affected by the agrarian laws had received some compensation and of the others the majority had become German citizens after the passage of the original Agrarian Law of 1919.[68] Thus the German government at once began negotiations for the trade treaty which was eventually signed in March 1929, leaving the few outstanding cases of dispossessed German landowners to be settled in private negotiations between Tallin and the Germans concerned.

The drawn-out nature of German-Baltic negotiations to reach a point of understanding through the settlement of old issues testifies to the extent of the political problems behind economic relations between Germany and East Europe after 1919. These larger issues, rather than the delays caused by the changing governments in both the Weimar Republic and the Baltic states throughout the 1920s provide a better explanation for the prolonged negotiations between Germany and the Baltic countries. Preventing Polish hegemony in the Baltic was the main motive of Berlin's trade treaty policy. Such larger aims help to explain why Germany was prepared to make so much effort to maintain and develop economic ties with the Baltic countries, but it would be quite wrong to minimise the value to the weakened Weimar Republic of the *economic* benefits of good relations with the Baltic countries. Moreover, Germany's economic policy cannot be seen simply in terms of disrupting Poland's plans for a Baltic bloc. Whilst Germany's trade treaties with Estonia, Latvia and Lithuania defused the Baltic clause, and thus effectively helped to undermine the wider regional alliance plans, it is clear that economically such a closed system would have been disastrous for the border states because of their somewhat similar and predominantly agrarian structures.[69] Since economic progress was in many respects the acid test of survival for Baltic leaders, Germany's contribution to that survival can hardly be seen in a wholly negative light.

All of these considerations are reinforced by recalling the effort expended both by the German government and the Baltic German leaders on the spot to preserve large German minorities in Latvia and Estonia, with whom Germany had no revisionist claims. Although Baltic public opinion on the question of German minorities remained exceedingly sensitive throughout the 1920s, the policy of constructive collaboration favoured by the main Baltic German leaders and by Germany's general policy towards the *Auslandsdeutsche*, again provided no small contribution to the economic development of both Latvia and Estonia.[70] And if due importance is accorded to the German minority as a whole in the Baltic states for the conduct of Weimar *Ostpolitik*, then the support of Baltic independence by Germany was more than just a corollary of its anti-Polish policies.[71] Indeed the whole question of the sovereign independence of the Baltic states was intimately linked with the continued survival of the German element, just as the removal by evacuation of that element under Hitler was the prelude to the ending of Baltic independence. In the 1920s, German trade policies in the border states functioned to modify and restrain the more extreme revisionist strategies current in the Weimar Republic. The attempt to prevent a Polish-led Baltic bloc in the interests of the Weimar Republic's revisionist aims clearly involved Russia, but after Rapallo it was increasingly difficult to reconcile the logic of German trade treaty policies in the Baltic states with Russian pressures against the small republics. Thus by 1931 German Foreign Minister Curtius was able quite accurately to reassure the Estonian Foreign Minister at a meeting in Geneva and to stress Germany's effort 'to encourage the independence of the Baltic states, since we were hardly keen to see them becoming dependent on Russia or joining a Polish led bloc'.[72]

The continued study of less familiar aspects of Germany's foreign relations after 1919 will help to offset the tendency to short-change the Weimar Republic's achievements in this field, which the stress on continuity of German foreign policy has brought in its wake. The recovery of Germany's economic weight and political influence in the Baltic area was indeed part of the Republic's drive to revise the Treaty of Versailles. Yet the methods used to achieve this goal, although dictated by German weakness after the First World War and revolution, contained much potential for peaceful change. The fact that those changes were unwelcome, to Poland for example, or to France and even Britain, who, during the 1920s, were unable in the last resort to match their political contribution to Baltic independence with a sufficiently powerful economic contribution, is another problem. In itself, it simply underlines the need to re-examine more closely the inter-relations of all the powers, large and small, in the inter-war years. Notwithstanding the violence of the criticism within Germany of a policy of revision in conjunction with, rather than against, the Western powers, Weimar *Ostpolitik* worked within a fairly tightly defined framework and this was only broken by the limitless ambitions nourished in the Third Reich.

Notes

1. Text of the agreement in G. Albat, *Récueil des principaux traités conclus par la Lettonie avec les pays etrangères, 1918-1928* (Riga, 1928), pp. 77-9.

2. Documents on British Foreign Policy (hereafter DBFP), first series (London, 1961), vol II, no. 413; G. Niedhart, 'Die westlichen Alliierten und das bolschewistische Russland, 1917-21', *Neue Politische Literatur*, 15 (1970), p. 466.

3. Auswärtiges Amt (hereafter AA), Akten betr. Wiederaufnahme des Warenaustausches, Baltenland, Nr. 4, Frieden II, Wirtschaftliches, Bd. I, Bundesarchiv Koblenz (hereafter BAK), AA to Nordexport Robert Schnabel, 20 Feb. 1919.

4. W. Lenz, 'Zur britischen Politik gegenüber den baltischen Deutschen' in R. v. Thadden *et al.* (eds.), *Das Vergangene und die Geschichte* (Göttingen, 1973), p. 273.

5. B. Siew, *Lettlands Volks- und Staatswirtschaft* (Riga, 1925), pp. 45ff.; E. Kroeger, *Die rechtliche Stellung des Ausländers in Lettland* (Berlin-Grunewald, 1930), pp. 16, 21, 44-5.

6. D. Kirby, 'A Great Opportunity Lost? Aspects of British Commercial Policy towards the Baltic States, 1920-24', *Journal of Baltic Studies*, no. 4 (1974), p. 365.

7. Ibid., pp. 364-5.

8. H. F. Crohn-Wolfgang, 'Die Republik Lettland und ihre wirtschaftliche Zukunft', *Jahrbücher für Nationalökonomie und Statistik*, 118 (1922), p. 422.

9. D. Groener-Geyer, *General Groener. Soldat und Staatsmann* (Frankfurt, 1955), p. 146.

10. H. Müller-Werth (ed.), *F. Rosen. Aus einem diplomatischen Wanderleben* (Wiesbaden, 1959), p. 288.

11. G. Stresemann, *Vermächtnis*, (Berlin, 1932), vol. I, p. 64

12. AA, Akten betr. politische Beziehungen Deutschlands zu Lettland, Bd. 2, London Foreign Office Film (hereafter FO), K2331/K663749-51, Wever to AA, 29 Jan. 1921.

13. AA, Akten betr. Wirtschaftsabkommen Estland, Wünsche, Deutsches Zentralarchiv Potsdam (hereafter DZA), 66301, Memorandum by Blücher, 11 Nov. 1921.

14. AA, Akten betr. politische Beziehungen Deutschlands zu Estland, Bd. 1, FO, K2325/K662143-7, Maltzan to Hentig, 17 Mar. 1922.

15. Reichsschatzministerium, Akten betr. Estland, Bd. 2, DZA 7175, Protocol of AA Meeting of 5 Feb. 1923.

16. Brockdorff-Rantzau Papers, Packet 14, Nr. 2, FO, 9101H/H 225582-86, Maltzan to Brockdorff, 31 May 1923.

17. See R. Frommelt, *Paneuropa oder Mitteleuropa* (Stuttgart, 1977).

18. H. Lippelt, ' "Politische Sanierung". Zur deutschen Politik gegenüber Polen', *Vierteljahrshefte für Zeitgeschichte*, 19 (1971), p. 330.

19. R. Brenneisen, 'Aussenhandel und Aussenhandelspolitik der baltischen Staaten mit besonderer Berücksichtigung der Beziehungen zu Deutschland', *Weltwirtschaftliches Archiv*, 30 (1929), pp. 384-5.

20. H. F. Crohn-Wolfgang, *Lettlands Bedeutung für die östliche Frage* (Leipzig-Berlin, 1923), pp. 42-3.

21. J. W. Hiden, 'The Weimar Republic and the Problem of the Auslandsdeutsche', *Journal of Contemporary History*, 12 (1977), pp. 280-1.

22. AA, Akten betr. politische Beziehungen Estlands zu Deutschland, Bd. 1, FO, K246/K075748-49, Maltzan to Wedding, 12 July 1923.

23. See K. -H. Grundmann, *Deutschtumspolitik zur Zeit der Weimarer Republik* (Hannover-Döhren, 1977), pp. 106 ff.

24. Ibid., pp. 229, 232.

25. Ibid., pp. 233-4.

26. AA, Akten betr, die Agrarreform in Estland, Bd. 3, DZA 66372, AA to Verband Sächsischer Industrieller (Dresden), 20 Apr, 1928.

27. See the immensely detailed reports in Reichsministerium des Innern, Akten betr. Nachrichten über politische Vorgänge, Estland, DZA 16617.

28. Brockdorff-Rantzau Papers, Packet 14, No. 1, FO 9101H/H225049-51, Maltzan to Brockdorff, 22 Dec. 1922.

29. Grundmann, *Deutschtumspolitik*, pp. 258-64.

30. W. O. v. Hentig, *Mein Leben. Eine Dienstreise* (Göttingen, 1965), p. 225.

31. AA, Akten betr. politische Beziehungen Deutschlands zu Estland, Bd. 1,

FO. K2325/K661987-92, Keyserling to Maltzan, 4 July 1920.
32. Brockdorff-Rantzau Papers, Packet 14, No. 2, FO, 9101H/H225587-91, Maltzan to Brockdorff, 24 May 1923.
33. AA, Akten betr. Probleme (Randstaatenbund einschl. Finnland und Polen), Bd. 2, FO, K243/K071349-56, Report of 7 Dec. 1923.
34. Ibid., K071364-76, Memorandum by A. Köster, 8 Dec. 1923.
35. F. L. Carsten, *Reichswehr und Politik, 1918-1933* (Cologne, 1964), p. 155.
36. H. I. Rogers, *Search for Security* (New Haven, 1975), p. 10
37. H. Pogge v. Strandmann, 'Grossindustrie und Rapallopolitik', *Historische Zeitschrift*, 222 (1976), pp. 298 ff.
38. Ibid., pp. 314 ff., on the problems with Russia. For a report on the German firms in the border states, see AA, Gesandtschaftsakten betr. Estland, 1919-22, Geheim 2B, Paket 21, Politisches Archiv Bonn (hereafter PAB), Report of 10 Jan. 1922.
39. AA, Akten betr. politische Beziehungen der Randstaaten zu Deutschland, FO, K1752/K429137, Maltzan to AA, 21 Apr. 1922.
40. AA, Akten betr. Neutralisierung der Ostsee, Bd. 1, FO, K154/K017379-97.
41. On the general problems, M. Walsdorff, *Westorientierung und Ostpolitik* (Bremen, 1971).
42. AA, Akten betr. Estland, FO, 3015/D594776-77.
43. AA, Büro von Stsekr. von Schubert, Akten betr. Ostprobleme, Bd. 4, FO, 4556, Memorandum by Wallroth, 17 Apr. 1925.
44. AA, Akten betr. politische Beziehungen zu den Randstaaten, Bd. 1, FO, 4561/E153689-93.
45. Ibid., E153694-95.
46. AA, Büro von Stsekr, von Schubert, Akten betr. politische Beziehungen zu den Randstaaten, Bd. 1, FO, 4561/E153741-43, Schubert's account of conversation with Voits on 25 June 1925, n.d.
47. Ibid., Memorandum by Schubert, 3 July 1925.
48. Ibid.
49. Reichsfinanzministerium, Akten betr. Kriegsschäden der Deutschen in Estland, Bd. 1, BAK, RZ/Zg 29/1959/742.
50. AA, Akten betr. Agrarreform in Estland und die aus derselben entstandenen Reklamationen, Bd. 5, DZA, 65956, Memorandum by Dittmar (AA), 16 Jan. 1926.
51. G. v. Rauch, 'Der Revaler Kommunistenputsch', *Baltische Hefte* (1955), pp. 19-23; on Meierovics's tour see AA, Akten betr. politische Beziehungen Deutschlands zu Lettland, Bd. 4, FO, K2331/K664204-5, Köster to AA, 5 Aug. 1925.
52. Rogers, *Search for Security*, p. 45.
53. AA, Akten betr. politische Beziehungen Deutschlands zu Lettland, Bd. 4, FO, K2331/K664219-21, Köster to AA, 10 Nov. 1925.
54. AA, Büro von Stsekr, von Schubert, Akten betr. politische Beziehungen zu den Randstaaten, Bd. 1, FO, 4561/E153666-68, Memorandum by Schubert, 10 Nov. 1925.
55. Akten zur Deutschen Auswärtigen Politik, Serie B, Bd. 2, I, pp. 177-9; H. I. Rogers, 'Latvia's Quest for an Eastern Locarno', *East European Quarterly*, 5 (1975), pp. 103-13.
56. AA, Akten betr. politische Beziehungen Deutschlands zu Lettland, Bd. 4, FO, K2331/K664223-26, Köster to AA, 8 May 1926.
57. AA, Akten betr. Sicherheitspakt, Bd. 2, FO, K244/K073052-53, Stresemann to Brockdorff, 29 Apr. 1926; Akten zur Deutschen Auswärtigen Politik,

Serie B, Bd. 2, I, pp. 459-62, 471-2; Bd. 2, II, pp. 232-4.

58. Rogers, *Search for Security*, p. 58.

59. Ibid., p. 50, where Rogers shows the dangers of a purely diplomatic study by failing to realise the full implications of German economic policy.

60. Albat, *Récueil*, pp. 359-73; Reichskanzlei, Akten betr. baltische Staaten, Bd. 4, BAK, R4 31/50, Schubert to Reichskanzlei, 26 Aug. 1926.

61. R. Brenneisen, *Lettland. Das Werden und Wesen einer neuen Volkswirtschaft* (Berlin, 1936), p. 108.

62. B. Gernet, 'Lettlands auswärtige Handelsbeziehungen', *Lettlands Ökonomist* (1929), p. 25.

63. E. Anderson, 'The USSR Trades with Latvia', *Slavic Review*, 21 (1962), p. 311.

64. Gernet, 'Lettlands auswärtige Handelsbeziehungen', pp. 27-31. See also the tables in A. Bilmanis, *Latvijas Werdegang vom Bischofsstaat Terra Mariana bis zur freien Volksrepublik* (Leipzig, 1934), pp. 130-1; J. v. Hehn, 'Lettland zwischen Demokratie und Diktatur', *Jahrbücher für Geschichte OstEuropas*, Beiheft 3 (1957), p. 15.

65. A. N. Tarulis, 'Baltic Ports. Soviet Claims and Reality', *Baltic Review*, 24 (1962), pp. 17-30.

66. Brenneisen, *Lettland*, pp. 378-81; U. Knaur, *Wirtschaftsstruktur und Wirtschaftspolitik des Freistaates Estland, 1918-40* (Bonn, 1962), pp. 130-2; I. Romas, *Die wirtschaftliche Struktur der baltischen Staaten und die Idee einer Zollunion* (Rytas, 1934), pp. 138-9, 164-7.

67. AA, Akten betr. die Agrarreform in Estland, Bd. 5, DZA, 65956, Lerchenfeld to Dittmar, 20 Feb. 1926.

68. Reichskanzlei, Akten betr. Handelsverträge mit den baltischen Staaten, Bd. 1, BAK, R4 31/1122, AA Memorandum, 21 June 1929.

69. G. v. Rauch, *The Baltic States* (London, 1974), p. 125.

70. Grundmann, *Deutschtumspolitik*, pp. 677 ff.

71. The danger of seeing German minorities outside the Reich simply in terms of helping German revisionism is underlined by K. Düwell, *Deutschlands Auswärtige und Kulturpolitik, 1918-1932* (Cologne, 1976), p. 243.

72. W. Hubatsch, 'Die aussenpolitischen Beziehungen des Deutschen Reiches zu Lettland und Estland', *Deutsche Studien*, 13 (1975), p. 306.

8 PARAMILITARISM AND SOCIAL DEMOCRACY: THEODOR KÖRNER AND THE SCHUTZBUND

Martin Kitchen

Theodor Körner will long be remembered as an outstanding mayor of occupied Vienna in the difficult years after 1945, and as much loved President of the Austrian Republic from 1951 until his death in 1957. This handsome and dignified old man seemed to many Austrians to be a living symbol of the political compromises of the new Republic. He had been a senior staff officer in the Imperial Army, but was later to become a Social Democrat. The frugality of his daily life and his earthy sense of humour gave him all the appearance of a man of the people, and yet the power of his personality and the strength of his deeply felt convictions commanded immediate respect and gave him unquestioned authority. He combined the attributes of the ascetic and the grand seigneur and was thus in many ways an ideal President. Yet although Körner was widely regarded as a Great Man, his true greatness was misunderstood. That he could have been one of the major theoreticians of 'Austro-Marxism' was almost inconceivable to most of his contemporaries. On his death five crates of manuscripts and books were taken from his official residence and given to a scrap-paper merchant. Similarly, books and papers were removed from his private apartment and sold for pulping. Fortunately a number of Körner's writings have survived, enough to establish beyond all shadow of doubt that he was one of the greatest socialist writers on military affairs, belonging in the same rank as Engels, Mao and Giap.[1]

Körner was born in Szönyi, Hungary, on 24 April 1873, the son of an artillery captain. He had a distinguished record at the military academy and then joined the Engineers. A poor, hard-working and ascetic officer, he first made his mark when attached to the telegraphic section of the General Staff where he soon attracted the attention of the Chief of the General Staff, Conrad von Hötzendorf. During the war he showed both bravery and efficiency and was an outstanding staff officer. At the end of the war he was chief of staff to the 1 Isonzo Army, with the rank of colonel.

During the war Körner had shown little interest in politics. He was unquestioningly patriotic and was deeply shattered by the defeat of the Central powers. He had no sympathy for socialism, or indeed for any other political movement. He was solely concerned with the technical problems of fighting the war, and even events as momentous as the October Revolution passed without recorded comment. At first sight it is surprising that he agreed, almost without hesitation, in November 1918, to help Julius Deutsch with the formation of a new Republican Army. Körner was still not a socialist, his sympathies lay with the left wing of the Greater Germans. Although he was often accused by his enemies of being a hopeless dreamer and an intellectual who was incapable of understanding the real world, Körner was always a realist. That so many of his contemporaries refused to accept the given state of affairs explains why they could so easily dismiss him as a misguided ideologue or an uncomfortable Cassandra. It was this realism that made him accept the Republic and put aside any dreams of a revival of the Dual Monarchy. In November 1918, in spite of the bitterness of defeat, Körner was convinced that the new state deserved his support and that his loyalty as a patriotic Austrian must be given to the Republic.

Körner believed that for an army to be effective it had to be an integral part of society. This was the living legacy of the great Prussian reformers of the period after 1806 and particularly of his idol Clause-witz. Thus the new state needed a new army. Any attempt to restore the old army in the Republic would be bound to lead to disaster. The democratic state needed a democratic army in which leadership was based on respect and on ability and in which the officers were convinced democrats. From the outset he was sharply critical of the 'unpolitical' *Reichswehr*, which he saw as a foreign body in the Weimar Republic and a menace to the infant democracy. Once he accepted the Republic he devoted all his energies to the creation of a truly republican army. In a memorandum written in 1923 Körner summed up his ideas on the Republican Army: 'The contradiction between the people and the army is nowhere more dangerous than in a democratic republic. The people must regard the army as a part of itself, the army must feel itself to be a part of the people and place itself at their service.'[2]

Although Körner had not yet become a Social Democrat he was in full agreement with Julius Deutsch, the Secretary of State for Defence for the first two years of the Republic.[3] Deutsch was deter-mined not to be the Austrian Noske. He was convinced of the necessity of a complete break with the old army, even at the risk of creating an army that was initially of dubious military value, and unlike Noske he knew that the danger from the reactionaries was far greater than the danger from the extreme left. Most officers found such ideas anathema, and regarded Körner at best as a lunatic, at worst as a traitor. That a colonel of the old army should favour trade unions for soldiers and the political indoctrination of the army seemed to them evidence of an unhinged mind and a frontal assault on law, order and common decency.

The Kapp Putsch of 1920 helped to convince many Austrians that Deutsch and Körner were perfectly correct in their analysis of the dangers of an 'unpolitical' army. Körner argued that the *putsch* was clear evidence of Noske's disastrous mistake in not removing reactionary officers and showed that an army must have a clear idea of what it is defending. The refusal of the *Reichswehr* to defend the Republic was proof that poltiical education was essential. Such was the impact of the Kapp Putsch on Austria that although the fortunes of the Social Democrats were rapidly waning, Deutsch was able to get the new Army Bill passed.[4] Shortly afterwards the government coalition fell apart and the Social Democrats were never again to form a government.

Carl Vaugoin, who was War Minister from 1922 to the end of 1933, was determined to rid the army of the influence of Social Democracy and to make it an effective instrument of the Christian Social Party. He agreed with Körner that an 'unpolitical' army was not possible, and with the help of his legal adviser, Dr Robert Hecht, he set about the systematic destruction of all Deutsch's and Körner's work.[5] Körner was not the man to accept this without a fight, and a running battle developed between the two men. Körner objected to Vaugoin's acquiescence to the reductions in the Army demanded by the Geneva Treaty of 1922. He protested against the emphasis on military parades and on the cavalry which he saw as a sentimental hankering after the glories of the Empire. Above all, he saw his dream of a democratic and republican army fading. His memoranda to Vaugoin were incredibly outspoken, and it is doubtful if a Minister has ever been addressed in such a tone by a military adviser. By June 1924 Körner was totally frustrated and handed in his resignation. He retired with the rank of general. Shortly afterwards he joined the Social Democratic Party.

Körner had now burnt his boats. The 'Red General' was cut dead by his fellow officers, and yet in the party he was always regarded as something of an outsider by the leadership, a tiresome prophet who was always at odds with official policy. In early 1923 the party had formed the Republican Defence League (Republikanischer Schutzbund) on the basis of the self-defence organisations that had sprung up spontaneously in the weeks immediately after the war. The party had been prompted to take this step by its failure to maintain control over the army, by the growth of paramilitary groups on the right, particularly the Heimwehr, and by the rise of Fascism in Italy. The avowed aims of the Schutzbund, spelt out in the statutes of 12 April 1923, were to defend the constitution, to help the authorities maintain law and order, to provide assistance in times of national crisis, to protect meetings held by republican organisations, and educate the minds and bodies of the membership.[6]

The party argued that the Schutzbund should help to maintain what Otto Bauer called the 'equilibrium of class forces' by acting as a kind of party police force, serving as umpires between the party and the police and restraining the *radikalinskis* within the party as much as the extreme right.[7] At the same time it was argued that the Schutzbund should raise the military consciousness of the proletariat. Thus from the outset there was a profound contradiction in party attitudes towards the Schutzbund. Some insisted that it should be a highly trained and disciplined military force that should unquestioningly serve the directives of the party, while others hoped that it would form a highly politicised and militant elite. The argument was soon to become one between the traditional ideas of ex-officers who thought along strictly conventional military lines, and those who were determined to formulate a new philosophy appropriate to the needs of a socialist party. The leading spokesman for these two sides were Major Alexander Eifler and General Theodor Körner.[8]

The confusion over the role of the Schutzbund was typical of the paramilitary organisations of the left in the inter-war years. The *Reichsbanner Schwarz Rot Gold*, the paramilitary organisation of the German Social Democrats (SPD), was intended almost exclusively for propaganda purposes. The leadership was unequivocally opposed to any kind of military training, although some radical local units ignored these injunctions.[9] An organisation that was packed with radical pacifists and was opposed to military training, and which was unarmed until the very last moment before the Fascists took power, was hardly a paramilitary organisation at all in the strict sense of the term. It was not until 1930 that Karl Höltermann formed an elite anti-Fascist organisation, the Schutzformationen (Schufo), but even the Schufo was not supposed to be armed, or do military training, although this stricture was ignored in some districts.[10] The Schufo was effective in organising ambulance units and courier services, and in providing intelligence reports on Nazi activities. In some areas, mostly in Prussia, they were even trained by the Reichswehr and the police. By 1932 there were between 250,000 and 400,000 members, so that it could no longer be regarded as an elite.[11] Unlike the Schutzbund the Reichsbanner could not conceive of having to fight the Army and the police. Its intention was to act as a reserve for the authorities in the event of a civil war.

The German Communists' Roter Frontkämpferbund (RFB) was hardly more radical in its approach. It was designed as a highly organised and permanent mass demonstration rather than as a party army.[12] Although some radicals argued that the RFB should be the military arm of the party, it was agreed that it should be an agitprop organisation to which non-Communists could belong. Parades were designed for propaganda effect and not for any military purpose. The RFB was given virtually no military training and it was in no sense an elite party army as was the SA. It was not until 1931 that Erich Wollenberg, a man of considerable ability, acting on Moscow's orders, began to re-organise the RFB, which was then illegal, into the nucleus of a German Red Army. Wollenberg soon came into conflict with Thälmann and the party leadership who supported the more cautious policies of the 'Anti-Fascist Association' (Kampfbund gegen den Faschismus) and the 'Anti-Fascist Young Guards'. Wollenberg was arrested, possibly tipped off by a comrade, and in April 1933 was dismissed from the party.[13] Thus the RFB remained a propaganda organisation designed to maintain 'proletarian discipline', and it was hoped that it would miraculously become an effective military organisation in the heat of battle. After the disastrous setbacks of the party in 1921 and 1923 in which revolutionary attempts had miserably failed, such a naive belief in spontaneity is truly astonishing. Mass demonstrations by uniformed comrades might create a temporary euphoria, but they were no substitute for hard organisational work and careful planning. The military section of the Communist International might claim that armed insurrection was the sole means of establishing the dictatorship of the proletariat without which Marxism degenerates into Social Democracy, but such radical ideas had no effect whatsoever on the German party.[14]

The Schutzbund leaders were well aware of the powerful attraction of uniforms, parades and military bands and saw the value of a 'demonstration army'. A bizarre regiment, the 'Republican Deutschmeister', was formed to win over the nostalgically inclined to socialism. Julius Deutsch argued that military rigmarole and sentimentality should not be monopolised by the extreme right, and called for an 'intelligent exploitation of naive popular sentiments.'[15] But unlike the Reichsbanner or the RFB, the Schutzbund leadership never questioned the need for military training. The constitution could not be defended nor law and order maintained unless the Schutzbund was properly trained. The problem arose over the type of training that was needed, and for what purpose. Was the Schutzbund a kind of proletarian Home Guard, or was it a vanguard determined to fight for a new society?

By 1926, when the Social Democratic Party met for its conference in Linz, it was generally agreed that the Schutzbund had to accept the need, in certain circumstances, for 'defensive violence'. But although the leadership argued that a civil war in defence of democratic freedoms against the violence of the right was a distinct possibility, they recoiled in horror from the consequences of such a thought. The profound humanist convictions of Austro-Marxism is one of its greatest legacies, but a deep horror of violence can all too easily hamstring a movement that is faced with an opponent that has no such scruples. Körner, who detested violence as much as any man, realised that in certain circumstances it could not be avoided, and that to fight a war with an army of pacifists was a certain recipe for failure.[16] The right could use this talk of violence as evidence of the sinister revolutionary intentions of the Social Democrats, and the party, by protesting its innocence, weakened its own position and increased the frustration of the rank and file who were engaged in constant violent clashes with the extreme right, and who feared that the day of reckoning was not too distant. Talk of defensive violence seemed to be oddly out of tune with the policy of defensive conciliation followed by the party in its dealings with the Christain Social Party which, under Seipel's able leadership, was slowly undermining the democratic achievements of 1918/19.

The first major test of the Schutzbund came on 15 July 1927 when an angry crowd burnt down the Palace of Justice in Vienna in protest against the acquittal of the men who had been charged with killing an invalid and a child during a clash between the Schutzbund and the right-wing Frontkämpfer in Schattendorf, a small village in the Burgenland.[17] Units of the Schutzbund were sent to the Palace of Justice in an attempt to control the crowd, to stop the violence and to protect the workers from the violence of the police. The Schutzbund was thus placed in an intolerable position. Being unarmed, it could do nothing to restrain the police or control the crowd. Although they tended wounded policemen, and although a small group under Körner entered the blazing building and saved the lives of a number of policemen and civilians, the police did not hesitate to fire on the unarmed *Schutzbündler*. Realising that their position was hopeless, they were forced to retire. The party argued that the Schutzbund had done its best, but most people realised that this was not enough.

At the national conference of the party, held shortly after 15 July, the Schutzbund came under attack from a number of delegates. The left argued that recent events proved that the Schutzbund had to be properly armed and trained and that an effective military policy was essential. The right, whose leading spokesman was Karl Renner, insisted that the weakness of the Schutzbund was proof of the need for compromise, for a realisation of the appalling risks of civil war and for 'internal disarmament'. Otto Bauer argued convincingly that compromise was impossible, because the Christian Socials refused to have any dealings with the 'men of July', whom they accused of plotting to overthrow the government by force. In such circumstances, to disband the Schutzbund would be sheer folly.[18]

In October 1927 the Schutzbund held its fifth conference at which the delegates accepted Alexander Eifler's new programme unanimously.[19] Eiflers's ideas were simple and precise. The Schutzbund should become the fully militarised executive organ of the political leadership. It should avoid all political issues and be the unthinking, unquestioningly obedient armed wing of the party. It would serve a dual purpose of restraining the rank and file and maintaining iron discipline, thus avoiding any repetitions of the mindless violence of 15 July, while at the same time it would protect the democratic republic against any threats from its enemies.

From the outset Körner was strongly opposed to such ideas. He was convinced that unless the Schutzbund was highly politicised it would be militarily useless. He stressed the need for individual initiative, which was only possible if members were fully aware of the political implications of their actions. Eifler's ideas were, he felt, an attempt to dress up old-fashioned militarism in a Social Democratic guise. At the conference he summed up his thinking in the slogan 'The Schutzbund must not only be the most determined section of the proletariat, it must also be the furthest thinking.'

It was not until spring of the following year that Körner wrote a detailed memorandum criticising Eifler's plan for the reorganisation of the Schutzbund.[20] He insisted that the Schutzbund should only fight in defence of democratic freedoms, and that it should never attempt to seize state power. But this did not mean that it should be merely a passive executive organ of the party. The Schutzbund should be a means of mobilising the full potential of the class-conscious proletariat by encouraging self-reliance, self-discipline and self-esteem.

This could not happen if the Schutzbund were organised on traditional military lines, emphasising blind obedience, deference to authority and rigid training methods. It was precisely in this emphasis on individual initiative and by making a conscious break with tradition that the Schutzbund could become both an effective military force and an important means of heightening the political consciousness of the working class. Körner was convinced that if the Schutzbund were forced to fight the army and the police using traditional methods it was bound to be defeated. The superior training and equipment of the government forces made any such direct conflict an almost certain recipe for disaster. The political dimension was thus critical. Government forces had to be demoralised and undermined from within, subjected to endless pinpricks and made uncertain of their role. Imitating the methods of the government forces would mean having to fight according to their rules, and thus the Schutzbund would be placed at a distinct disadvantage. Conversely, the Schutzbund would gain an enormous advantage by forcing the Army and the police to fight in a manner that they had not expected and for which they had not been trained.

Körner always insisted that the political and social dimension of warfare was of far greater importance than technical military considerations. His studies of Clausewitz strengthened this belief. He particularly liked Clausewitz's remark that: 'Of all the factors under consideration in the art of war new inventions or new ideas are the least important, and the most important are new social conditions and relationships.'[21] His vital concern was thus to harness these new social and political forces and to use them for military purposes. Such forces can only be used if the purpose for which they are devoted is in the true interests of the majority of the people. Seen in this light, victory would go to the side that was the most progressive.[22] The Schutzbund would have been invincible if only the leadership had tapped the massive strength that lay slumbering in the working class.

Alexander Eifler refused to even consider such criticisms. He was convinced that the Schutzbund, strengthened by recent reforms, could defeat the Army and police in a head-on collision, and that it should remain depoliticised. At the conference Eifler's position had not been seriously challenged, and he remained convinced that he was on the right track, confident that he had the support of Deutsch and of Bauer. Körner also had some reason for optimism. The conference had agreed that an open confrontation with the enemy should be avoided and all possible methods should be used in any future struggle. Particular emphasis was placed on the need for a general strike, which Körner believed was an essential weapon to use against the class enemy. The conference was thus something of a stalemate between Körner and Eifler. Eifler had the support of the leadership, but Körner had considerable support from the rank and file. For the moment the struggle between the two had been postponed, but the opportunity to have a serious look at the shortcomings of the Schutzbund during the crisis of 15 July had been missed.

The militarisation of the Schutzbund continued apace. Greater emphasis was placed on drill and infantry tactics, and manoeuvres were held, including one massive affair close to Vienna. In early 1929 a plan was produced for the defence of Vienna which bore the unmistakable imprint of Alexander Eifler's ideas.[23] It was assumed that in the event of a Heimwehr *putsch* the insurgents would try to seize the main government offices in the inner city. As the Army and the police were likely to be opposed to such drastic action by the Heimwehr, it was further assumed that the Schutzbund would be able to act as a reserve, controlling a ring around the centre of the city from which postion they would be able to force the Heimwehr out of their strongholds and cut them off from any relief from outside.

Although Eifler later claimed that he had developed the plan in close collaboration with Körner, in fact the General was never consulted. Eifler refused to attend a meeting that Körner called to discuss the plan, which he felt was 'rubbish', the typical unimaginative and conventional plan of a hidebound militarist.[24] By now Körner was hopelessly isolated and the Schutzbund leadership was overflowing with confidence. At the Schutzbund conference in October 1929 Otto Bauer gave a rousing speech, saying that the Schutzbund was ready to fight against Fascism at any time, and Karl Höltermann, visiting from Germany, pledged the support of 100,000 members of the Reichsbanner in such an eventuality. This radical talk lulled most of the delegates into a feeling of false security, and when the Schober government was forced to make some important concessions in its plans for far-reaching consistutional reform, this feeling was further strengthened.[25]

It was not long before this feeling of euphoria gave way to the more familiar one of uncertainty and willingness to compromise. The Schober government fell on 25 September 1930, and the new government under Vaugoin included two prominent members of the Heimwehr, Starhemberg as Minister of the Interior, and Hueber as Minister of Justice. Elections were called for November, and there were persistent rumours that the Heimwehr was planning a *coup* and that the government was about to ban the Schutzbund. In spite of the fact that these rumours were totally unfounded, Starhemberg being fearful of a direct confrontation with the Social Democrats, the Schutzbund made frantic preparations to organise illegally, and in marked contrast to the bombastic rhetoric of the conference only one year ago it was decided that this was not an issue over which the Schutzbund should fight. The government attempted to discredit the Social Democrats by ordering a series of searches for small arms. In fact very little was found, and the party gained 41 per cent of the popular vote at the election, thus getting the largest number of seats. Placing Wiener Neustadt virtually under military rule and bringing in the artillery in a show of strength at Linz merely made the government appear somewhat ridiculous, and the Heimwehr was bitterly disappointed at not getting the chance to have a crack at the Schutzbund.

This excitement soon died down, and the Schutzbund devoted most of its efforts to helping to organise the Workers' Olympic Games in Vienna. Suddenly, in September 1931, came the Pfrimer *putsch* in Styria. The Schutzbund was immediately placed on the alert, and the party leadership warned the government that unless decisive action was taken it would not be able to hold back the Schutzbund from acting on its own. In point of fact the leadership did everything possible to restrain the Schutzbund, some units of which, like the Bruck-an-der-Mur division under the militant Koloman Wallisch, were straining at the leash and longing for a showdown with the Heimwehr. Bauer and Deutsch argued that if the Schutzbund were to act alone, the Army and the police would probably support the Heimwehr, and that the only hope was to force the government, however reluctantly, to crush the *putsch*.[26]

The policy of the Schutzbund during the Pfrimer *putsch* was a dramatic confession of the total inadequacy of the Eifler plan. Eifler, unlike Körner, assumed that the Army and the police would always oppose an attempted Heimwehr or Nazi *putsch*, and that the Schutzbund would thus serve as a reserve to the government forces. Now it appeared that this calculation was not necessarily true, and that the Schutzbund was quite incapable of dealing with a situation in which the Army and the police did not act decisively against attacks on the republic by the right. The Schutzbund, far from being the impressive military force that Eifler and Deutsch claimed it to be, was little more than a bargaining counter in negotiations between the party leadership and the government. For the first time there was also clear indication that the rank and file was getting increasingly impatient with the empty rhetoric and the timid practice of the leadership.

Körner had resigned from the Schutzbund in 1930 after endless clashes with Eifler, who had joined the organisation on a full-time basis after the Palace of Justice affair, and who enjoyed the uncritical support of Julius Deutsch. Eifler felt that Körner was an unrealistic intellectual with a misplaced faith in the masses, and Deutsch tended to agree.[27] Körner, as usual, was outspoken in his criticisms of Eifler, referring to his plan for the defence of Vienna as 'hair-raising rubbish'. Although he had resigned, Körner was not the man to sulk. Many provincial leaders had enormous respect for his judgement, and the more the policies of the leadership were questioned, the more they turned to Körner for advice. He also wrote numerous articles for journals such as *Der Freie Soldat*, *Reichsbanner* and *Der Schutzbund*, articles that were widely read and discussed and which are of considerable interest even today.[28] His resignation from the Schutzbund was not widely publicised, and many members felt that he was still in a leading position.

The disagreements between Körner and Eifler flared up once again when Eifler's plan for action in Upper Styria was first discussed, a plan that was soon adapted for other regions of Austria for use in the event of a repeat performance of something like the Pfrimer *putsch*. Eifler's plan is largely concerned with an analysis of the relative strength of the Schutzbund and the Heimwehr in Styria, and the section dealing with appropriate action is remarkably sketchy.[29] Körner's devastating criticism of the paper was far more detailed than the original, and provides an excellent summary of his views on the role of the Schutzbund.[30]

Throughout his life Körner studied Clausewitz, and the main lesson he drew from these studies was the critical importance of the political dimension of warfare. He was thus able to rescue Clausewitz from his vulgarisers in the 'Schlieffen School' who saw him as the philosopher of the decisive battle.[31] Thus Körner liked to quote Clausewitz's remark that 'war does not belong to the arts or the sciences, but to the field of social life.'[32] The field of social life was, for Clausewitz, politics, which thus included 'humanity and all the expressions of philosophical understanding'.[33] When the *Militärwissenschaftlicher Rundschau*, the official journal of the German Ministry of War, published two letters from Clausewitz to General von Müffling written in December 1827, Körner wrote a lengthy exegesis on these remarkable summaries of Clausewitz's thought.[34] He was particularly struck by Clausewitz's point that:

we should not be led into believing that war is a simple act of violence and destruction, but we must realize that war is a political act, that it does not exactly follow its own laws, but is a truly political instrument that does not control itself, but is directed by a hand. That hand is politics.

It was precisely this refusal to see that war, and particularly civil war, was a political instrument that was the fundamental weakness of Eifler's approach. Körner felt that Eifler was as narrow-minded and unimaginative as Pfrimer, both men thinking that a *putsch* was a purely military affair in which neither the army nor the people were involved. Eifler, who prided himself for his practical approach to military problems, was thus in Körner's eyes a sandbox strategist who refused to take into account the importance of political and social factors, which to any student of Clausewitz were the vital elements in any strategy. The strength of the Schutzbund was certainly not in its effectiveness as a military unit. There could be no question that it was no match for the army in training and in equipment. Eifler's figures, which were obviously inaccurate, suggested that the Heimwehr in Upper Styria had twice the number of men, more than six times the number of rifles and 163 machine guns to 25. If this indeed were so, it is difficult to see how the Schutzbund could hope to fight the Heimwehr in a conventional confrontation. Unless there was a radical change of policy the Schutzbund was heading for a disaster even more serious than that suffered on 15 July.

The great advantage of the Schutzbund was that it could exploit the enormous reserves of strength in the party and the trade unions. The belief that there could be a simple military solution to the problems facing Austrian democracy was typical of old-fashioned militarism with its belief in the superiority of the military over the political. The Schutzbund had to use its political power to win over units of the Army and the police to the defence of democracy.[35] Social Democratic officials should use their positions to protect the Republic against the Heimwehr. The unions should resort to strike action to halt the movement of men and supplies. But Körner did not believe that there was any serious threat of a Heimwehr 'March on Vienna', dismissing this as idle chatter by 'dilettantes like Eifler and ignoramuses like Pfrimer and Steidle'. In his view the Heimwehr was no more capable of mounting such a complex military operation than was the Schutzbund, under its present leadership, of stopping them. Körner knew that the key to any civil war is state power. If the Fascists could not seize state power then they were powerless. This meant that Vienna was the key to the whole situation. A new plan was urgently needed for the capital to replace the wholly inadequate scheme suggested by Eifler. But the basis of all Körner's criticism was the belief that unless the masses supported the political stand of the party the Schutzbund would have no chance. It was thus the political dimension that was decisive, a dimension wholly lacking in Eifler's plan.

In his introduction to the 1891 edition of Karl Marx's *Class Struggles in France* Engels argued that the time of barricades and direct armed confrontation with organised state power had passed and that the struggle between the bourgeoisie and the proletariat would be decided at the political and not the military level. Körner strongly endorsed this view. He felt that the militants among the Schutzbund, among whom he singled out Koloman Wallisch, were as blinkered in their view of the situation as Eifler or the Heimwehr leaders. All of them felt that a solution could be found in violence alone, whereas Körner was convinced that if the Schutzbund were forced to fight in such circumstances it was bound to be defeated. The events of 12 February 1934 were to prove him right, and even Deutsch, who had refused to listen to Körner, had to admit that he had been correct.[36]

Körner never had the opportunity to work out an alternative plan to Eifler's. He could only sketch in the outline of such a scheme. In place of rigid centralisation, with all orders coming from the party headquarters in the Wienzeile in Vienna, he wanted a decentralised and flexible command structure that could react quickly to changes in the local situation. In place of a blind faith in a purely military solution, Körner called for a skilful use of political power. Flexibility, the exploitation of situations in which the Schutzbund had local advantages and reliance on the determination of the politically mobilised masses, were the keys to success. But such radical ideas were dismissed as hopelessly unrealistic by Eifler and his superiors, who regarded Körner as an impractical dreamer.

Having resigned from the Schutzbund, Körner devoted most of his efforts to journalism, hoping that he could influence professional soldiers and members of the Schutzbund by drawing lessons from the experience of the past. From 1928 Körner wrote articles for *Auf Vorposten*, a monthly supplement to *Der freie Soldat*, the journal of the Social Democratic Military Association (Militärverband). After 1930 these articles appear more frequently, in an attempt to change the policy of the Schutzbund. The articles are written in a clear and lean prose, the points made forcefully in short and direct sentences, and they are completely free from jargon and pretension. Reading these vivid pieces it is hard to imagine how Körner could have been accused of being a 'bottle green philosopher' and an arrogant intellectual.[37]

The theme of all these articles is the need to consider the political dimension of any military situation so that the full potential of the people can be exploited for military purposes. Thus in his study of the revolution of 1848 in Austria, he concentrated on the political aspects of the struggle and on the relationship between the Army and the people. The experience of Hungary showed that regular officers who fought for the revolution were incapable of understanding and using the revolutionary strength of the masses, and although they made many significant contributions to the struggle, they were too hidebound by conventional training to be effective as revolutionary leaders.[38]

His study of the Russian Revolution of 1905 concentrated on the importance of strikes in the revolutionary struggle, a factor largely ignored by Eifler and the Schutzbund leadership. For Körner a revolutionary strike was much more than a refusal to work: 'The strike uses all possible methods: it calls, it persuades, it plots, it threatens, it frightens, it throws rocks, and finally fires from a Browning pistol.'[39] The vital factor in 1905 was the attitude of the Army. In 1905 it remained loyal, in 1917 it collapsed. Thus, as his study of the Kapp Putsch showed, an army in a democratic republic must have a clear idea of what it is defending, and must in this sense be a 'political' army. The lesson from this was obvious. The Social Democrats should pay particular attention to gaining political influence over the Army, particularly among the rank and file, as an essential part of its anti-Fascist struggle. The Schutzbund could not hope to save Austria from Fascism if the Army had no desire to defend democracy.

The experience of France in 1830 showed vividly that a corrupt government and a demoralised army were powerless against a people determined to resist an attempted *coup*.[40] If an Austrian Polignac were to be frustrated, then the Social Democrats would clearly have to step up their political campaign, or it was at the political level that any future struggle would ultimately be decided.

Körner's warnings fell on deaf ears. The government continued to harass the Schutzbund with continuous raids on party centres. Eifler, now promoted to the position of Chief of Staff, increased the military training of the Schutzbund. Map reading and drill were emphasised, and in the summer of 1932, 16,000 men took part in impressive manoeuvres. But anxious not to provoke the authorities, there was very little actual weapons training. The Schutzbund had been forced on to the defensive, but Eifler still continued to talk confidently of it as a viable military force capable of standing up against the army. Such confidence was wholly unfounded.

In March 1933 Dollfuss closed parliament, and many *Schutzbündler* felt that the time had come to fight in defence of democracy. A few days later Dollfuss banned the Schutzbund. The party had already decided that if the Schutzbund were banned there should be no resistance, and a new organisation was formed under the same leadership. The illegal Schutzbund was a shadow of its former self. Many of its most determined members had left, fed up with its conciliatory policies. Government pressure on the Schutzbund was steadily increased. It had lost any power to threaten the government, and was terrified of taking any initiative. On 3 February 1934 Eifler, and Körner's admirer Rudolf Löw, were arrested. In the following days other leaders were rounded up. On 5 February Otto Bauer, Julius Deutsch and Friedrich Adler turned in desperation to Körner and asked him to take over the leadership of the Schutzbund.[41] Körner visited some units in Vienna and was horrified at what he found. It was generally accepted that a general strike would be the signal for military action, but no one seemed to have any idea what to do once they had assembled for action. As the organisation of the Schutzbund was chaotic, and planning hopelessly inadequate, Körner felt that to fight would be sheer madness. Even a general strike was unlikely as the railway workers, probably the most important single group in the event of a civil war, were totally demoralised after the failure of their strike in 1933. Convinced that the Schutzbund would be defeated, Körner refused the offer to lead it, and joined a delegation of moderates which visited President Miklas on 11 February in an attempt to negotiate a compromise solution. The time for compromise had passed. On the following day fighting began in Linz, spread to other centres, and within three days the Schutzbund and the Social Democratic Party had been destroyed. With no leaders, no plan, inadequate training and a ruthless opponent, the Schutzbund was doomed. Democracy was quickly defeated.

Körner's moderate position in February 1934 should not obscure the truly radical nature of his thinking. He attacked the party left for taking an essentially idealist position by failing to analyse the objective conditions, and he liked to quote Marx's remark that 'instead of taking real conditions they make naked will the drive-wheel of the revolution'. Clausewitz had also insisted that there is no point in using violence unless there is a clear understanding of precisely for what purpose it is to be used. Calls for an armed struggle and for a fight to the death are all very well, and may have a temporary bracing effect on morale, but they will lead nowhere unless the precise ends to which the struggle is to be devoted are clearly conceived.[42] To fight a hopeless fight was madness in his view, and he had no sympathy for socialists like Liebknecht or Rosa Luxemburg who, in a similar situation, had argued that a glorious failure could be an inspiration to later generations. Körner detested violence, and knew how precious is human life, but he knew that there were times when it could not be avoided. It was the duty of a military leader to use violence as effectively and as sparingly as possible, and this in turn was only possible if all factors were taken into consideration.

Although Körner stressed the political and social dimensions of armed conflict, he never discounted the importance of rigorous professional military training. All the great socialist writers on military affairs from Engels to Mao have scorned romantic anarchist notions of the invincibility of an ill-trained but inspired mob, and Körner was no exception. But he was also in the great tradition in that he knew that professionalism alone was not enough. He believed that a democratic society needed a democratisation of armed force, and that such a democratisation would strengthen rather than weaken the military power of the people.

At first sight it might seem that Körner's ideas have little relevance in the modern world. The days of paramilitary politics seem to have gone for ever, the heroic struggle against Fascism a thing of the past. Körner's Cassandra-like warnings thus may seem to be of merely antiquarian interest. But his insistence on the social dimension of warfare led him to predict that Nazi Germany could never defeat Soviet Russia because a Fascist regime, in spite of its talk of *Volksgemeinschaft*, could never unleash the full energies of the people in the way that a socialist state, even with its Stalinist deformations, was able to do. Similarly he argued that wars of national liberation against the imperialist powers would soon lead to the spectacular defeat of the mighty nations, for within the weakest of peoples there lies incredible hidden strength. The bankruptcy of modern military planning and the ghastly prospect of nuclear destruction are gradually causing a rethinking of strategic and tactical doctrines. In this long overdue process writers like Körner have much to offer to those trying to find a way out of the impasse.[43]

Lastly, there is Körner the socialist. When pressed to define his position he described himself as a 'democratic bolshevik'. This phrase

is a typical expression of 'Austro-Marxism'. It is a political position
that finds few supporters. From the left it is denounced as pseudo-
revolutionary rhetoric that misled the proletariat and made impossible
any genuine alternative to bourgeois democracy.[44] The right feels that
doctrinaire Marxisms blinded the party to the need for compromise
and flexibility.[45] At its worst 'democratic bolshevism' was merely a
balancing act between the left and right wings of the party, but its
essential message was that socialism and democracy should never be
separated. The experience of a socialism without democracy is a terrible
warning that without genuine democracy socialism quickly degenerates
into a non-capitalist but also non-socialist form of state power.
Democracy without socialism cramps individual initiative and self-
fulfilment and gives the people little control over their own destiny.
Körner was a passionate democrat with an unshakable belief in humanity, but he realised that democrats might well have to use violence to
preserve their freedom. Without an inspiring political vision such a
struggle would almost certainly be lost. For Körner only violence
that served genuinely humane ends could be justified, not only in moral
terms, but also from the purely military standpoint. There are times
when violence cannot be avoided, but even then respect for humanity
should not be forgotten. Körner believed that these two opposites
could be reconciled and that every socialist had to come to terms with
the problems of humanity and of power: of 'democracy' and 'bolshevism'. The unity of these two apparent opposities is a source of strength
rather than weakness, both in politics and in its 'continuation by other
means' — in armed conflict.

Notes

1. E. C. Kollman, *Theodor Körner. Militär und Politik* (Munich, 1973)
provides the basic facts of Körner's life but is lacking in analysis. I. Duczynska,
Der demokratische Bolschewik: Zur Theorie und Praxis der Gewalt (Munich,
1975), is a marvellously lively book that stresses the significance of Körner as a
military thinker. A shorter English version entitled *Workers in Arms: The
Austrian Schutzbund and the Civil War of 1934* (New York, 1978), has a useful
introduction by E. J. Hobsbawm setting the problem in context. Ilona Duczynska
gave me considerable help in writing this chapter. I am deeply saddened that I
am no longer able to show it to her.
2. Kollman, *Körner*, p. 118
3. On the Army and the republic see L. Jedlicka, *Ein Heer im Schatten der
Parteien* (Graz, 1955); A. Staudinger, 'Die österreichische Wehrgesetzgebung
1918-1938', *Oesterreichische Militärische Zeitschrift* (1971), pp. 151-5, 219-24.
4. Jedlicka, *Ein Heer*, p. 25.

5. P. Huemer, *Sektionschef Robert Hecht und die Zerstörung der österreichischen Demokratie* (Vienna, 1975).

6. The best work on the Schutzbund is C. Vlcck, 'Der Republikanische Schutzbund in Oesterreich. Geschichte, Aufbau und Organisation', unpublished PhD thesis, Vienna, 1971.

7. It would appear that these ideas were largely the work of Rudolf Löw: Duczynska, *Der democratische Bolschewik*, p. 72. Löw had been a captain in the Austro-Hungarian Army. He was Körner's closest associate in the Schutzbund. Later he fought with the Haganah in Palestine. On the equilibrium of class forces see O. Bauer, *Die österreichische Revolution* (Vienna, 1923), and 'Das Gleichgewicht der Klassenkräfte', *Der Kampf*, 17 (February 1924).

8. On Eifler see H. Tober, 'Alexander Eifler. Vom Monarchisten zum Republikaner', unpublished PhD thesis, Vienna, 1966; J. Deutsch, *Alexander Eifler, Ein Soldat der Freiheit* (Vienna, 1947) is too uncritical. Eifler was a man of considerable ability and courage. Sent to Dachau after the *Anschluss* he was a source of inspiration to his comrades. He died in the camp in 1945.

9. K. Rohe, *Das Reichsbanner Schwarz Rot Gold. Ein Beitrag zur Geschichte und Struktur der politischen Kampfverbände zur Zeit der Weimarer Republik* (Düsseldorf, 1966), p. 164.

10. Ibid., p. 366

11. Ibid., p. 374.

12. K. G. P. Schuster, *Der Rote Frontkämpferbund 1924-1929* (Düsseldorf, 1975), p. 44.

13. Ibid., p. 235.

14. For their ideas see the remarkable book: A. Neuberg, *Armed Insurrection* (London, 1970).

15. J. Deutsch, *Antifaschismus! Proletarische Wehrhaftigkeit im Kampfe gegen den Faschismus* (Vienna, 1926).

16. Duczynska, *Der demokratische Bolschewik*, p. 91.

17. On the Schattendorf affair see G. Botz, *Gewalt in der Politik* (Munich, 1976), pp. 107-11. On 15 July: R. Neck and A. Wandruszka, *Die Ereignisse des 15. Juli 1927* (Vienna, 1979).

18. The best summary of the right wing's arguments at the conference is in O. Trebitsch, *Der 15. Juli und seine rechte Lehre* (Vienna, 1927). For comments on the conference see Vlcek, *Der Republikanische Schutzbund*, p. 161.

19. 'Verhandlungsbericht der fünften Reichskonferenz', *Der Schutzbund* (November 1927).

20. Körner's 'Principles for the Use of Violence and of Civil War' are discussed in detail in Duczynska, *Der demokratische Bolschewik*, pp. 120-32.

21. Quoted in: Theodor Körner, *Auf Vorposten: Ausgewählte Schriften* (Vienna, 1977), p. 215.

22. Ibid., p. 222.

23. At his trial after February 1934, Eifler argued that the plan was largely the work of Körner. As Körner violently objected to the plan, this claim is clearly absurd. Duczynska is wrong in attributing the violent ultra-left 'Tactics for Streetfighting' to Eifler. See Duczynska, *Der demokratische Bolschewik*, pp. 349-62 for the text, and pp. 125, 153, 188, 222, 229 and 345 for comments. It would seem that this curious document was based on Eifler's ideas but spiced with wild terroristic notions. The document was not used at the Schutzbund trial, and was thus clearly thought by the police to be the work of an isolated fanatic.

24. Vlcek, *Der Republikanische Schutzbund*, p. 228.

25. *Der Schutzbund* (November 1929) for details of the conference.

26. *Arbeiter-Zeitung*, 14 Sept. 1931 for the party's attempts to justify its tactics.

27. Deutsch, *Eifler*, p. 28.

28. Some of the most important articles are collected in: Körner, *Auf Vorposten*.

29. Text in Vlcek, *Der Republikanische Schutzbund*, pp. 512-24.

30. Ibid., pp. 525-47. Characteristically vivid commentary by Duczynska, *Der demokratische Bolschewik*, pp. 157-65.

31. H. -U. Wehler, 'Der Verfall der deutschen Kriegstheorie: vom "Absoluten" zum "Totalen" Krieg von Clausewitz zu Ludendorff' in *Krisenherde des Kaiserreichs 1871-1918* (Göttingen, 1970).

32; C. v. Clausewitz, *Vom Kriege* (Bonn, 1972), Book 2, Chapter 3, p. 303.

33. Ibid., Book 8, Chapter 6, p. 993.

34. *Militärwissenschaftliche Rundschau* (March 1937). Körner's article in Körner, *Auf Vorposten*, pp. 235-58.

35. Lenin wrote: 'Of course, unless the revolution assumes a mass character and affects the troops, there can be no question of serious struggle.' V. I. Lenin, *Collected Works*, vol. 11, p. 174 ('Lessons of the Moscow Uprising').

36. J. Deutsch, *Putsch oder Revolution?* (Karlsbad, 1934), p. 26.

37. Bottle-green was the colour of the Austro-Hungarian General Staff.

38. Körner, *Auf Vorposten*, pp. 41-100.

39. Ibid., p. 119.

40. Ibid., pp. 178-94.

41. Duczynska, *Der demokratische Bolschewik*, p. 179.

42. *Österreichisches Staatsarchiv: Allgemeines Verwaltungsarchiv*, Polizeidirektion Wien, Akten Februar 1934, Zl. Pr. IV 2606/1934 Karton 1.

43. One of the most imaginative efforts in this field is by the commander of the Austrian Army. See Emil Spannocchi, 'Verteidigung ohne Selbstzerstörung' in *idem, Verteidigung ohne Schlacht* (Munich, 1976). Similar ideas are expressed in G. Brossollet, *Essai sur la non-bataille* (Paris, 1975). H. Afheldt, *Verteidigung und Frieden* (Munich, 1976) is a brilliant analysis of modern strategic thinking. A. Roberts, *Nation in Arms: The Theory and Practice of Territorial Defence* (London, 1976) is an excellent study. I have summarised some of these arguments in 'The Traditions of German Strategic Thought', *The International History Review*, 2 (April 1979).

44. The most recent attack from the left is R. Loew, 'The Politics of Austro-Marxism', *New Left Review*, 118, (November-December 1979).

45. N. Leser, *Zwischen Reformismus und Bolschewismus: Der Austromarxismus als Theorie und Praxis* (Vienna, 1968) is the outstanding book on Austro-Marxism. It is strongly sympathetic to Renner's right-wing position.

9 DEMOCRACY AND THE POWER VACUUM: THE PROBLEM OF THE PARTY STATE DURING THE DISINTEGRATION OF THE WEIMAR REPUBLIC*

Karl Dietrich Bracher

Since the early 1920s, from the seizure of power by Mussolini, Hitler and Franco in Europe to the Latin America of today, the history of democracy has been overshadowed by the threat of self-destruction. Each example is an instance of functional problems and the failure of pluralistic democracies to deal adequately with socio-economic and ideological crises which the political powers and institutions of a free society are unable to solve. A crisis of confidence is followed by the transition to dictatorship which, in the German and Italian cases, did not even require a *coup d'état*: democracy was destroyed by apparently democratic and legal means and the 'new legality' legitimised by presuasion and force in plebiscitary one-party elections.[1]

Even after half a century the German case of the crisis and decline of the Weimar Republic is still a prime example of this process, an almost perfect model and a permanent warning. When I wrote my book on the end of the Weimar Republic in the 1950s I was impressed by two major factors. First, that the complexity of the phenomenon cannot be reduced to a simple formula, but is part of a lengthy process of the 'dissolution' of democracy itself that can only be explained by means of a careful structural analysis. Secondly, the development itself is determined by clear decisions and distinct phases which I have described in detail and which I have tried to explain with the concepts of the loss of power and the power vacuum.[2] 'Dissolution' and 'power vacuum' express two aspects of the Weimar catastrophe which have subsequently stimulated the controversy that on the one hand an apparently inevitable decay originating from the foundation and early history of the Republic is observable; but on the other hand there is the realisation of the possibility of alternative decisions existing until the very end when Hitler was appointed Chancellor on 30 January 1933. The apparently hopeless situation which resulted from the developments of 1930-2 opened the way to dictatorship which seemed to be the only way out of the paralysis of a democracy. But it was the concrete decisions of the political leadership after the collapse of the Grand Coalition in March

*Translated by Martin Kitchen.

1930 that made the solution of 1933 inevitable.

This combination of inevitability and chance in the destiny of the Weimar Republic shows up the inadequacy of a one-sided analysis and contradicts any monocausal explanation, whether this be making the role of the economy (Marxist) or the actions of the individual (historicist) the key to events. The same is true of all approaches that go back to a single main cause or explanatory model: economics (the economic crisis), institutions (constitutional weakness), sociology (petty bourgeoisie), ideology (the authoritarian tradition) and explanations based on political economy, social psychology or the role of personality. Such models give important suggestions and are of value when taken in a historical and political perspective.[3] Their real value can be seen in the decisive stage of the crisis in 1932 that is here characterised with the concept of the power vacuum.

This concept illuminates the situation of political deadlock, a self-induced blockade of the state and society – a situation in which the political forces neutralised one another and paralysed the work of parliamentary institutions. The extreme polarisation and radicalisation of political life disturbed the formation of a consensus and a majority, and finally opened the way to power of an anti-system – parties which promised to fill the vacuum with a new content. The collapse of the legitimation of democracy and the mounting influence of militant dictatorial movements are two sides of the same phenomenon which can be described as the 'Weimar syndrome'. The same thing is meant with today's warning and admonitory formulae: 'Bonn is not Weimar,' or 'Italy should not become Weimar.'

Recently a remarkable book was published which contains a series of comparative studies on the breakdown of democratic states in Europe and Latin America called *The Breakdown of Democratic Regimes*, edited by Juan Linz and Alfred Stepan.[4] This substantial volume not only enriches our knowledge of empirical details, but also attempts a systematic investigation of the general problematic. The analysis of the Italian case of 1922 by Paolo Farneti[5] also speaks of a 'power vacuum', and Juan Linz uses the term in a lengthy chapter comparing the collapse of different democratic systems.

Looking at Italy in 1922 the following aspects are emphasised: the crisis of the parliamentary system involves a disturbance of the balance of power and the division of political functions creating what I have described as a democratic 'loss of power'.[6] The autonomy of political society is lost, extreme polarisation takes place, street politics and the intrigues of various power groups dominate the scene. As long as this does not result in a *coup d'état* or revolution the loss of democratic autonomy results in the stalemate of a power vacuum, and the initiative rests with small groups and people who control decisions.

The phase of a disturbance of the political balance of power follows a shrinking of the political arena. That political force which can organise enough power behind its schemes to overcome the stalemate or vacuum is able to seize power. This concentration and aggregation of forces occurred in Italy not through revolution, but partly by a putschist seizure of institutional power, and above all by the use of violence.

Juan Linz's comparative summary of European and Latin American experiences[7] includes the following points: insoluble problems, a disloyal opposition that is hostile to the system and which exploits its problems in the struggle against democracy, the collapse of responsibility in parties that remain loyal to the system, the weakening of the authority of the government and trust in the ability of the government to find the solution to these problems and provide a defence against violence, all of which leads to a loss of legitimation and to a general atmosphere of tension, to hectic politicisation and finally to the widespread feeling that something new must be tried. The results are wild rumours and conspiracy theories, mobilisation in the streets and the toleration or justification of violence by sections of society, and also the increasing pressure of the anti-system opposition and a general insecurity and uncertainty.

There are three ways in which a solution to this crisis situation is attempted. The first possibility is a strengthening of the executive by constitutional change, emergency powers, suspension or interruption of parliamentary activity, intervention in regional and local government, and change or inclusion of the military leadership. This first possible solution can be successful if all the democratic parties can be included, and if they avoid working with the opposition which is antagonistic to the system.

The second possibility is the attempt to give government a broader base by bringing in a part of the hitherto disloyal opposition that is antagonistic to the system. But this usually leads to a transformation of the state and more often to the handing over and taking over of power, as in Italy in 1922, Germany in 1933 and Czechoslovakia in 1948.

The third possibility is a continuation of the polarisation in a kind of civil war until one of the forces that is opposed to the system tries to seize power. Then the government has two possible courses of action:

either it gives power to the military in the hope of a merely temporary suspension of democracy;[8] or it appeals to the nation and tries to mobilise organisations such as the trade unions on its behalf (like the Spanish Republic in 1936).[9] But in a highly politicised society this means civil war, and is only successful when victory is swift, and thus the danger is avoided that democratic legitimacy is lost in a revolutionary transformation. In Spain between 1936 and 1939 this was unsuccessful, but it was successful in France during the changeover from the Fourth to the Fifth Republic in 1958.[10] The particular problem of the German power vacuum in 1932 was obviously that the government itself hardly had a democratic base.

Attempts such as the book by Juan Linz and his collaborators are of interest in two ways. The historical question of how far the dissolution of the First German Republic can be explained in terms of the specific factors and conditions of the German national state is here posed in a comprehensive explanatory context. This leads to the further equally fundamental and relevant question of the inherent weaknesses and dangers of modern democracy that, under different conditions, constantly lead to dictatorship, either of a traditional authoritarian or of a revolutionary totalitarian type. Even if, like the author, one regards current theories with critical scepticism, whether they are Marxist or systems oriented, one must acknowledge the value of a meticulous comparative study of crises, if this helps to get the controversy over the decline of Weimar democracy out of the impasse.

In spite of the incredible number of specialised studies and new sources it seems to me that the number of interpretations and explanations of the great crisis from 1930 to 1933 has remained remarkably constant in the last twenty-five years.[11] Disregarding an often abstract and demanding terminology, they are still concerned with fundamental questions that have always been asked: the attitude of the government and the president, the role of the parties in parliamentary government, and the attitudes and behaviour of the people. Nowadays these are expressed in more impressive terms: political culture and the ability to govern, fragmentation and functional disequilibrium, legitimation crisis and the overthrow of the system. In spite of the amount of specialised historical and social scientific research we are still faced with the threefold question: the weight of historical and political burdens on the political democracy of Weimar, the significance of the dualistic relationship between party-political and presidential components, and the room for manoeuvre and decision-making powers of the people involved.

This does not mean that the crisis of the Weimar Republic can be reduced to a simple or deterministic model. Scholars cannot be satisfied with the acceptance of the idea of an inevitable functional incapacity of Weimar democracy since 1918,[12] or the suggestion of a definitive end of parliamentary democracy in 1930 as in the crude interpretation of my controversy with Werner Conze.[13] The methodological contrast and confrontation between structuralist and individualistic, of typifying and historical approaches, and particularly between determinism and voluntarism does not help us understand the problem with which we are concerned. It is much more a question of how, and in what ways, historical analysis should deal with the problem of political alternatives, or whether it should only describe the past and concentrate on strictly straightforward explanations. However one interprets the often misunderstood quotation from Rankes: 'Simply show how it actually was,'[14] it should be kept in mind when dealing with all forms of monocausal explanatory models, such as present-day theories of capitalism, Fascism or democracy which threaten to dominate historical writing on the Weimar Republic, and particularly to remember the multitude of factors and possibilities that make up the historical process. Only a careful, subtle and at the same time comparative approach can counter the temptation of monocausal historical explanations and meet the actual needs of empirically based and truly open historical research.

In spite of the greater distance, and in spite of changes in the times and generations, the Weimar Republic still remains relevant, and often to a disturbing degree. None of the great controversial questions of conventional and structural history are yet as adequately answered as one might expect, given the amount of specialised research. On the contrary, the Weimar Republic and its failure — the decay and collapse of a democracy from within and without — remains a hotly disputed paradigm, used by different political and social scientific tendencies. In Germany and abroad it is brought up whenever the preservation and maintenance of democracy against authoritarian and totalitarian temptations and threats is on the agenda. The critics and proponents of the struggle against extremism use the example of Weimar, the latter for good reasons, whereas the former often distort the facts.[15] Weimar is also in the background of the crisis which faces Italy since the 1970s: the power vacuum and the paralysis of the political process are indicators of the collapse of power which helps the extremist movements of the left and the right and their promise of a 'new order'.[16]

The constantly controversial state of research and interpretations of the problems of the Weimar Republic appear in several key areas: in the dispute over the nature of the revolution of 1918/19 and over the question of democracy and the soviets; in the discussion of the constitutional and power structures which paved the way for political developments; in the debate about continuity and discontinuity in German history from the Empire to the Republic and then to dictatorship; on the role of people and groups in the political power process, which is particularly important at the beginning and end of the Republic, and which calls for a combination of conventional and structural history; and lastly the factors in the actual process of dissolution which from 1929/30 seem to develop inevitably and yet depend on a series of decisions and were in no sense unavoidable. Each of these 'cases' show how questionable are monocausal or definitive explanations and demonstrate the need for more research and the discussion of minor themes, possible alternatives or lost causes which crop up later on and which make the apparently inevitable decisions relative, and show the questions of cause and pre-conditions, freedom, chance and necessity, in a new light. No arguments are taboo, as the proponents of final historical explanations would like us to believe, whether this is the 'good' concept of revolution opposed to the 'false' comparison of totalitarian regimes, or the idea of history as a hanging judge whenever it suits their own interpretation. It makes no difference if events and the connections between them are presented from the outset or afterwards as logical and consistent, or even as historically necessary and socially determined.

On the question of soviet democracy it must be pointed out that it was directed against the parliamentary democratic principle of a pluralistic representative system, and has shown itself to be a problematical dual system (as in Russia before the October Revolution), and as a step towards the totalitarian one-party state (as in the consequences of Lenin's seizure of power), or as a means of holding up a federal and apparently democratic system that does not permit an opposition (as in the present-day Yugoslavian model). The claim that the soviet state can be combined with parliamentary democratic principles remains, in spite of many brave attempts even in empirical studies, in the realm of the hypothetical.[17] On the contrary, all great historical examples since the Paris Commune show the fundamental difference between representative pluralist parliamentary democracy and the plebiscitary and unique concept of democracy (as in Rousseau) with its anti-pluralist, anti-representative and finally totalitarian consequences. Then there are the parliamentary forms which are a sort of disguise and deception and not a true democratic synthesis. They are either in the name of a concept of democracy which rests on the fiction of the complete unity of the people, or democracy as the dictatorship of a single party or leader.

When judging the Weimar Republic as a whole and looking at the causes of its failure, this provides important suggestions. It seems no longer possible to dismiss the structural problems and the unfortunate history of the first German Republic as the inevitable consequence of a fundamental anti-revolutionary decision in 1918/19. The question whether a thoroughgoing and genuine revolution, instead of parliamentarisation, would have guaranteed democracy in Germany does not provide a useful answer which would explain from the outset the crises and failure of the Weimer Republic. The trouble is not the lack of a 'complete' revolution, the parameters and points of reference of which appear to be uncertain if one looks at the dictatorial results of a socialist idea of revolution in Russia, but rather the reluctance to have a fully parliamentary regime to establish a definite multi-party democracy.[18] Along with the burden of the war and the opposition of the left and the right there was the original flaw of the Weimar Republic: its ambivalent power structure, a mixture of parliamentary and presidential systems, which had disastrous consequences later on. It was not the question of revolution and soviets as is suggested by the historical legend which is partly nostalgic and partly agitatory, and which often goes hand in hand with a glorification of the dictatorial seizure of power by Lenin as the prototype of a democratic revolution.

That the combination of representative and plebiscitarian elements, i.e. the fundamental problem of modern democracy, was not successful in the Weimar Republic, is due largely to the power of the presidential system over parliamentary democracy. The need for the parties to compromise was diminished because there were two ways to power and the formation of a government: either the parties could withdraw their support, or the realm of presidential power could be extended. The formation of parliamentary majority governments in the normal way was not the rule. In the event of a crisis the dictatorial presidential 'reserve constitution' became a parallel constitution which stabilised the crisis and made a democratic solution less likely because of the continually present temptation to establish a dictatorship.[19] Such potential consequences escaped the eager eyes of the fathers of the constitution. They thought that they could bring together elements from different political systems and traditions without considering their differing *rationes constitutionis* which could lead to weakness or to a conflict between the two popularly elected powers, parliament and the president. The thoroughly negative effect of this synthetic constitution on the relationship between parliament and the government hindered the ability of the parties to get used to the functions of government and opposition and to the need for compromise and co-operation. Nor did it counteract the formation of many divergent ideological and interest groups when, before the great crisis, this was still possible, and parliamentary majorities were not yet destroyed by the radicalism of the left and the right.

The realisation that parliaments and parties in the Weimar Republic did not play the role and did not fulfil the functions which are allotted to them in a parliamentary democracy is a vital explanatory model. The well known sociologist M. Rainer Lepsius describes the German development in the work mentioned above under the heading 'From Fragmented Party Democracy to Government by Emergency Decree and National Socialist Takeover'.[20] He feels that the fragmentation of the parties, the retreat from government and the use of emergency powers for crisis management were the main reasons for the collapse of democracy. Thus the fact that the Weimar parties were class and ideological parties became exacerbated. And by reference to the emergency regime we can also pin-point the political and constitutional traditions which formed the self-image, aims and attitudes of the parties. They made the fatal unfolding of the great crisis possible and even determined its course.

These two great problems were brought together in the discussion of the 1950s in the hypothesis that the parliamentary multi-party system was nearing its end in 1929/30 and that a presidential solution was on the cards. In other words, the *actual* development became at the same time a *necessary* development. This is how Werner Conze, in tune with the dominant interpretation of the failure of the parties and thus of parliament which he described in 1954 in the formula of the end of the party state, interpreted the crisis, providing an excuse for the establishment of a presidential regime. His question sounds very categorical, even deterministic: 'Why did the parliamentary multi-party system *have to fail* in Germany in 1929/30, even *before* Hitler appeared to be a serious candidate for power in Germany?'[21]

This widely held opinion overlooks two basic factors in these developments:

(1) the importance of a pre-democratic understanding of the

nature of parties, and of a deep-rooted antipathy to parties among
the ruling classes which had an effect on electoral behaviour and
hampered the role and self image of the parties;[22]

(2) the significance of the dualistic structure of the Weimar
constitutional and governmental systems was particularly great
in these circumstances, in that it led to a reduced responsibility
of parties and parliament and exerted a negative influence on the
confrontation between party politics and government policy, and
on both parliamentary and presidential power.

The question is not only that the Weimar parties, in Max Weber's
sceptical words of 1917, were ill-prepared 'to take over the responsibility of government *at all*'.[23] It is also a question of what was the
influence from the beginning, and even more so in moments of severe
socio-economic or political crisis, of the fact that these parties were
neither constitutionally nor politically forced or obliged to take on
political responsibility and to practice in parliament and government
the role which was accorded to them in a parliamentary democracy.
Herein lies the importance of the presidential 'reserve constitution',
which started as an emergency constitution and became the main
constitution. And this was in turn related to the question of the political and especially the psychological effect exerted by the fact that the
necessary pre-condition of a positive attitude by the parties and of
the functioning of a parliamentary democracy – its firm anchorage
in the system of government – was weakened and even destroyed by
the above-mentioned dualism. This vitiated the 'education' of the
parties and voters, which Max Weber demanded of a constitution
(even though he too favoured a strong president in contradiction to
his own idea).[24]

In stressing the emergency situations in which presidential power
must intervene it is easy to overlook the fact that there was not only
a fundamental difference between the revolutionary situation of 1923
and the growing economic crisis of 1930, but also that the crisis was in
large part due to the reluctance to form parliamentary majorities and
governments, and that the easy way out which was provided by a
presidential minority or emergency government merely strengthened
the trend towards extra-parliamentary non-party government. There
was hence no incentive to overcome the cleavages within political
society and the fragmentation of the parties. Social and ideological
demarcation lines were certainly strong, but there could be no encouragement of compromise or an integrating effect stemming from

an attitude towards the constitution and government which was based partly on a non-parliamentary legitimation of political power, and what is more, which was actually directed against the parties and gave this anti-party effect fresh encouragement and justification. At the very least the obligation to arrive at decisions in a parliamentary fashion was being called into question; after all, whan a coalition broke up it was always possible to consider the alternative, non-parliamentary, solution.[25] In this way the lack of responsibility of parliaments and parties in the Empire had become no more than a semi-responsibility. Certainly, there was considerable room for manoeuvre.

In the light of these questions it is possible to see that during the vitally important government crisis of March 1930, which was caused by a relatively minor disagreement, no attempt whatever was made to form a government based on a parliamentary majority. Brüning's minority government could be immediately constituted with the emphatic support of presidential power. The inactivity of the parties and of parliament, their failure to work out an alternative coalition policy (in which effort they were hindered rather than encouraged), is not simply the result of a single and controversial 'structural crisis' of party behaviour or of the 'party state', but rather of the widely accepted view that non-parliamentary government was a normal state of affairs. It was not only constitutionally possible; it was very popular with its anti-party and anti-parliamentary thrust; it was, finally, actively encouraged by the President and his advisers after March 1929. As early as 15 January 1930, six weeks before the beginning of the Brüning crisis, Hindenburg had an interview with the leader of the Conservative People's Party, Count Westarp, and suggested a right-wing presidential Cabinet. According to his State Secretary Meissner, it would be 'anti-parliamentary' and formed without the usual coalition negotiations and agreements, and apparently was to involve a similar change of government in Prussia, the stronghold of the Weimar coalition. It was a design which went beyond the provisions of the constitution, and threw a light on the intentions behind the *putsch* in Prussia on 20 July 1932. A year previously, on 18 March 1929, Hindenburg had assured Westarp that he was determined to break with the tradition of appointing the Chancellor after consultation with the parties. He had added that he would use his right to dissolve the Reichstag to the full: Hindenburg 'did not intend to proceed according to this practice ever again'.[26] In what genuine parliamentary democracy would such an openly anti-parliamentary and yet constitutionally correct policy by the head of state be possible? Although it would not lead to an immediate government crisis, it was certainly an anticipation of one.

The hypothesis of the all-important failure of the party state, a failure which allegedly gained a powerful impetus in 1929/30, is hence based on a number of dubious assertions which do not take into account the power structure and the decision-making process. It overlooks the fact that a true 'party state' did not exist, even before 1930; its realisation was hindered by the views of most German constitutional lawyers and by the dual character of the government system which encouraged the formation of Cabinets that were 'above party' and which thought of the parties as 'extra-constitutional' institutions.[27] The presidential system rested on non-parliamentary decisions and on a rejection of a democratic party solution. After 1930 the parliamentary alternative was no longer attempted. The pressure to form a coalition was gone, and the avoidance of responsibility, which it would otherwise have been hard for all parties to maintain during the economic crisis, eased the way for a presidential solution. Thus an authoritarian experiment in accordance with the wishes of the President and his entourage, which in 1930 seemed to be a possible option, became apparently inevitable.

This is not to deny that as early as 1929/30 the problems were very serious. But Brüning's solution occurred at a time when parliamentary majorities were still possible (this was, after all, before the National Socialist electoral victories). Yet, no attempt was made to find a majority because a presidential minority government was an apparently easier and more effective solution. Here lies the whole tragic history of the Weimar governmental crisis, but this should not be seen simply in terms of a definitive failure of the 'party state', but rather as a result of the constitutional dualism and the earlier demands for an anti-party presidential solution by influential forces which had lined up against parliamentary democracy. It was for this reason that in 1930 a parliamentary solution was not attempted, although it was numerically possible. The rapid formation of Brüning's government occurred without consultation of the parties, and particularly of the strongest party, the SPD, also because Hindenburg and his advisers did not think of the possibility of this alternative; they were not interested in a parliamentary solution.[28]

The important difference, in my view, is that the assumed inevitability of the presidential-authoritarian policy of Brüning which gave parliament a secondary role (*nolens volens* in the true sense of the term) and led to disaster is unproven, even if the reality of the crisis and the complexity of the situation are undeniable, which later resulted in the 'power vacuum' and made possible a quasi-legal seizure of power by the Nazis. One cannot see this controversy simply as an allegedly fundamental difference between the methodologies of history and political science; it is much more a question of whether or not one accepts the fluidity of the historical situation in a traditional as well as a structural historical sense.

Even when one speaks of the capitulation of the 'party state' one should concentrate on the role of people and interest groups while not underestimating the constitutional and psychological dimension as well as the continuation of anti-party and anti-parliamentary structures. It was those factors which hindered the development of a tradition of parliamentary government and the growth of a sense of responsibility among the parties and tempted them to shy away from political power at a decisive moment. The policy of the theoreticians and practitioners of the authoritarian state around Hindenburg, in business, among the military and in the universities did not allow them to put up an effective defence because the presidential alternative to parliamentary government always offered itself an easy way out. It was particularly attractive given the unpopular measures taken to deal with the crisis, and because it was apparently legitimised by the continued possibility of an authoritarian-plebiscitarian government within the political system of the republic. The First German Republic was for far too many people a 'provisional republic'.

Notes

1. On the importance of the Italian example: A. Lyttelton, *The Seizure of Power. Fascism in Italy 1919-1929* (London, 1973), pp. 77 ff.; E. Nolte, *Die Krise des liberalen Systems und die faschistischen Bewegungen* (Munich, 1969); W. Schieder (ed.), *Faschismus als soziale Bewegung* (Hamburg, 1976), pp. 11 ff. For a criticism of current theories of Fascism: K. D. Bracher, *Zeitgeschichtliche Betrachtungen* (Munich, 1979), pp. 13 ff., 62; R. de Felice, *Der Faschismus. Ein Interview* (Stuttgart, 1977), pp. 29 ff., and the postscript by Jens Petersen, ibid., pp. 125 ff. See also J. Petersen, 'Die Entstehung des Totalitarismusbegriffs in Italien' in M. Funke (ed.), *Totalitarismus* (Düsseldorf, 1978), pp. 105 ff.

2. *Die Auflösung der Weimarer Republik*, 6th edn (Düsseldorf, 1979), Part 1: 'Probleme der Machtstruktur', Part 2: 'Stufen der Auflösung'. On the power vacuum see my essay, 'Auflösung einer Demokratie' in *Faktoren der Machtbildung* (Berlin, 1952), pp. 45 ff.

3. K. D. Erdmann, *Die Zeit der Weltkriege* (Stuttgart, 1976), pp. 145 ff., 327 ff., also the bibliography; V. Hentschel, *Weimars letzte Monate* (Düsseldorf, 1978), pp. 7 ff., with important sources and documents. A fundamental study of the role of the Reichswehr: F. L. Carsten, *Reichswehr und Politik 1918-1933*

(Cologne-Berlin, 1964). I am most grateful for the many stimulating discussions I have had with Francis Carsten over the course of the last twenty years.

4. J. Linz and A. Stepan (eds.), *The Breakdown of Democratic Regimes* (Baltimore, 1978).

5. See R. de Felice, *Mussolini* (3 vols., Turin, 1965 ff.) and *Le interpretazioni del fascismo* (Bari, 1971).

6. P. Farneti, 'Social Conflict, Parliamentary Fragmentation, Institutional Shift, and the Rise of Fascism' in Linz and Stepan (eds.), *The Breakdown of Democratic Regimes*, Part 2, p. 4.

7. J. Linz, 'The End of Democracy', in *The Breakdown of Democratic Regimes*, Part 1, pp. 75 ff.

8. Whether this was a possibility has always been discussed in terms of the roles of Schleicher and Hammerstein. Bracher, *Auflösung*, pp. 592 ff., 639 ff.; Th. Vogelsang, *Reichswehr, Staat und NSDAP* (Stuttgart, 1962), pp. 335 ff.; Hentschel, *Weimars Letzte Monate*, pp. 79 ff.; Carsten, *Reichswehr*, pp. 418 ff.

9. W. Schieder and Ch. Dipper (eds.). *Der spanische Bürgerkrieg in der internationalen Politik* (Munich, 1976), pp. 7 ff., 55 ff.; also the major work of H. Thomas, *The Spanish Civil War* (London, 1961); R. Carr, *Spain 1808-1939* (Oxford, 1966); and R. Carr (ed.), *The Republic and the Civil War in Spain* (London, 1971).

10. For the change-over from Guy Mollet to de Gaulle: G. Ziebura, *Die V. Republik* (Cologne-Opladen, 1960), pp. 56 ff.; P. Viansson-Ponté, *Histoire de la République gaullienne* (Paris, 1970), vol. 1, pp. 61 ff.

11. I differ from current interpretations on three points: the effect of proportional representation remains uncertain and therefore questionable; the 'failure' of the parties must always be seen in terms of the dualistic system of government; Hindenburg was not always in favour of a majority government, as is shown by his decision in 1930 which marks the beginning of the end.

12. See particularly A. Rosenberg, *Geschichte der deutschen Republik* (Karlsbad, 1935), pp. 6, 239.

13. K. D. Bracher, W. Sauer and G. Schulz, *Die nationalsozialistische Machtergreifung*, 2nd edn (Cologne-Opladen, 1962), pp. 35 ff., also my postscript in G. Jasper (ed.), *Von Weimar zu Hitler 1930-1933* (Cologne, 1968), pp. 69 ff.

14. L. von Ranke, *Vorrede zur Geschichte der romanischen und germanischen Völker von 1491 bis 1514*, 3rd edn (Leipzig, 1885), pp. V-VIII.

15. A dreadful example of slanted writing: F. Duve and W. Kopitzsch (eds.), *Weimar ist kein Argument* (Reinbek, 1976), which contains excerpts from historical literature that are taken out of context so that the meaning is often reversed.

16. In this context belongs the present discussion about the legitimisation and the ability to rule of liberal parliamentary democracies: P. Graf Kielmansegg and U. Matz (eds.), *Die Rechtfertigung politischer Herrschaft* (Freiburg/Munich, 1978); W. Hennis, P. Kielmansegg and U. Malz (eds.), *Regierbarkeit* (2 vols., Stuttgart, 1977-9), particularly the detailed historical and political analysis of R. Lill, 'Italiens "Schwerregierbarkeit" ', vol. 2, pp. 334-74.

17. This is also true of the fundamental historical studies of E. Kolb, *Die Arbeiterräte in der deutschen Innenpolitik 1918-1919* (Düsseldorf, 1962), and P. von Oertzen, *Betriebsräte in der Novemberrevolution* (Düsseldorf, 1963), which have been followed by a massive literature. See as a contrast the critical systematic study of the Yugoslav model by P. Kevenhörster, *Das Rätesystem als Instrument zur Kontrolle politischer und wirtschaftlicher Macht* (Opladen, 1974), pp. III ff., 95 ff.

18. On the concept of revolution: P. Noack, *Die manipulierte Revolution* (Munich, 1978), pp. 23 ff., 111 ff.; a critical empirical study in F. L. Carsten, *Revolution in Central Europe 1918-1919* (London, 1972), pp. 323 ff.; by con-

trast G. A. Ritter and S. Miller (eds.), *Die deutsche Revolution 1918/19* (Frankfurt, 1968). The Communist revolutionary legend as presented in the East German 'Zeitschrift für Geschichtswissenschaft' is contradictory to the idea of parliamentary democracy, and thus the vast revolutionary literature of the GDR provides no help in this matter.

19. The idea of a 'reserve constitution' does not show up clearly enough the dualistic nature of the parliamentary and presidential systems, in which the latter was the most important. Constitutional experts began to discuss the possibility of a change-over to dictatorship as early as 1923. Carl Schmitt talked of 'measures' that were not bound by constitutional law but were 'breakthroughs' by the President using article 48, although he did not become completely anti-democratic until much later: *Veröffentlichungen der Vereinigung der deutschen Staatsrechtslehrer 1* (Berlin, 1924), p. 97. See Bracher, *Auflösung*, pp. 43 ff., 325 ff.; K. D. Bracher, *Deutschland zwischen Demokratie und Diktatur* (Bern/Munich, 1964), p. 37. An excellent study of article 48, the self-destruction of the parliamentary system and the Nazi seizure of power: F.K. Fromme, *Von der Weimarer Verfassung zum Bonner Grundgesetz* (Tübingen, 1960), pp. 122 ff.

20. R. Lepsius in Linz and Stepan (eds.), *Breakdown*, Part 2, p. 46, which is an excellent summary of the problems in terms of a historically based political sociology.

21. W. Conze, 'Die Krise des Parteienstaates in Deutschland 1929/30', *Historische Zeitschrift*, 178 (1954), pp. 47 ff. (italics by K. D. B.). This important essay appeared while my book was in print, so that a debate was not possible at that time. His short and sharp criticism of my '*Auflösung*' appeared in the *Historische Zeitschrift*, 183 (1957), pp. 378 ff., and many other historians agreed (viz. W. Besson, *Württemberg und die deutsche Staatskrise* (Tübingen, 1959), p. 11). A second review, *Historische Zeitschrift*, 187 (1959), pp. 407 ff., took back a number of mistaken ideas and interpretations, of which little notice was taken. This is the reason for the stereotyped judgements of the unhistorical and even deterministic character of the book, which in fact stresses the possibilities that were open until 30 January 1933, and which argues against the so-called necessity of the events (see p. 638, the last page). In fact the difference is about the alternatives in 1930 and their consequences. This controversy still seems to me important and fruitful for both history and social science.

22. Typical are statements from those close to the Stahlhelm. The basic study is V. R. Berghahn, *Der Stahlhelm, Bund der Frontsoldaten* (Düsseldorf, 1966), pp. 211 ff.

23. M. Weber, 'Parlament und Regierung im neugeordneten Deutschland' in *Gesammelte Politische Schriften* (Munich, 1921), p. 184.

24. See the critical judgement of W. Mommsen, *Max Weber und die deutsche Politik 1890-1920* (Tübingen, 1921), pp. 330 ff., 379 ff.

25. Noticeably in the period of normalisation from 1924 to 1929, when it was not possible to talk about a *putsch*: M. Stürmer, *Koalition und Opposition in der Weimarer Republik 1924-1928* (Düsseldorf, 1967), pp. 78 ff., 248 ff. ('the unfinished parliamentary system').

26. Westarp papers in K. D. Bracher, *Deutschland*, pp. 42 ff., and *idem*, *Auflösung* pp. 271 ff.; E. Jonas, *Die Volkskonservativen 1928-1933* (Düsseldorf, 1965), pp. 63 ff.

27. See the influential book of H. Triepel, *Die Staatsverfassung und die politischen Parteien* (Berlin, 1928), pp. 33 ff.

28. This fact is not emphasised enough in K. D. Erdmann's balanced account: *Zeit der Weltkriege*, p. 314.

THE THIRD REICH AND THE PROBLEM OF
'SOCIAL REVOLUTION': GERMAN OFFICERS
AND THE SS

Gunnar C. Boehnert

Shortly after Hitler's *Machtergreifung* on 30 January 1933, Reichsführer SS Heinrich Himmler asked a number of retired senior military officers, well established landowners, leading professionals and industrialists to attend a special meeting in Munich.[1] The speech which Himmler delivered to these invited representatives of the traditional elite groups in German society is of considerable importance, as it outlined his concepts of elitism.

Himmler stated that every state required an elite and that the SS was to be the elite of the new regime. To bring this about it was necessary to link up the National Socialist Revolution with the established traditions in Germany, thereby 'merging everything genuine which had survived from the past and shown itself capable of confronting the future'.[2] Himmler was well aware that without the co-operation of the existing elites in Germany, it would be a difficult task for the SS to establish itself as the new elite. Hence he issued an invitation to members of the traditional elite groups to join the SS so that they could provide the 'genuine military tradition, the bearing and breeding of the German nobility, and the creative efficiency of the industrialist'.[3] It is this attempt of trying to bring about a merger of the old established elite with that of the new aspiring elite, a process also referred to as the silent revolution ('die geräuschlose Revolution') that this chapter intends to examine.

The Reichsführer's invitation was eagerly taken up by the traditional elite groups. The offer to wear the smartly tailored black uniform with the silver runes was difficult for many to resist. The ensuing rush of the *Akademiker* to join the ranks of the NSDAP and other NS organisations has been the subject of a number of studies.[4] The haste with which German jurists joined the SS Führerkorps after January 1933 has been dealt with by this author.[5] Joachim Fest expressed the opinion that the success which the National Socialists enjoyed among the professionals and *Akademiker* 'casts grave doubts upon the proposition that the high ranking officers and big industrialists had shown themselves the weakest point in withstanding the regime's seduction and blackmail'.[6]

The attitude of the active Reichswehr officer corps towards National Socialism has been investigated in a number of studies. Most agree that it was impossible to speak of any corps solidarity of cohesiveness either for or against the Hitler government by 1933.[7] It is generally accepted that a minority of active officers was favourably inclined towards Hitler, another minority was opposed to Hitler, while the bulk of the corps viewed the political events of 1933 with remarkable passivity. A further cleavage in the corps was produced by the generation gap, with younger officers generally favouring the new regime, 'whereas the majority of the older generation probably remained sceptical'.[8] Joachim Fest wrote that by 1933 the German officer corps was composed of 'vanquished men'.[9]

It is the purpose of this paper to investigate the position adopted towards National Socialism of an elite group in German society so far largely ignored, that of the retired professional military officer corps. The investigation makes use of both quantitative as well as qualitative data.[10] The questions which this study attempts to answer are: was there a rush among the retired officers similar to the one found among the intellectuals and professionals to join the NSDAP and other NS organisations after the Machtergreifung? during what period did the majority of ex-officers join the SS? and what contributions did the retired officers make once they joined the SS in the consolidation of the Hitler regime; in other words, were many prepared without reservations 'to realise the aims of the leadership?'[11]

The statistical part of this study is based on 200 case histories of former military officers who donned the black uniform between 1925 and 1939.[12] All of them had received their regular commissions in the Wilhelmine Army or Navy, all had fought in the Great War and with only two exceptions all had resigned or retired from the Army or Navy prior to the *Machtergreifung*. Table 1 shows the joining pattern of the former officers and compares it to that of jurists,[13] senior private employees,[14] professors and secondary-school (*Gymnasium* and *Oberschule*) teachers,[15] professionals (*Freiberufliche Akademiker*)[16] as well as the total corps sample.[17]

The table shows that compared to the total corps sample, the former officers as well as all the other professional groups of the *obere Mittelstand* were underrepresented in the SS Führerkorps during Phase I (April 1925 — December 1930). Even during the first part of Phase II, that is during the final two years of the Weimar Republic, the officers and the *obere Mittelstand* remained underrepresented. It was the *Machtergreifung* which appears to have been the watershed for many of the professional groups of the *obere Mittelstand*. Whereas 25.2 per cent of the sampled senior private employees joined the

Table 1: Percentages of Elite Groups Joining SS, 1925-39

	percentage of Total Corps	Military Officers	Jurists	Professors and Secondary-school Teachers	Senior Private Employees	Profes-sionals
Time Periods						
Sample percentage		3.8	10.7	1.7	5.0	11.0
Apr. 1925 – Dec. 1927	2.3	–	0.4	–	–	–
Jan. 1928 - Dec. 1930	10.4	4.0	2.1	2.2	9.2	5.0
Total Phase I	12.7	4.0	2.5	2.2	9.2	5.0
Jan. 1931 – Jan. 1933	27.8	19.1	10.7	17.6	25.2	20.8
Feb. 1933 – June 1934	29.5	22.1	42.6	44.0	38.5	46.9
Total Phase II	57.3	41.2	53.3	61.6	63.7	67.7
July 1934 – Dec. 1936	12.6	23.6	16.8	15.4	13.4	11.9
Jan. 1937 – Sept. 1939	17.4	31.2	27.5	20.9	13.7	15.4
Total Phase III	30.0	54.8	44.3	36.3	27.1	27.3

SS between January 1931 and January 1933, 38.5 per cent joined between January 1933 and June 1934. More dramatic were the joining patterns of the jurists, the professionals and the professors. Whereas only 10.7 per cent of the sampled jurists had decided to don the black uniform between January 1931 and January 1933, 42.6 per cent did so during the first 17 months of the Hitler regime. Of the *Freiberufliche Akademiker* only 20.8 per cent joined the SS between 1931 and 1933, while 46.9 per cent joined after the *Machtergreifung*. For the same time periods the percentage of professors joining the SS rose from 17.6 to 44 per cent.

The table suggests that the *Machtergreifung* had little impact on the joining pattern of the ex-officers. Whereas 19.1 per cent of the sample joined during the two years prior to January 1933, only 22.1 per cent joined between the date that Hitler became Chancellor and the murder of Röhm on 1 July 1934. If one looks at the joining pattern of the *obere Mittelstand* from April 1925, the table shows that by the end of Phase II (30 June 1934) only 45.2 per cent of the sampled ex-officers had joined the SS as compared to 55.8 per cent of the jurists, 63.8 per cent of the professors and secondary-school teachers, 72.7 per cent of *Freiberufliche Akademiker*, and 72.9 per cent of the senior private employees. When one compares the joining pattern of the *obere Mittelstand* with that of the total corps sample one can see that by 30 June 1934 members of the *obere Mittelstand*, with the noticeable exception of the former officers, had begun to dominate the SS Führerkorps.

The joining pattern of the one-time 'erster Stand in Lande'[18] as revealed in Table 1 is of some interest as it has been asserted that 'in spring 1933 fresh blue blood was inserted into SS veins . . . hardly one distinguished name in Prussian-German military history was missing, they all joined.'[19] Among the 'blue blood' that came to the SS in the spring of 1933 were, according to Höhne, the Prince von Hohenzollern-Emden,[20] von Daniels,[21] von Nathusius,[22] von der Goltz[23] and von Treuenfeld.[24] By maintaining that many of the ex-officers joined the SS in the spring of 1933, Höhne assumes that the joining pattern of the officers did not differ from that of other professional groups of the *obere Mittelstand*. Table 1, however, demonstrates clearly that the watershed for the officers was not reached until Phase III or until the July 1934-September 1939 period.[25] It was during Phase III that 54.8 per cent of the sampled ex-officers joined.

An explanation for this unusual joining pattern is not too difficult to find. A very important reason for the reluctance of the ex-military officers to commit themselves to the new regime was undoubtedly Röhm, the SA *Stabschef*. Soon after Hitler assumed power and while the *Akademiker* rushed to join the NSDAP, Röhm voiced ambitious plans to merge his three-million-strong storm trooper army with the Reichswehr for the purpose of using the professional Reichswehr soldiers as mere training cadres for his SA.[26] This was an open challenge to the professional officer corps. The involvement of the Reichswehr leadership in the plot to eliminate Röhm has been well documented.[27] Only after the Hitler regime had dealt with Röhm to the satisfaction of the professional military establishment did the retired officer corps deem it right to join the new elite of the Third Reich.[28] The fact that many of the ex-officers would henceforth proudly wear the uniform of the formation which was responsible for the murder of von Schleicher and von Bredow further suggests the moral bankruptcy of the erstwhile 'first estate of the land'.

Now that it has been demonstrated that the joining pattern of the ex-officers differed from that of the other professional groups of the *obere Mittelstand*, several other questions come to mind. One obvious one is, what function, other than a purely cosmetic one, did the ex-officers fulfil in the SS? That is, how far, beyond lending their illustrious names and wearing the newly acquired black uniform on public occasions, did the officers go in helping to establish the SS as the new elite? An equally important question is, what concessions did Himmler make in order to facilitate the merging of the old elite with the new one? While these are obviously very complex questions, it is hoped that a more detailed examination of some selected personnel files may provide some answers to them.

When Himmler asked the former General der Artillerie a.D. Dr Heinrich von Maur,[29] holder of the highest award for bravery, the *pour le mérite*,[30] to join the SS, it was obvious that Maur's membership would add prestige to the new elite. Maur, who began his illustrious military career in 1881, was 73 years old when he donned the black uniform in 1936. It gave him the dubious honour of being 'the oldest SS man of all'.[31] But the old general was also a proud and loyal member of the SS. He always signed his correspondence with his SS rank first, then with his military rank a.D. He also was able to write to his 'verehrter Kamerad und Reichsführer-SS' as late as 1943 when many had begun to doubt in a German *Endsieg*, 'even if setbacks should happen now and then, final victory is now a certainty, and will be even more certain if every clear-sighted and decent German supports him [Hitler]'.[32] The letter was written a few days after Maur celebrated his eightieth birthday.

A retired naval officer, Admiral a.D. Franz Claassen,[33] who was admitted to the SS in 1937 because Himmler felt that as 'Director of Labour for the Pomeranian Economic Area', Claassen could 'make an important contribution to the SS in this capacity as an SS leader',[34] also expressed firm belief in a German *Endsieg*. As late as January 1944 Claassen requested to be given an active command in the Waffen SS. Himmler thanked the 63-year-old former admiral, but stated that he could not employ a senior naval officer in the Waffen SS.[35]

After the *Anschluss* the former Austrian Generalmajor Karl Ritter von Kurz[36] joined the SS. In 1943 the 60-year-old general wrote to Himmler, 'Please grant the heartfelt request of an old soldier and fighter for the movement to be allowed to take part in the German people's struggle for freedom.'[37] Himmler had to inform von Kurz that he could not use him in the Waffen SS. Undeterred, the former major-general renewed his request for an active combat command in 1944. This time Himmler informed the old warrior that he could best serve the Fatherland by giving speeches in the *Steiermark*.[38]

It should be emphasised that not all ex-officers showed such eagerness to participate in the final stages of the 'freedom fight of the German people'.

The former First Lieutenant Herbert Edler von Daniels[39] had advanced to 'Oberregierungsrat und Leiter der Führerschule des Berliner Hochschulinstituts f. Leib. Uebg.' after resigning his regular commission in 1919. In 1942 he was posted to Prague where he headed the Amt für Leibesübungen im SS-Hauptamt.[40] It appeared that the former Oberleutnant would spend the war years in the relative safety and comfort of Berlin and Prague. Daniels, however, had the misfortune of being the younger brother of Generalleutnant Edler von Daniels who, along with the Sixth Army, was captured at Stalingrad. It soon came to Himmler's attention that the SS Standartenführer von Daniels in Prague was a relative of the captured Generalleutnant von Daniels, now a prominent member of the *Freiheitskommittee* set up by the Russians. Himmler was outraged and his justice swift. He ordered SS Standartenführer von Daniels to the front 'so that the shame that his brother, the *Freiheitskommittee* member, Generalleutnant von Daniels, has brought to the family [Sippe] could be atoned'.[41] Daniels, however, did not appear too eager to rehabilitate his family's honour at the front at this late stage of the war. His friends in Berlin were able to postpone his posting to the front for many months. When it appeared that his combat posting could no longer be held up, it was 'discovered' that he did not have the qualifications to lead a regiment.[42] He was, therefore, posted in January of 1945, at a time when many young people died in the futile last-minute fighting, to a regimental commanders' course at the *Panzergrenadierschule* in Kienschlag.[43]

Himmler was well aware that he had to relax the strict SS admission standards applied to ordinary applicants when it came to the ex-officers and other representatives of the *obere Mittelstand*. While Himmler remained inflexible in the enforcement of the racial[44] and marriage rules,[45] there were instances when he ignored unfavourable political reports on candidates which his own security office had prepared. When, for instance, the *Sicherheitshauptamt* found the former Oberst-leutant a.D. von Kretschmann[46] to be the 'reactionary German national type' for whom 'there was no evidence at all of National Socialist reliability',[47] Himmler chose to ignore the report. Although one could hardly consider the report a suitable recommendation for an aspiring member of the new elite, Himmler not only commissioned von Kretschmann, but also promoted him on four subsequent occasions.[48]

Himmler also ignored the political assessment compiled by the *Sicherheitshauptamt* on the former Hauptmann Dr von Lossen.[49] Lossen, the son of the well known historian and Secretary of the Academy of Science, Professor Max von Lossen, was described in the report marked 'strictly confidential' as 'a very nationalistic man'. But the security branch felt that he was 'presently too much of a snob' ('mit Standesdünkel behaftet') and that he was still rooted too deeply 'in the non-political point of view of the officer corps'. He lacked the proper understanding for 'Volksgemeinschaft' and therefore 'cannot be regarded as a National Socialist'.[50] Himmler read the report, then wrote with green pencil, 'to be promoted'.[51]

In a similar fashion Himmler demonstrated considerable tolerance in his dealings with officers already admitted to the Black Order. When SS Oberführer von Petersenn, a former Commander in the Navy, openly stated during an *SS-Schulungsabend* that Alfred Rosenberg was unfit to speak in public and should be dismissed from the Party, Himmler ignored the recommendation of the SS-Oberabschnitt to dismiss him.[52] And when SS Obersturmbannführer von Festenberg-Packisch advised a former wartime fellow officer who was half-Jewish not to surrender certain incriminating documents to the Gestapo, but to hide them, Himmler handed Festenberg-Packisch a minor reprimand.[53]

In March of 1933, Sepp Dietrich[54] received orders from Hitler to establish a new *Stabswache*. Although the *Stabswache* numbered at first only 120 men, it was to form the core of a new branch in the SS, the *Verfügungstruppe*, later called the Waffen SS. The *Stabswache*, renamed 'Leibstandarte SS Adolf Hitler' in September 1933,[55] soon distinguished itself in a rather macabre way. It formed the principal element in the liquidation of the SA leadership in June 1934. As a reward for the loyal services rendered, Hitler promised to enlarge the Leibstandarte to regiment size.[56] But not only did Hitler keep his promise to enlarge the Leibstandarte, by March of 1935 when general conscription was introduced in Germany, the *Verfügungstruppe* had grown to 6,383 officers, NCOs and men.[57]

In order to ensure that the military units of the SS would be led by competent officers, three SS *Junkerschulen* or SS officer academies were established. They were the SS *Junkerschule* Bad Tölz established in 1934, the SS *Junkerschule* Braunschweig established in 1935, and after the *Anschluss* of Austria a third *Junkerschule* was created in Klagenfurt.[58]

The most urgent problem which the infant *Verfügungstruppe* had to solve was not how to attract young recruits, but how to attract experienced military instructors. These were to train the young officer cadets in the *Junkerschulen* and the raw recruits in the SS training depots. Several methods were used to obtain the military experts. The first was to ask the regular army to second a number of senior NCOs to the *Verfügungstruppe*. Secondly, commissions in the *Verfügungstruppe* were offered to senior NCOs with above-average service records. It was also hoped, and here the SS was not disappointed, that a number of regular army officers would accept SS commissions. SS Oberstgruppenführer Paul Hausser[59] and SS Obergruppenführer Felix Steiner[60] were perhaps the best-known SS commanders during the war who had transferred from the army. The SS also called upon the pool of retired officers to accept active SS commissions. SS Brigadeführer Goetze[61] was one retired officer who accepted the offer of lecturer of tactics at the *Junkerschule* in February 1935.

As the case of Goetze demonstrates, Himmler was forced to make certain allowances even with those former officers who now held active SS commissions. A short time after coming to the *Junkerschule*, Goetze's questionable political activities prior to 1933 came to light. It appears that he had been an active member of the *Tannenbergbund*, a right-wing organisation which looked upon the NSDAP 'as undesirable competition'.[62] One of the men who remembered Goetze as particularly hostile towards the SS and SA was also a teacher at the *Junker-*

schule. SS Sturmbannführer Dr Koster[63] stated 'that it is particularly shocking to see a man again as a senior SS officer who previously talked about our Führer in an offensive manner as a wretched foreigner and opposition speaker'.[64] Himmler ordered no disciplinary action against the former *Tannenbergbündler*. Instead he gave Hausser, Commandant of the *Junkerschule*, the authority to deal with the matter. Hausser reported, 'I have pointed out to Dr Koster that all officers in the school, irrespective of their past, must now work together in a comradely fashion.' Hausser emphasised, 'I consider it to be my particular and special responsibility to make sure that this principle is carried out.'[65] Himmler concurred. Goetze, whose military expertise was obviously valued more than his past political connections, was made Commandant of the *Junkerschule* in January 1937.[66]

In spite of the leniency shown by Himmler on occasions, it would be erroneous to assume that he would not use more severe measures in his dealings with the ex-officers. This was especially true in time of war. Two officers, who in the late 1930s had accepted SS commissions, then reverted to their army ranks in September 1939, discovered that even as army officers they were not exempt from the harsh SS justice.

Major von Salviati[67] was a well known equestrian who through the Reiter SS became head of Himmler's remount office and 'Leiter der SS-Reitschule in Hamburg'.[68] When war broke out Salviati did not join the Waffen SS, but preferred to serve in the Army. For four years he served as adjutant to Field Marshall von Rundstedt.[69] Over the years Salviati became increasingly disillusioned not only with the Nazi regime but also with what he considered the political cowardice of the Army High Command. He made the grave error of recording his increasing estrangement from the regime in his diary. When this diary was discovered in the Gestapo investigations after 20 July 1944, the material in it was used as evidence against him.

Although Salviati was not directly implicated in the assassination plot, Himmler declared to Kaltenbrunner after reading the diary, 'I can say right now that if the People's Court does not condemn him I shall have Mr Salviati shot as a dishonourable SS man.'[70]

Another officer who unfortunately was too late in recognising the true nature of the regime to whose elite he belonged, was Generalleutnant Moser.[71] Moser, who retired from the regular Army in 1937, joined the SS when he was 'Inspekteur der Ordensburgen der NSDAP'.[72] The event which brought Moser face to face with the stark reality of the Hitler regime was his posting to Lublin as *Oberfeld-*

kommandant in 1942. On his arrival in Lublin, Moser's predecessor, General von Altrock, informed him of the 'camp . . . on the Southside of the Cholmer Chausee'.[73] There was a strict *Wehrmachtsbefehl* that no member of the armed forces was to go near the camp. Von Altrock had scrupulously obeyed this order. Moser, however, was bothered by the camp, especially by the 'smell of corpses' which often penetrated to the city. Moser conducted his own investigation and there is no reason to doubt the sincerity of his words when he wrote, 'I have no words to express my horror at these unheard-of barbarities.' Once Moser established with certainty that the camp which Himmler referred to as 'a concentration camp for Jews'[74] was the extermination camp Majdanek in which hundreds of thousands of prisoners were killed, the old general, who described himself as 'an honest and decent soldier', knew what he had to do. In the *Freies Deutschland*, Moser wrote, 'every decent German must disavow a government that has ordered such an organised mass murder.'[75] The 64-year-old general, after serving some 42 years in the German Army, severed his ties with the regime. When the Russians approached Lublin in July 1944, he walked towards the Russian lines and captivity with his hands raised.[76]

When Himmler was informed of Moser's surrender, he wrote to the *Chef des SS-Personalhauptamtes*, 'There can be no doubt that Moser has surrendered to the Soviets and has not shot himself.' Therefore, he ordered Moser stripped to the rank of ordinary SS man and 'cast him out of the SS in disgrace because of cowardice'.[77]

This chapter has shown that while the retired officers did not distinguish themselves from the rest of the *obere Mittelstand* in their eagerness to join the SS, it was their joining pattern that set them apart from the other professional groups. The quantitative data revealed that whereas the watershed in the joining pattern for most professions occurred after January 1933, the turning point for the retired officers was not reached until after June 1934. Undoubtedly Hitler's decision to silence the ambitious Röhm in June of 1934 made the new regime and its various organisations more appealing to the ex-military officers.

When one takes a closer look at the functions which the officers fulfilled in the SS, one has to conclude that they varied considerably. There were those officers who were admitted to the SS largely for ceremonial reasons. These men allowed their illustrious names to be associated with the SS for the privilege of wearing the black uniform of the new elite on public occasions. This aspect of establishing the SS as the new elite cannot be overrated. After the war, when the horrors of the Third Reich were being revealed, the Archbishop of Freiburg confessed that in Freiburg the SS was always considered the most respectable of all NS organisations.[78] The retired officers must assume partly the responsibility for creating in Germany the image that 'the better type of people' could be found in the Black Order.[79]

In a more direct manner the retired officers provided invaluable assistance in shaping the military branch of the SS. By doing so they inadvertently helped to create the branch of the SS which in a few years would successfully challenge the military's traditional right as the sole bearer of arms. The importance Himmler placed on the development of the *Verfügungstruppe*, a branch he called 'the finest section that I have in the SS',[80] can be seen from the fact that he tolerated men as military instructors of potential SS officers whose political views were hardly compatible with those of National Socialism.

It can be seen that the willingness of the retired officers to allow themselves to become linked with the elite formation of National Socialism greatly benefited the SS. That Himmler in the process had to admit men into his organisation whose views were irreconcilable with those of the new regime was not that important. When the well known and frequently respected men of the former 'first estate of the country' appeared in their elegant black uniforms they became paladins of the new Reich regardless of their political beliefs. A few would recognise the mistakes they made, but in most cases their gestures of opposition came too late and were futile. The fact that the SS was able to establish itself as the new elite in such a short period of time demonstrates that the silent revolution was successful.

Notes

1. H. Höhne, *Der Orden unter dem Totenkopf: Die Geschichte der SS* (Gütersloh, 1967), p. 125. See also F. Kersten, *The Kersten Memoirs, 1940-1945*, trans. from the German by Konstantine Fitzgibbon and James Oliver (New York, 1957), pp. 244-5.

2. Ibid., p. 246.

3. G. Graber, *The History of the SS* (New York, 1978), p. 66.

4. Joachim Fest wrote that 'one asks oneself in amazement what were the causes of the success which the blatantly anti-intellectual movement of National Socialism enjoyed among poets and thinkers' (J. Fest, *The Face of the Third Reich*, trans. from the German by Michael Bullock (London, 1972), p. 376.) Michael Kater in his article wrote that a large number of academics in the early 1930s 'um sich abzusichern nicht gerade Mitglied der egalitären NSDAP, weniger noch der SA, wohl aber der äusserlich attraktiven und gut organisierten SS werden wollte' (M. Kater, 'Zum gegenseitigen Verhältnis von SA und SS in der Sozial-

geschichte des Nationalsozialismus von 1925-1939', *Vierteljahresschrift für Sozial- und Wirtschaftsgeschichte*, no. 2 (1971), p. 357. For a more general treatment of the SS membership after 1933, see R. Koehl, 'The Character of the Nazi SS', *The Journal of Modern History*, no. 2 (1962). See also G. Boehnert, 'An Analysis of the Age and Education of the SS Führerkorps', *Historische Sozialforschung*, no. 12 (October 1979).

5. G. Boehnert, 'The Jurists and the SS Führerkorps, 1925-1939', paper delivered at the Anglo-German Historical Conference, Cumberland Lodge, May 1979. The article will shortly be published in the collection of conference papers by the German Historical Institute, London.

6. Fest, *Face of the Third Reich*, p. 376.

7. F. Carsten, *Reichswehr und Politik, 1918-1933* (Köln, 1964), p. 453. See also R. O'Neill, *The German Army and the Nazi Party, 1933-1939* (New York, 1966), p. 5; J. Wheeler-Bennett, *Nemesis of Power; The German Army in Politics, 1918-1945* (London, 1954), pp. 291-5.

8. Carsten, *Reichswehr und Politik*, p. 451.

9. Fest, *Face of the Third Reich*, pp. 355-6.

10. This article is based on the author's unpublished PhD dissertation, 'A Sociography of the SS Officer Corps, 1925-1939', University of London, 1977. For the study 5,250 case histories were selected from the 61,340 SS officer personnel files housed in the Berlin Document Centre.

11. W. Johe, *Die gleichgeschaltete Justiz; Organization des Rechtswesens und Politisierung der Rechtssprechung 1933-1945, dargestellt am Beispiel des Oberlandesgerichtsbezirks Hamburg* (Frankfurt am Main, 1967), p. 197.

12. The former officers made up 3.8 per cent of the 5,250 selected case histories.

13. In this category were classified all SS officers who had completed their law degrees.

14. Managers, directors, heads of major departments were classified in this category.

15. Because in social prestige the gap between secondary-school teachers (*Gymnasium* and *Oberschule*) and professors is smaller than between secondary-school teachers and elementary-school teachers, secondary-school teachers were classified with professors.

16. Normally jurists would fall into this category, but because the jurists were subjected to a more detailed examination in the dissertation they received a separate category.

17. The above-named professional categories belong to the *obere Mittelstand*. They are therefore compared to the former officers.

18. Carsten, *Reichswehr und Politik*, p. 452.

19. Höhne, *Der Orden*, p. 127.

20. Personnel File: SS Sturmbannführer Prinz Franz Josef von Hohenzollern-Emden, SS no. 276,691, born 30 August 1891, in Heiligendamm. According to the personnel file Hohenzollern-Emden did not join the SS until June 1936.

21. Personnel File: SS Standartenführer Herbert Edler von Daniels, SS no. 258,002, born 31 March 1895, in Arolsen. According to the personnel file von Daniels did not join the SS until July 1935.

22. Personnel File: SS Oberführer Engelhard von Nathusius, SS no. 250,071, born 18 July 1892, in Freienwalde/Oder. According to the personnel file von Nathusius did not join the SS until September 1935.

23. Personnel File: SS Gruppenführer Friedrich Freiherr von der Goltz, SS no. 293,076, born 25 October 1873, in Berlin. According to the personnel file von der Goltz did not join the SS until April 1938.

24. Personnel File: SS Gruppenführer Karl von Treuenfeld, SS no. 323,792,

born 31 March 1885, in Flensburg. According to the personnel file von Treuenfeld did not join the SS until May 1939.

25. Fest without the benefit of quantitative evidence arrived at the same conclusion when he wrote that the decisive landmark in Army-Party relations was not 30 January 1933 but 30 June 1934. He based his conclusion on the Army's 'unprotesting readiness to toe the line' during the Röhm crisis, when the slaughter of the SA leadership was 'so openly celebrated by the military leaders that Blomberg had to remind them it was not fitting to rejoice over those "killed in battle" as he put it' (Fest, *Face of the Third Reich*, p. 372).

26. O'Neill, *The German Army*, pp. 34-5. In early 1934 Reichenau, recently promoted to major-general and head of the Armed Forces Office, received a letter from Röhm which stated, 'I regard the Reichswehr now only as a training school for the German people. The conduct of war, and therefore of mobilization as well, in future is the task of the SA' (ibid., p. 38).

27. Wheeler-Bennet, *Nemesis*, pp. 314-32. See also O'Neill, *The German Army*, pp. 31-54.

28. Höhne, *Der Orden*, p. 122.

29. Personnel File: SS Obergruppenführer Dr Heinrich von Maur, SS no. 276,907, born 19 July 1863, in Ulm/Donau.

30. 'Abschrift der Begründung des Vorschlages zu einem Allerhöchsten Gnadenbeweis für den Generalmajor v. Maur', 22 May 1917. Ibid.

31. SS-Personalhauptamt, Amt II A2, 'Prüfungsblatt', 20 June 1944. Ibid.

32. Letter from SS-Gruppenführer Dr H. von Maur to Reichsführer-SS, 22 July 1943. Ibid. In the letter Maur compared Hitler to Ghengis Khan, stating, 'Was Tschingis Khan für den Osten war und für ihn getan hat, erstrebt unser Führer wenn auch mit allerdings humaneren Mitteln für Europa.'

33. Personnel File: SS Brigadeführer Franz Claassen, SS no. 288,638, born 15 November 1881, in Goldbeck, Pommern.

34. Letter of SS-Oberabschnitt Nord to Chef des SS-Hauptamtes, 28 June 1937. Ibid.

35. Personal letter to SS-Brigadeführer Franz Claassen from SS-Gruppenführer und Generalleutnant d. Waffen-SS v. Herff, 14 Jan. 1944. Ibid.

36. Personnel File: SS Brigadeführer Karl Ritter von Kurz, SS no. 323,046, born 24 December 1873, in Wien.

37. Personal letter to Reichsführer-SS Heinrich Himmler from SS-Standartenführer und Generalmajor z.V. Karl Ritter v. Kurz, 19 July 1943. Ibid.

38. Personal letter to SS-Brigadeführer Karl Ritter v. Kurz from Reichsführer-SS Heinrich Himmler, 23 Aug. 1944. Ibid.

39. Personnel File: SS Standartenführer Herbert Edler von Daniels, SS no. 258,002, born 31 March 1899, in Arolsen.

40. Master Card. Ibid.

41. Letter to SS-Personalhauptamt from Chef des SS-Hauptamtes, 8 Nov. 1943. Ibid.

42. Letter to SS-Brigadeführer und Generalmajor d. Waffen-SS Dr. Katz from SS-Hauptamt – Amt AI, 29 Nov. 1944. Ibid.

43. Master Card. Ibid.

44. SS Untersturmführer Dr Arnold Bacmeister had to resign from the SS because 'Sein Urururururgrossvater war Jude.' It did not seem to matter that Bacmeister's ancestor was baptised in 1725. Personnel File: SS Untersturmführer Dr Arnold Bacmeister, SS no. 277, 480, born 13 Nov. 1907, in Heilbronn.

45. SS Obersturmbannführer Dr Hohl was unceremoniously dismissed from the SS when he refused to obtain Himmler's permission for his marriage. The report stated further that the SS found the moral life of the 56-year-old widower

unacceptable. Alone in the SS Oberabschnitt Elbe Hohl was supposed to have fathered seven illegitimate children, while the SS officer admitted to a further fifteen illegitimate children scattered throughout Germany. The report concluded 'Man mag über diese Betriebsamkeit denken wie man will; sie erscheint SS-mässig gesehen nicht tragbar.' Report of SS-Hauptamt – SS-Gericht, 18 Dec. 1941. He was officially released from the SS on 19 December 1941. Personnel File: SS Obersturmbannführer Dr Hans Hohl, SS no. 192,635, born 17 July 1885, in Dresden.

46. Personnel File: SS Brigadeführer Ernst von Kretschmann, SS no. 277,320, born 12 November 1874, in Hergisdorf/Mansfelder Seekreis.

47. Report to Reichsführer-SS, Personalkanzlei from Chef des Sicherheitshauptamtes, 27 Nov. 1936. Ibid.

48. Kretschmann was promoted Obersturmbannführer on 30 January 1937; Standartenführer on 20 April 1937; Oberführer on 9 November 1937; and Brigadeführer on 9 November 1942. 'Dienstlaufbahn', ibid.

49. Personnel File: SS Standartenführer Dr Oscar von Lossen, SS no. 309,503, born 17 June 1887, in Munich.

50. Report to SS-Personalhauptamt from Gauleitung München-Obb., 13 July 1937. Ibid.

51. Ibid.

52. Statement made by SS Oberführer von Petersenn, see 'Antrag auf Entlassung des SS-Standartenführers v. Petersenn aus der SS wegen mangelhafter weltanschaulicher Eignung.', 29 July 1936. The report stated that Petersenn had demonstrated on several occasions 'dass er geistig nicht in der Lage ist weltanschaulich in unserem Sinne zu denken'. Personnel File: SS Oberführer Walther von Petersenn, SS no. 276,141, born 30 April 1882, in Rittergut Janopol (Kurland). Petersenn was promoted to Oberführer on 20 April 1938.

53. Himmler's instructions read, 'Das SS-Personalhauptamt wird den SS-Sturmbannführer Festenberg-Packisch auf die Unmöglichkeit seines Verhaltens hinweisen.' Letter to Chef der Sicherheitspolizei from Reichsführer-SS Heinrich Himmler, June 1939. Von Packisch was promoted to Obersturmbannführer in September 1939. Personnel File: SS Obersturmbannführer Hermann von Festenberg-Packisch, SS no. 273,742, born 8 January 1880, in Flensburg.

54. Personnel File: SS Oberstgruppenführer Josef Dietrich, SS no. 1,177, born 28 May 1892, in Hawangen.

55. H. Buchheim, *Anatomie des SS-Staates; Die SS – das Herrschaftsinstrument, Befehl und Gehorsam*, Bd. I (München, 1967), p. 161.

56. Ibid., p. 162. By a decree dated 20 July 1934 Hitler also made the SS an independent organisation. Until then the Reichsführer SS came under the jurisdiction of the SA Stabschef.

57. By 1935 the Leibstandarte had grown to 2,544 men. In addition the SS Standarte 'Deutschland' numbered 2,589 men, the SS Standarte 'Germania' numbered 698 men, the SS Pioniersturmbann had 139 men and the SS Junkerschulen had 413 officer cadets. Altogether the *Verfügungstruppe* numbered some 6,383 officers, NCOs and men. *Statistisches Jahrbuch der Schutzstaffel der NSDAP, 1937* (München, 1938), p. 47.

58. Buchheim, *Anatomie*, p. 164.

59. Personnel File: SS Oberstgruppenführer und Generaloberst der Waffen-SS Paul Hausser, SS no. 239,795, born 7 October 1880, in Brandenburg/Havel.

60. Personnel File: SS Obergruppenführer und General der Waffen-SS Felix-Martin Steiner, SS no. 253,295, born 23 May 1896, in Stallupönen, Ostpreussen.

61. Personnel File: SS Brigadeführer Friedemann Goetze, SS no. 261,405, born 26 February 1871, in Stade.

62. Letter to Chef der Personalkanzlei from Führer SS-Oberabschnitt Mitte,

8 Feb. 1938. Ibid.

63. Personnel File: SS Standartenführer Dr Paul Koster, SS no. 3,700, born 20 April 1905, in Kellberg/Eifel.

64. Report marked 'Persönlich' to Reichsführung-SS from SS-Oberführer Paul Hausser, SS-Führerschule Braunschweig, 8 Apr. 1935. Personnel File: Goetze.

65, Ibid. When Goetze applied for party membership in early 1938 his application was turned down on the grounds 'dass Goetze vor der Machtübernahme Tannenbergssündler war und sich keineswegs im Sinne der Bewegung betätigte'. Ibid.

66. 'Dienstlaufbahn' of SS Brigadeführer Goetze. Ibid.

67. Personnel File: SS Sturmbannführer Hans von Salviati, SS no. 277,083, born 23 August 1897, in Stuttgart.

68. Report to SS-Personalhauptamt from Chef der Sicherheitspolizei und des SD, 17 Sept. 1944. Ibid.

69. Ibid.

70. Letter to Chef der Sicherheitspolizei und des SD from Reichsführer-SS Heinrich Himmler, 14 October 1944. Ibid.

71. Personnel File: SS Gruppenführer Hilmar Hermann Moser, SS no. 309,713, born 5 November 1880, in Langenorla/Kr. Roda.

72. Master Card. Ibid.

73. Moser's 'Erklärung' in the newspaper *Freies Deutschland*, 2. Jahrgang, Nr. 37, 10 Sept. 1944. Ibid.

74. Letter to Chef der Sicherheitspolizei und des SD from Reichsführer-SS Heinrich Himmler, 11 Sept. 1944. Ibid.

75. Moser's 'Erklärung' in *Freies Deutschland*, dated 11 Sept. 1944. Ibid.

76. Eye-witness report of the surrender of Generalleutnant Moser given to the SD at 'Heeresstandortverwaltung Zamosc', 9 Aug. 1944. Ibid.

77. Letter to Chef des SS-Personalhauptamtes from Reichsführer-SS Heinrich Himmler, 12 Oct. 1944. Ibid.

78. Höhne, *Der Orden*, p. 125.

79. W. Schellenberg, *Hitler's Secret Service*, trans. from the German by L. Hagen (New York, 1956), p. 7.

80. *Trial of the Major War Criminals before the International Military Tribunal* (Nüremberg, 1947-9), vol. XXIX, document 1918-PS, p. 107.

11 GERMAN REACTIONS TO MILITARY DEFEAT, 1945-1947: THE BRITISH VIEW

Barbara Marshall

Commemorating the fortieth anniversary of the outbreak of the Second World War the new President of the Federal Republic, Karl Carstens, spoke of the 'grave guilt' with which the Germans had burdened themselves, because they were responsible for the death of millions of people. But he also mentioned 'a difference of opinion that runs throughout the nation. Some, particularly young people, are not prepared to accept that the motives and actions of those who fought... in the war...were honourable.' And he went on to say that German soldiers who fought in the Second World War had been exposed to an inner conflict of fighting for their country and of maintaining a wrongful system in doing so. The German soldiers who fell deserved as much an honourable memory as the killed civilians.[1]

These words seem revealing in several ways. The past still continues as a live and divisive issue in West Germany today; the past also still produces a kind of defensive response which indicates that those who lived through it have not come to terms with it. Indeed, such was the impact of defeat on the Germans that a more thorough investigation into attitudes and motives underlying the German infatuation with Hitler and the massive repression of this experience by the population was not possible until twenty years after unconditional surrender, and then it was undertaken by non-historians.[2] Historians after the Second World War when dealing with the Third Reich remained largely concerned with organisation, structure and the way in which state power was exercised, or with Hitler personally. The treatment of the post-war period tended to concentrate on reconstruction leading to the emergence of two German states. Only recently have important studies appeared which analyse the way in which Hitler was enthusiastically supported by a majority of Germans and how the lives of ordinary people were affected by National Socialism.[3] There is need for closer investigation of German reactions to military defeat and the collapse of the Third Reich, if only because attitudes as reflected in the President's statement were shaped in the immediate post-war period.[4]

This essay throws some light on the motives for German behaviour in the period 1945-7, as they appeared to the British occupiers. It is based on reports from Germany by the British 21st Army Group (for 1945), on evidence collected by the BBC (1945/6) and on information produced by Information Services Control (ISC), the branch of the British Element of the Control Commission which — with special responsibility for the licensing and supervision of the mass media in Germany — was directly concerned with re-education and 'the mood of the German people'.[5] The reports of 21st AG were often written by 'intelligent young men' with considerable knowledge of Germany which they had acquired during their wartime service with Psychological Warfare of SHAEF or with Military Intelligence. Although much of this material is not quantified and therefore allows only general conclusions as to the spread of certain opinions, it was taken seriously at the time. The Foreign Office, the main recipient of this information, considered it the only way by which it could obtain some knowledge of 'what was going on in Germany'.[6] The BBC had by the summer of 1946 evaluated some 18,000 listeners' letters per month and reckoned to have a more balanced view of German opinion than many journalists writing on the subject.[7] The image of Germany which emerges from these British sources is therefore seen through British eyes and British preconceptions naturally colour this image. Thus the Germany of 1945 is constantly compared with that of 1918 as indeed many of the occupation policies have to be seen in this light. The reports also reflect the fact that, particularly in the early phase after the end of hostilities, British observers made no distinction between Nazi and non-Nazi Germany; to them the whole German nation was collectively responsible for Nazi crimes. But there seems to have also been a genuine attempt, notably in the BBC and ISC, to penetrate the mysteries of the German 'national character' more deeply, and many results of this first analysis have been confirmed in later sociological and social psychological investigations.

All witnesses of the German military collapse in 1945 and of the mood of the German population agree that the German people reacted with passivity; they seemed to be in a state of shock. There was no attempt to repeat what had happened at the end of the First World War, namely to create by revolutionary means a 'new Germany' which could dissociate itself from the militarism and the policies of the previous regime. But there was also little revulsion from National Socialism among individual post-war Germans, once the Allies had, in a massive information campaign, made the extent of Nazi inhumanity common knowledge. According to a British observer in the autumn of 1945, the Germans were undergoing a process 'from self-exculpation, to self-justification to self-assertion'.[8]

German reactions to defeat in 1945 are closely linked to the degree to which National Socialism and Hitler had become rooted in German Society. This is not meant in the sense that most Germans accepted National Socialist ideology, but it signifies rather the broad consensus over certain Nazi measures. The abolition of the republican form of state, the destruction of the political parties and the trade unions were welcomed by the mass of the German bourgeoisie who had come to consider the parties ineffectual squabblers and the trade unions as representing the dangerous 'left'.[9] The republic had failed on all counts: it had been unable to fight effectively for German 'national' interests against the Treaty of Versailles; it was incapable of maintaining an adequate standard of living when grappling with the economic crisis of the early 1930s; it appeared helpless when dealing with public disorder in the streets. The majority of Germans desired change, and when this change took place, when the 'left' was eliminated, Hitler could count on the massive support of the bourgeoisie. His popularity reached a pre-war peak when, in order to restore 'law and order', he moved against his own SA and when unemployment figures dropped.

However, a distinction needs to be made between different elements of National Socialism. The party and its local officials were frequently made responsible by the population for the shortcomings of the regime. Indeed, as has been shown for rural Bavaria in the Third Reich, party functionaries were often not socially integrated into their local community, unless they were a member of the traditional establishment (i.e. priest, teacher, burgermeister).[10] They therefore came in for an increasing amount of criticism. Hitler, on the other hand, towered above every criticism. This is evidenced by the almost standard phrase which accompanied adverse comments about the regime, 'Wenn das der Führer wüsste.' The average German was thus conformist and non-conformist at the same time.[11] Conformist and profoundly loyal to the person of the *Führer*, who represented a conservative concern for 'law and order'; non-conformist *vis-à-vis* the party which for the average citizen often embodied the worst, 'revolutionary' aspects of National Socialism.

The cult of the personality, the intense worship of the powerful leader figure is, of course, a well known phenomenon in German history. It was one of the weaknesses of the Weimar Republic that it had not been able to build up such a figure on which irrational beliefs could focus and with which the average German could form an emotional bond. For politics needed this emotional appeal to the

German masses, admirably phrased by the Kaiser in 1914: not political parties but German *Vasallentreue* would save the Fatherland in its hour of need. Hitler thus rendered the majority of Germans a service by delivering them from the 'perplexities of democracy'.[12] The sense of enthusiastic relief after his accession to the Chancellorship in 1933 is amply evidenced. Hitler was the means of effective social integration which had eluded the republic. Just as before 1933 Hitler had been the means by which the divergent elements of the NSDAP could be held together, after 1933 he embodied the 'new Germany'. He could speak as the ordinary chap from experience of the trenches and of unemployment; he personified selfless 'service', 'duty', 'sacrifice' to and for the nation. He was one with his people. In this sense German society became indeed a *Volksgemeinschaft:* the almost mystic experience of 'one for one'. It was this theme, skilfully manipulated by Goebbels' propaganda, which resulted in the widespread identification of the individual with the policies of the *Führer*. He embodied 'infantile dreams of omnipotence',[13] he was making Germany prosperous internally and powerful externally.

From this process of identification of self with the leader of the masses two things follow: the leader needs to maintain dynamic policies to sustain the blind faith of his followers; the masses abandon their independence. Both were evident in the Third Reich: dynamism was kept alive by the self-manifestation of the regime in countless mass meetings and campaigns against 'the enemy' — the left, the Jews, the Bolsheviks and, lastly, by war. The German masses, including the left, had always to some extent lived in a world of make-believe. This is demonstrated by the great importance attached to 'national' issues before and after the First World War, often at the expense of a constructive interest taken in the 'social question'.[14] This emerges also from the actions of the Social Democrats in 1918 who failed to create their own real power base in the pious hope that the rest of the nation would become loyal to them. Throughout the Weimar Republic political realism was not rewarded. Political parties which took on the arduous task of running the country through participation in government lost steadily at election time. Controversial issues, such as the Treaty of Versailles or the Dawes or Young plans were never put to the people for a decision and they therefore never had to live with the consequences of decisions which they themselves had made. Demagogues of all shades had an easy game. This blindness to reality continued under Hitler. The measures against the left were acclaimed by many, their unlawfulness often excused. The murder of the SA leadership was greeted as an act of liberation, the cynical disregard for the law was frequently overlooked. The reality of the treatment given to the Jews was ignored because it was presented as 'orderly' and administrative measures – in contrast to euthanasia and the violent excesses against the Jews such as the *Kristallnacht*, which were not approved by a majority of the German people.[15]

Lack of realism also characterises German attitudes to Hitler's foreign policy. On the one hand the Germans wanted peace above all else and Hitler's foreign policy successes were applauded because they were achieved peacefully. However, the implication that this policy would lead to war was not seen, although the Munich crisis had given the population a disturbing warning. Yet, when war did break out, it did not lead to the massive drop in Hitler's popularity which one might have expected; military victories came too easily and quickly and enhanced Hitler's standing with the population. War seemed to heighten both realism and unreality at the same time. As enemy bombs dropped on German cities and enemy armies advanced towards Germany, so Hitler increasingly became the only hope and means of survival. Loss of faith in Hitler would indeed be to admit defeat. The officers' attempt to kill Hitler on 20 July 1944 therefore was not welcomed by a majority of the people.[16] Loyalty to Hitler – as well as Nazi terror – explain the prolonged and dogged resistance when military defeat was already a virtual certainty. When Hitler and the Third Reich finally collapsed there was nothing left to fight for, hence the almost completely passive acceptance of Allied occupation.

Many of these German attitudes emerge again from British observations of German reactions to military defeat after 1945. One could divide these observations roughly into three categories:

(a) the mood of the German people in general in 1945, compared to their reactions to military defeat in 1918;

(b) the collapse of National Socialism and Hitler's disappearance left an enormous void in people's consciousness which only gradually came to be filled by new 'authorities';

(c) the inability of the Germans to accept guilt or responsibility for crimes committed during the Third Reich.

As far as the first category is concerned, references abound in the sources to the dazed, stunned state of the German population when the Third Reich collapsed. There seemed little interest in the life around them, or in the future of Germany.[17] Housing, food, clothing and the reunification with lost members of their families preoccupied the Germans, and these priorities were to remain for many years. The Germans had feelings only for themselves; it seemed that the general situation was too awful to cope with. Concentration on one's personal problems meant often shocking indifference towards all those who had suffered under National Socialism. Cripples who came home from the war found it difficult to find work; former concentration camp inmates were often not welcomed back into their communities.[18] When in October 1945 Jews were given the status of 'victims of Fascism' which entitled them to extra food rations, this was resented by the German population. 'There is a tendency among civilians to treat these people either unsympathetically or callously: I don't want to have anything to do with them. I want to forget them.'[19] British impressions of this mood in the German population had not changed eighteen months later:

> Whenever one observes ordinary Germans...the first thing that strikes one is their complete disregard of one another, their ruthlessness, and above all the complete and utter absence of any consideration for their neighbours...I had occasion to see German officials at work... The contempt, rudeness and lack of interest that were encountered defy description.[20]

First German reactions to military defeat as such appeared to the occupiers as a neat amalgam of surviving Nazi ideology and attitudes which had been encountered before, after the First World War. As after the First War Germans seemed to consider themselves undefeated. Although the reality of their defeat was inescapable, the Germans seemed to have convinced themselves that they had succumbed only to the massive material superiority of the Allies. There was excessive pride in the population that they had been able 'to hold out for so long'. German superiority showed itself again in the idea that the German fighting forces had been very small; their successes were all the more impressive, indeed German victories were due entirely to 'brilliant planning and the matchless skill and audacity' of these few German soldiers. German ideas of superiority particularly persisted towards the Russians. 'A few German soldiers beating off the attack of hordes of "sub-human asiatics" is a popular conception of the war in Russia.' British observers could only note with irritation that the Germans, in their manic preoccupation with themselves, seemed to be unaware of 'the degree of organisation of our production and supply behind our armed forces and. . .the bitter engagements we fought before we were in a position to gain and exploit superiority'. A year later German superiority had been reinforced by the experience of Allied occupation. 'They speak with contempt of the Russians. They dislike the French. . . They prefer the English if there has to be an occupation.'[21] But the British also came under increasing criticism. Given the persistent feeling that Germany had been 'morally unde-feated', the Germans had to find other explanations for defeat than the material advantages of the Allies. The Allies encountered an old favour-ite — betrayal. 'This is the most common reason put forward by both troops and civilians for the German failure to invade Britain in 1940. Everything was ready. . .but the plan was betrayed to the British and could not be carried out.'[22] The betrayal theory of the Germans was particularly often focused on the unsuccessful *putsch* of July 1944. 'Just as the *Führer* was about to complete his master plan to throw the Allies into the sea he was nearly killed by a clique of traitors, and when he recovered it was just too late; the Allies had seized their opportunity and had swept up to the German frontiers.'

Other variants were the idea that Germany had possessed secret miracle weapons which by betrayal had fallen into enemy hands. This did, however, not apply to the V1 and V2 which were considered by the Germans 'somewhat surprisingly. . .as almost playthings', but to the atom bomb which had just been dropped on Japan. 'More and more reports have been received concerning the theory that the atomic bomb was a German invention, the secrets of which were captured by the Allies and rapidly exploited against Japan.' It seemed to the British that here was a new legend in the making.

> The seriousness of a spread of this belief is clear. If large numbers of Germans now come to believe that there really was a weapon of unprecedented power ready, or almost ready, to knock out the Western powers, they will clearly see excuses for many of the actions of their leaders which they have so far condemned — the desperate resistance of Berlin, the defence of the Ruhr. . . They will come to see the end of the war not so much as a defeat, but as a cruel trick of fate which robbed them of victory when it was almost within their grasp.

None of these reports are in any way quantified; it is not known how many Germans really believed that victory was in their grasp. Other sources suggest[23] that the mass of the population was utterly dejected and profoundly disillusioned with National Socialism. To some extent therefore the concern of the British observers seem to reflect their own attitudes which were shaped by what they knew German behaviour to have been after the First World War. However, in a survey carried out in 1950 and 1952 among 1,000 people in the FRG and in West Berlin 25 and 23 per cent respectively still believed the reason for Germany's military defeat in 1945 to have been 'betrayal, sabotage'.[24]

Military defeat thus seemed on the surface to have changed little of the most unpleasant characteristics of the Germans. The population emerged miserable and stunned, but also cantankerous, selfish and arrogant. The Germans remained a puzzling nation.

Many of our pre-conceived ideas about Germany were shattered in the course of our journey: especially our rather black and white conceptions of Nazis, anti-Nazis, PGs [Party members], etc. After a few days we came to the conclusion that there is nothing black and white and clear-cut and simple in connection with Germany and the Germans.[25]

The figures given above indicate some of the feelings which prevailed among Germans even after the war about National Socialism and Hitler. As has already been said, the Nazi Party had always come in for a measure of criticism. Military defeat brought the manifestations and presumptions of National Socialism crashing down. The disaster which the Nazis had brought upon the nation was for all to see. In this sense no 're-education' was needed. The Allies underestimated the enormous sense of relief with which the mass of the German people welcomed their advance because it signified the end of what had become a futile struggle. National Socialism had indeed been a dynamic movement which derived much of its strength from the psychological impact it had on the people. It could not survive defeat, as Hitler himself had predicted many times. The Allies therefore moved into a vacuum. But military defeat also removed the focal point around which the German nation had rallied most loyally: Hitler. The reality of his responsibility or of his disappearance as such was simply rejected. Thus, in the autumn of 1945, the BBC, in a careful analysis of thousands of listener's letters came to the conclusion that one-third of the population blamed 'alle möglichen Umstände' for the catastrophic situation in which Germany found itself, but never Hitler, and this figure was put by individual members of the BBC from their own observations as high as 60 per cent. German letter-writers put the figure as high as 60 per cent among civilians and 90 per cent among members of the armed forces.[26]

Similar conclusions were reached in a survey in the summer of 1947 among 1,250 civilian internees who had all been Party members. Only 10-20 per cent considered Hitler a criminal, whereas 70-80 per cent thought that he had not committed criminal acts. The attempts of this large number of men to find excuses for Hitler struck British observers as 'pathological'. Among the 250 youths of this group (18-20 years old), 70-80 per cent did not believe Hitler committed criminal acts or 'don't admit it for fear of personal pain'. There was a tacit agreement among the internees who professed to have been against 'the principle of dictatorship' and for this reason, they claimed, they had disapproved of Italian Fascism. Their relationship with Hitler was one of devotion 'to the man', not to the principle which he represented.[27] That this infatuation with Hitler survived the end of the Third Reich is demonstrated again in a survey among 2,000 Germans in 1952 where the following views were expressed about Hitler: 10 per cent thought he was the greatest statesman this century and that his true greatness would be recognised only much later; 22 per cent believed that Hitler had made 'a few mistakes', but that he had been an excellent state leader; 40 per cent were of the opinion that Hitler had achieved many good things but that his fatal actions and qualities outweighed his achievements considerably; only 28 per cent held Hitler to have been a politician without a conscience who had been responsible for many crimes.[28] Already in 1948 57 per cent of those asked had answered 'yes' to the question, 'Do you think National Socialism was a good idea, badly carried out?',[29] which seems to support British conclusions that the Germans reacted to the reality of military defeat with massive escapism.

It remained to be seen what the mass of the German people would escape to. One very obvious objective was the desire to reconstruct the country, which became the overriding preoccupation of post-war Germans. Although a perfectly logical aim in itself it became, in its 'manic exclusivity'[30] a substitute for the lost values of the past. No other objective could hope to unite the German people to this degree, and it is perhaps significant that this basic consensus disappeared at a time when the period of reconstruction in West Germany was completed and a new generation began to question certain underlying assumptions. Other attempts to fill the gap left by National Socialism remained somewhat at the periphery of people's interest. This applies, for instance, to the considerable religious revival at the end of the war which brought great numbers into the churches. Those who attended the churches did not always do so for entirely ulterior motives. The Catholic Bishop of Münster therefore decreed a period of probation for those who sought (re)-admittance to the Church, so that they could not hide in the folds of the Church from secondary justice.[31] But British observers agreed that given these reservations, there was certainly the need in a 'spiritually starved and disillusioned people' to seek 'in the Church a faith which will not only give them an answer to their personal problems but will also strengthen their sense of community'.[32] However, the churches themselves had been compromised by often too close involvement with National Socialism and could therefore not produce authoritative answers even for the church-going part of the population.[33]

Another device by which difficult problems of the past, such as Germany's excessive nationalism, could be overcome was a keen interest in the emerging internationalism. A wider international organisation of European states would absolve the Germans from having to make 'national' decisions again, and by co-operating in this wider framework Germans could begin to redeem themselves and become eventually acceptable partners again. German hopes in this respect were widely reported in 1945. Interest in the idea of European union was particularly strong among the more conservative elements of the population.[34] Churchill's Zürich speech of March 1946 did much to intensify this interest. In a survey among 825 inhabitants in the British zone, carried out by ISC[35] in the spring of 1947, 69 per cent of those asked thought that Churchill's proposals for the creation of the 'United States of Europe' were a good idea. It is perhaps revealing how strong an undercurrent of anti-Russian feeling was in the answers:

A considerable majority of the respondents in favour regard it [the United States of Europe] as the best guarantee for the preservation and continuance of European culture...it can be safely assumed that the majority of this group is comprised of people who consider European culture in danger from Russian bolshevism.

If on the one hand German nationalism was now replaced by a, for some, equally fervent internationalism, the anti-Russian tendencies showed not only that many Germans felt threatened from that direction, but also that certain aspects of Nazi ideology lingered on.

In general most Germans had only a vague idea about the political future of their country. As long as the Allies exercised control of Germany, dividing the country into their zones of interest, questions about the organisation of a German government and whether a German government should negotiate a peace treaty seemed irrelevant.[36] Indeed, now that military government was in control of their country, most Germans accepted this new authority unquestioningly. Obedience to Allied rule was another form of filling the void left by the Nazis. Attitudes to the Allies were identical to what they had been to state authority before: disciplined and orderly on the one hand with high expectations that 'the system' would provide.

> They have not got out of the habit of being led, pushed, bullied, exhorted and pressed to act in this way or that way. They excuse political indifference with the extremely hard conditions of life, and, to an astonishing extent, expect others to act for them, the 'others' being mostly Military Government... For many Germans the whole scale of values has broken down, a prolonged and bitter effort has failed and there is a feeling of hopelessness.[37]

But the real causes for their plight were again ignored by the Germans. If the Allies could not provide enough food, it was not because Hitler had started a war as a result of which agricultural production had been disrupted in many countries, or because of a world food shortage — in German eyes British malevolence was to be blamed. If not enough coal was produced to provide heating for every German house it was not seen as a result of Germany's military defeat, but as a conspiracy of the Allies with the intention of letting the Germans freeze to death.[38] The Germans thus not only accepted the Allies as 'Authority', but also became totally dependent on them, to the extent that the ills of the post-war situation appeared somehow only related to Allied actions or intentions.

British attempts gradually to build up a democratic system by investing local political parties and local government with slowly increasing powers therefore had an air of unreality for many Germans. Although these steps were not unwelcome, they were not enthusiastically embraced either — they were accepted like everything else as yet another manifestation of Allied authority. This equation of military government with 'democracy' led to a development in which failures and shortcomings in the Allied running of the zone were seen as failures of 'democracy'.

The great mass of those who classify themselves as disappointed anti-Nazis rejected National Socialism for its failure and welcomed the arrival of Democracy as the panacea to cure all Nazi ills and right all Nazi wrongs. Now, having experienced Military Government for a year, they are bitterly disappointed with Democracy. Just as they failed to understand the essential character of National Socialism and to realise the enormity of German crimes in recent years, so they are now unable to realise that their present wretched plight is the legacy of National Socialism and to understand the censure of the world... A truism such as a plain statement that Military Government is not Democracy comes to many Germans as a startling revelation.[39]

Essentially, therefore, the Germans in the first post-war years emerge as being as firmly wedded to authoritarian leadership as ever. Hitler continued to enjoy extraordinary respect, and he was only reluctantly supplanted by the new authority of the Allies. But authority has to be strong to be successful. Military government in the chaos of the immediate post-war period could not come up to German expectations and by advocating democracy it seemingly denied the very foundations on which it rested: authoritative leadership. German misunderstanding of 'democracy', in the eyes of the British observers, not only revealed a great deal about the psychological make-up of this nation, but also boded ill for a future democratisation.

For many British observers one of the most startling elements in German reactions to military defeat was the vehemence with which the great majority of Germans rejected the notion of guilt or responsibility for crimes committed under the Nazi regime. To some extent the Allies themselves had encouraged this process by the way in which they dealt with proven Nazis when they first moved into Germany. They had systematically discouraged all spontaneous German attempts to weed out National Socialism themselves; the numerous Anti-Fascist groups which sprang up in the country as Allied troops advanced were banned from operating.[40] The party political complexion of these groups was of course often 'left' and thus suspect to the conservative troop commanders. But British and American reluctance to use proven anti-Nazis in the running of their zone went far beyond fear of revolutionary excesses. Instead of trade unions, Social Democrats or other non-Nazis, the occupiers relied on representatives of the churches or on general 'respectable' figures. Often known Nazis remained in their posts when their expertise was needed.

The eradication of National Socialism on the other hand — the often proclaimed objective for which the Allies had fought the war — was treated as a long-term question. Delays and inefficiencies in the denazification programme underline this fact. The psychological impact on the German population of this inconsistent approach by the Allies was enormous.[41] No amount of Allied talk of German responsibility (or 'collective guilt' or 'guilt' — the terms were often used synonymously), or the widespread or efficient publicising of Nazi atrocities would make much impact on the population at large, as long as the Allies themselves went on compromising with the Nazis. The Allies, of course, could not run their zone without the help of the Germans, and most German experts had been experts under the Nazis and were thus implicated in the eyes of the public. But Allied exhortations that *all* Germans had been responsible for National Socialism and needed to change their ways remained unconvincing as long as prominent Nazis remained in their posts. To many Germans these contradictions smacked of intolerable hypocrisy and derived from an Allied assumption of moral superiority which in Geman eyes was all the less convincing as the Allies themselves had committed numerous atrocities of which the dropping of the atom bombs on two Japanese cities was only the last and most horrendous example.[42] Above all, the Allies failed to exploit the state of shock in which the population found itself in the first months of occupation for the purpose of 're-education'. Not only were Nazis not weeded out systematically enough, there was also no positive goal given to the Germans, except for the rather nebulous notion of 'democracy' which was to materialise in the distant future.

The Allied approaches intensified the already existing German tendency to reject the realities of military defeat and of Nazi atrocities. Just as the Germans paid lip-service only to the fact that National Socialism had brought about shortages of all kinds only to proceed to constant demands for the Allies to provide all amenities, the Germans paid only scanty tribute to atrocities committed. The showing of the film on the concentration camps, 'Todesmühlen' ('Mills of Death'), throughout the zone produced among the German audiences scenes of tears and expressions of regret and sorrow.[43] 'It would perhaps be understandable if the Germans expressed doubt at the truth of the atrocity stories ... but overwhelming evidence shows that they do believe what we have told them.'[44] There were massive demonstrations in a number of towns for the victims of National Socialism such as the one in Berlin where on 9 August 1945 more than 70,000 attended a mass meeting.

Making every allowance for German enthusiasm for public demonstrations of any kind ... and the common desire of all Germans to
free themselves of guilt by associating with the guiltless one could
nevertheless hardly fail to be impressed by the atmosphere of grief
and depression which pervaded the assembly.[45]

But this German reaction, so it seemed to British observers, did not
go far enough. 'Horror, shame and anger — there it ends. There is
scarcely ever any expression of personal guilt. The most usual argument is that the German people were ignorant of the cruelties inflicted
and therefore cannot be considered guilty.'[46]

It is of course true that the degree to which the Germans knew of
Nazi atrocities depended on the area where the individual lived. Thus
people in remote rural areas such as Bavaria heard only infrequent
rumours. But in other regions in Germany more was known, although
it is debatable what could have been done about this knowledge in
times of war and intensified Gestapo terror. However, the British
appear quite perceptive in their analysis that

The vast majority closed a shutter in their minds and refused either
to consider what they had already heard, or to allow access to
further suggestions or reports. Their ignorance, so far as it existed
was due to their own refusal to face the facts and their failure
to verify what they were almost too afraid to suspect.

Besides, now, after the war, is was easy to get all the necessary
information and, based on this information, the individual could reject
National Socialism and its excesses. However, according to British
sources, this did not happen. There was little interest in the trials
of major Nazi criminals such as the Belsen or Nuremberg trials,[47] the
reporting of which was moreover held to be one-sided.[48] The whole
idea of putting members of the now defeated ruling class of the enemy
on trial with the outcome a foregone conclusion appeared to be another
example of Allied hypocrisy. Other British sources speak of some
German opinions in favour of 'those responsible being punished', but
doubt whether these opinions were an expression of a genuine desire
of atonement for past wrongdoings or rather that by punishing the
'big fish' the small fry hoped to go free.

There were of course a great number of people, notably among
listeners to the BBC,[49] among whom a lively discussion about 'guilt'
etc. did take place. But for the vast majority of people these issues

were best forgotten. Ignorance of the past was only one example.

It is claimed that given similar circumstances, this could happen anywhere. As proof of this, the success of similar methods in foreign policy is quoted. It was not only inside Germany that men failed to stand up against Nazism. A German will admit a certain lack of moral courage on the part of his people. . .[but] it was wrong to believe that only Germans were capable of the brutality of the horror camps.[50]

One year later a report by a member of the Wiener Library on his impressions during a prolonged journey through the Zone came to similar conclusions:

I found no trace anywhere of a feeling of guilt or the consciousness that every individual or at least many of them, must bear part of the responsibility for the war and its attendant misery. Some with whom I spoke were only too ready to admit the guilt of some individual high up Nazis — hardly ever Hitler — but this guilt consisted, in their minds, not in having unleashed the war, but in having lost it. The Germans today seem but too ready to place the blame on almost anyone but themselves.[51]

In their rejection of guilt the German people found a powerful mouthpiece in the Catholic Church. The religious revival had widened its influence and it spoke with the authority of an organisation which had opposed some of the excesses of National Socialism such as euthanasia. However, the first pronouncements by German Catholic bishops revealed no deeper insight into the nature of National Socialism and no clearer recognition of right or wrong. These utterances caused considerable stir among British observers and were widely commented upon in the Foreign Office. They illustrate German attitudes so perfectly that they will be quoted at some length.

On 31 May 1945 Kurt Groeber, Archbishop of Freiburg, addressed 'the German people'.[52] After describing three classes of people who were forced to give their lives, a figure which amounted to thousands [sic!], he summarised:

All this was sanctioned by this 'new faith', by this German virtue of hardness, this devilish urge for vengeance and this obtuse fanaticism which caused men to trifle with the lives of their fellow men as if they were godlike, absolute masters. In this case is it not our vicarious duty to atone for these crimes against foreign blood and to pray for those who have been murdered by the thousand so that hated nations might either be totally exterminated or emasculated for all time?

Here was the reference to German guilt for crimes committed outside Germany which the British had expected. However this passage was disproportionately short and was followed by a lengthy description of the havoc and destruction which war had brought to Germany. Moreover, it appeared that National Socialism had befallen the Germans like a contagious disease leaving the Germans themselves quite helpless. '*They* wished to make you [German people] great and more powerful than all other nations. . . *They* knew only too well how to divide and disunite. . .*they* attempted. . .to bring to oblivion. . .the nation's spiritual character.' The Allies were asked to assist the Germans in their misery because otherwise Germany would be driven 'into the arms of despair' with an 'enormous danger for the rest of the Christian world'. Having given short attention to the thousands killed elsewhere, the Archbishop described at length the terrible fate which had befallen the Germans:

> German corpses. . .strewn over the whole of Europe and far beyond its borders and the flower of our manhood is decaying under the hillocks and graves of distant countries, or is bending its neck to an alien serfdom (*Fron*).

To British observers there seemed too little reference in this sermon to the link between National Socialism and military defeat, too much emphasis on the destruction in Germany, and the beginning of German cries for help in the expectation that the Allies would provide. Here 'the incessant flow of complaints' by the Germans about their conditions seemed to originate. That the Archbishop's view of the world did not coincide with those of the British was illustrated particularly by his reference to all those who had died through Nazi brutality: 'they join the ranks of those who only a few years ago in Spain [in support of Franco] sacrificed their lives for Christ and the sacred faith of the martyrs of ancient Christendom.'

Other Church pronouncements were even more outspoken. Thus Cardinal Graf Galen's rejection of any notion of 'guilt' or 'responsibility' to the British bordered on the polemic:

If it is represented now that the whole German people – every one of us – is to blame for the cruelties which have been committed by members of our race during the war, then this is unjust. If it is said that the whole German people – every one of us – participated in the guilt for the crimes committed abroad and in Germany, above all in the concentration camps, then it is for many of us an untruthful and unjust accusation. The very concentration camps themselves, with their numerous German inmates and sacrifices, show by what means every resistance to the oppressive measures of the rulers, indeed every free expression of opinion, was suppressed, punished and really made quite impossible. It is a denial of justice and love, if it is declared that every German person participated in the guilt of each criminal act and thus is deserving of punishment. The unavoidable results of war, the sorrow for our dead, for the destroyed cities, dwellings and churches, we will accept and patiently bear with God's help; but not unjust accusations and punishment for injustice and cruelty under which we sighed and suffered heavily.[53]

At the annual conference of Catholic bishops at Fulda in August 1945 the Anglo-American insistence on German guilt was heavily criticised; this insistence had a 'demoralising effect' on the German people. Moreover, '60% of the political prisoners in Allied custody were unjustifiably detained and should now be released.'[54] In later years it has often been said that the Allies placed too much emphasis on 'guilt' and that they failed to give the Germans a positive goal to aim for. While this is certainly a valid criticism, it is nevertheless noteworthy that the German rejection of guilt or responsibility set in immediately, as soon as the Germans realised that these views could be expressed with impunity and well before prolonged Allied insistence could have had its adverse effect. Moreover, these were not the views of the anonymous, ignorant 'man in the street'; much the same would be read from every Catholic pulpit in the land. Those who turned to the Catholic Church for guidance in troubled times would go away comforted but unenlightened.

Although this general refutation of responsibility for Nazi crimes and the inability of the Germans to look at their situation objectively seems consistent with their attitudes to political reality under the previous regimes, it nevertheless came as a profound shock to Allied observers. Somehow it had been assumed that, given enough information, the Germans would accept the Allied point of view. It was on this assumption that much soul-searching took place among the British as to who was to blame for the Germans' obvious failure to respond in the expected way to irrefutable evidence. The Foreign Office was particularly critical of the ineffectual way in which British propaganda was conducted in Germany. In refutation of these allegations but also as a result of prolonged observations of German reactions to a variety of issues, Information Services Control insisted that there was a flaw inherent in the Germans' psychological make-up which prevented them from absorbing unpleasant truths, however effectively they might be wrapped up.

The Germans are ignorant not so much because nobody has enlightened them as because they do not want to be enlightened. Indeed it is uncertain how far they are genuinely ignorant and how far they are feigning ignorance, more or less consciously. For they cannot admit awareness of that version of the facts which the Allies are seeking to force upon their consciousness without admitting responsibility or even guilt. There is a strong undercurrent of unwillingness to cooperate in disseminating these facts, which probably stems from two sources. In the first place they have a vague feeling that, if only they had as rich a wealth of evidence at their disposal as the Allies, they could produce a rational justification of German policy which would at least provide a basis for argument. And secondly, they have the usual psychopath's reluctance to face up to unpleasant facts. . . There is an underlying subconscious fear that to the misery of a lost war will be added the misery of having to confess that Germans were responsible for the war which was lost, not to mention for the losing of it. Hence there is a strong resistance, heightened by the customary tension between rulers and ruled, to any real effort to disseminate the facts.[55]

In the last analysis German reactions to military defeat could be comprehended only as manifestations of a psychologically deeply disturbed nation. ISC's conclusions as to how 're-education' could be carried out under these circumstances underline this verdict: the occupiers must gain the trust and confidence of the Germans, and treat them as equals. This meant rapid reconstruction of the country and the restoration of an adequate standard of living; the heavy emphasis on penalising the Germans by insisting on their guilt, on denazification and on dismantling must be ended. Clearly, these were not ideas which were practical short-term policies. Britain herself was too impoverished to provide for Germany on this scale; there would also have been few among the British public who would have supported such a 'soft' line towards a most brutal former enemy. The implication for any 're-education' policies seemed clear:

> any attempt to 're-educate' the German people is bound to fail because the German people are in no mood to be re-educated. Force is adequate to conquer the bodies of a people but sympathy alone can succeed in conquering their minds. Yet sympathy is too often expected by the Germans to manifest itself in perpetual concessions, and at the end the conversion which the sympathy was intended to produce remains as far off as ever. Here lies the final crux of the occupation which, like most final things, is spiritual rather than material. If only Military Government could win respect and admiration! But it does not because, apart from its more superficial defects, the qualities which the British prize in government are not respected by the Germans who look for quick results. As things stand, the choice seems to lie between ramming home a British version of the facts, thereby exciting considerable German bitterness and resistance but with some chance of preventing the Germans from evading things they find unpleasant, and alternatively keeping silence in the hope that the harmony thereby engendered will make possible a more fruitful and cooperative discussion later. It is not an enviable choice.

To the British, German reactions to military defeat thus combined to make a depressing account of human feebleness. Many of the British reports may have been coloured by the fact that individual writers were of Jewish origin — this is valid particularly for some of the BBC material — and that members of military intelligence often belonged to the moralising left. All reports were produced under the impact of the longest and bitterest fighting in European history and with the revelation of Nazi mass murder fresh in the observers' minds. Not much love could therefore be expected for the defeated enemy. But much of the evidence presented is supported by later German opinion polls and sociological analyses, although of course more detailed work needs to be done in Germany to test the validity of these results.

Such a view of German attitudes seems also to have had certain consequences for British policies in Germany, such as 're-education'. 'Re-education' was of course a low priority even for military government, and this was partly due to a lack of clarity in British minds as to what they wanted to achieve in Germany. Partly, however, it seems that to 're-educate' where 're-education' was such a hopeless task was a meaningless undertaking. This, as well as other factors, might also explain the far greater British reluctance to get involved in direct confrontations with the Germans — as the Americans frequently did — over issues such as the reorganisation of education.[56] The British believed that all they could provide was a general framework, but that ultimately the sick nation had to heal itself.

Notes

1. K. Carstens, 'When Germany Plunged into the Abyss' in *Report from the Federal Republic of Germany*, 3 Sept. 1979. Published by the Embassy of the Federal Republic of Germany.

2. R. Dahrendorf, *Gesellschaft und Demokratie in Deutschland* (München, 1968); A. Mitscherlich, *Die Unfähigkeit zu trauern* (München, 1967).

3. M. Broszat *et al.* (eds.), *Bayern in der NS-Zeit* (München, 1977 and 1979), vols. 1 and 2; I. Kershaw, 'The Führer Image and Political Integration: the Popular Conception of Hitler in Bavaria during the Third Reich' and L. Kettenacker, 'Sozialpsychologische Aspekte der Führer — Herrschaft', papers delivered at the conference 'The National Socialist Regime and German Society', 9-11 May 1979, Cumberland Lodge, Great Windsor Park. The literature on the Third Reich and on Hitler is so vast that detailed references have been omitted.

4. A first attempt was made in M. Balfour, *Four-Power Control in Germany* (London, 1956).

5. For 're-education' in general see K. Koszyk, ' "Umerziehung" der Deutschen aus Britischer Sicht', *Aus Politik und Zeitgeschichte*, B29/78, 22 July 1978.

6. For details on the source material see my article, 'German Attitude to British Military Government 1945-47', *Journal of Contemporary History* (1980)

7. FO371/46899-00338 FO Comment on Control Commission for Germany (British Element), Progress Report for Germany for the period 1 — 31 July 1945. Future references to Foreign Office files will omit the prefix FO371.

8. 46935-X/M 03623 BAOR, Fortnightly Intelligence Summary for period ending 6 Oct. 1945.

9. Kershaw, 'The Führer Image'.

10. E. Fröhlich, 'Die Partei auf lokaler Ebene. Zwischen gesellschaftlicher Assimilation und Veränderungsdynamik', conference paper, see note 3 above.

11. Kershaw, 'The Führer Image'.

12. J. P. Stern, *The Führer and the People* (London, 1975), p. 42.

13. Mitscherlich, *Die Unfähigkeit*, p. 34.

14. Dahrendorf, *Gesellschaft*, p. 16.

15. Kershaw, 'The Führer Image'.

16. M. Steinert, *Hitler's War and the Germans*, (New York, 1977), p. 271.

17. 46933 — X/M 03485, 21st Army Group, Weekly Political Intelligence Summary for week ending 4 Aug. 1945.

18. 46934 — X/M 03623, 21st AG, Wkly. Pol. Int. Sum. for wk. end. 4 Aug. 1945.

19. 46934 – X/M 03623, 21st AG, Wkly. Pol. Int. Sum. for wk. end. 24 Aug. 1945.

20. BBC Written Archives, Report on a Tour of the British Zone, by F. M. Blumenfield, 30 Dec. 1946.

21. BBC Written Archive, Report on a Group Visit to Germany, March 1946.

22. 46934 – X/M 03623 21st AG Wkly. Pol. Int. Sum. for wk. end. 7 Sept. 1945, for the following.

23. Steinert, *Hitler's War*, p. 324.

24. E. Noelle and P. Neumann (eds.), *Jahrbuch der Öffentlichen Meinung, 1947-55* (Allensbach, 1956), p. 137; 33% believed in 'Own weakness, superiority of the enemy' and about 15% in 'generally bad leadership'.

25. BBC Written Archive, Report on a Group Visit to Germany, March 1946.

26. BBC Written Archive, German Feature, Letter-Box Programme No. 9, 10 Sept. 1945 and No. 10, 26 Sept. 1945.

27. 64881 – C11379/9915/180, Report, 27 July 1947.

28. Noelle and Newmann (eds.), *Jahrbuch*, p. 136.

29. Ibid., p. 134.

30. Mitscherlich, *Die Unfähigkeit*, p. 19.

31. 46935 – X/M03623, *BAOR Intelligence Review* (new series), no. 12, 19 Nov. 1945.

32. 46933 – X/M03485, 21st AG, Wkly. Pol. Int. Sum. for wk. end. 28 July 1945.

33. 46933 – 02749, 21st AG, Wkly. Pol. Int. Sum. for wk. end. 14 July 1945.

34. 46935 – X/M 03623, BAOR, Fortn. Int. Sum. for per. end. 6 Oct. 1945 and BBC Written Archive.

35. 64515 – X/M 03757, German Reaction Reports, no. 17, 20 July 1947, for the following.

36. 64515 – X/M 03757, German Reaction Reports, no. 13, 10 Mar. 1947.

37. BBC Written Archives, Monthly Report from Germany, 6 Mar. 1946.

38. 55800-07690, ISC Report for per. end. 27 Nov. 1946.

39. BBC Written Archives, Monthly Reports from Germany, 6 July 1946.

40. See U. Borsdorff, L. Niethammer and P. Brandt (eds.), *Arbeiterinitiative, 1945* (Wuppertal, 1977), for details.

41. There are numerous references to this problem in the sources. See particularly: 46933 – X/M 03485, 21st AG, Wkly. Pol. Int. Rep. for wk. end. 14 July 1945; 46973 – C7200/483/18, Political Report No. 1, L Corps District of British Occupation Forces on Denazification, 12 Oct. 1945; 55613 – C4342/143/18, Notes on a Visit to Germany of Mr O. Harvey and Mr W. Strang, 26 Mar. 1946.

42. 46934 – X/M 03623, 21st AG, Pol. Int. Sum. for wk. end. 18 Aug. 1945.

43. 55512 – X/M 02889, Foreign Office Research Department, The Film Situation in all the Zones of Germany, 5 May 1946.

44. 46933 – X/M 03485, 21st AG, Wkly. Pol. Int. Sum. for wk. end. 14 July 1945.

45. 46969 – 02804, Gedenktag für die Opfer des Faschismus, 21 Sept. 1945.

46. 46933 – X/M 03485, 21st AG, Wkly. Pol. Int. Sum. for wk. end. 14 July 1945 for the following.

47. 46935 – X/M 03623, BAOR, Fort. Int. Sum. for per. end. 6 Oct. 1945 and 55798 – 07690, ISC Monthly Report for period ending 18 Apr. 1946.

48. 55800 – 07690, ISC Monthly Report for period ending 5 Nov. 1946, for the following.

49. BBC Written Archive, The Funkbriefkasten. A Review of its First Year. 6 July 1946.

50. 46935 – X/M 03623, BAOR, Fort. Int. Sum. for per. end. 6 Oct. 1945.

51. 55879 – X/M 02336, Report on a Recent Journey to Germany by L. W. Bondy, July 1946.

52. 46808 – X/M 03711, Archbishop of Freiburg Kurt Groeber, Pastoral letter to the German People, 31 May 1945.

53. 46933 – X/M 03485, 21st AG, Pol. Int. Sum. for wk. end. 28 July 1945.

54. 46935 – 02749 BAOR Fortnightly Int. Sum. for fortn. end. 22 Sept. 1945. The Protestant Church did not speak with one voice. Whereas there were appeals by the first zonal synod of the various branches inspired by Bishop Wurm and Pastor Niemöller to the German population to 'return to Christianity' and to recognise the guilt of all Germans, local branches of the Protestant Church remained under the influence of pastors favourable towards National Socialism. Ibid.

55. 55800 – 07690, ISC Int. Sum. No. 7 for per. end. 17 Sept. 1946, for the following.

56. A. Hearnden, *The British in Germany* (London, 1978), pp. 42-3. See also L. Niethammer, *Entnazifizierung in Bayern* (Frankfurt, 1972), p. 411 ff.

THE 'MISSING REVOLUTION' IN INDUSTRIAL
SOCIETIES: COMPARATIVE REFLECTIONS ON
A GERMAN PROBLEM

Richard Löwenthal

Revolutions, according to the famous statement of Karl Marx, are
the locomotives of history. He was, of course, thinking of the democratic revolutions of the West — of the Dutch, English and French
revolutions as well as the American one, which he described as 'bourgeois revolutions'. No similar 'locomotives' had as yet made their appearance in other parts of the world. He was also thinking of the 'proletarian' revolutions he foresaw for the future of the capitalist industrial
societies that had arisen from those bourgeois revolutions. As the
bourgeois revolutions had played a decisive role in overthrowing the
absolute monarchies, sweeping away the remnants of a feudal ruling
class and clearing the way for the rise of industrial capitalism and the
eventual development of democratic institutions, so the proletarian
revolutions of the future would overthrow the rule of the bourgeoisie,
however liberally disguised, expropriate the capitalist expropriators
and make room for the rise of a classless society and the eventual
withering away of any form of state. And as the first awakening of the
popular masses had culminated in revolutionary dictatorships directed
against the survivors of the old regime in England and France before
issuing into more liberal regimes, so the coming uprising of the workers
would be bound to culminate in a 'dictatorship of the proletariat'
over its former exploiters before the domination of men over men
could disappear altogether. Marx knew well enough that his 'bourgeois
revolutions' had in fact happened at different stages of economic and
social development and with different international complications
in different countries and that several of them had suffered equally
violent restorations before the end of the revolutionary cycle was
reached; but he remained firmly convinced that, as the goal of democracy could not have been attained without a bourgeois revolution, at
least not in the major nations, so the goal of the classless society could
not be attained without a proletarian revolution, although in politically
backward countries, like the Germany of his time, the two upheavals
might be telescoped into a single process of 'permanent revolution'.

It is beyond the scope of this chapter to re-examine the question of

how far the Marxian theory of revolutions is an adequate generalisa-
ation of the history of the great democratic revolutions of the West.
We are concerned here with the fact that, on the one hand, this theory
has influenced modern thought about the pre-conditions of democracy
far beyond the ranks of self-confessed Marxists, and on the other hand
has long played a vital part in the doctrine guiding the actions of the
Communist movements of our time. Our purpose, then, is to confront
the beliefs and doctrines derived from Marxian theory not with different interpretations of the evidence on which it was based – that of
revolutions in Western, pre-industrial societies – but with the new
evidence presented since Marx's time by the development of industrial
societies. That evidence goes to show that thus far, in no industrial
society has a political order been overthrown by a revolution of the
masses 'from below' – be it a 'bourgeois', democratic or a 'proletarian'
Communist revolution. Yet so strong is the hold of the Marxian theory
– or should we call it the Marxian revolutionary myth? – over public
imagination, that this seemingly obvious fact has up to now hardly entered the public consciousness.

The Alternatives of Modernisation

The first correction administered by the course of history to the
Marxian revolutionary vision took place in its author's lifetime and
was fully recognised by him: it was the experience that modern, industrial capitalism could in certain circumstances develop without a
'bourgeois' revolution under traditional monarchist rule and by virtue
of a compromise between the bourgeois and the pre-bourgeois landowning class. Marx identified this development in Prussia and Prussian-
united Germany as a 'revolution from above', and indeed Bismarck
himself once stated that 'in Prussia only kings make revolutions.'
A largely parallel development took place in Japan at the same time,
described alternatively as the 'Meiji Restoration' or the 'Meiji Revolution'. Both cases showed that 'modernisation' in the economic and
administrative, and largely also in the educational, sense could succeed
without a democratic revolution, and indeed without substantial
advances towards democracy. But in the eyes of Marx, and of his
followers in the Social Democratic movement, this did not prove that
in such countries the democratic revolution had become superfluous.
It had merely been postponed: the revolutionary role that the bourgeoisie had failed to play would eventually be taken over by the proletariat. In other words, whereas the 'classical' democratic revolutions

had appeared in the Marxian analysis as a *pre-condition* for the breakthrough of the new productive forces, they now came to be expected as an eventual *consequence*.

As the need for modernisation became urgent in more non-Western countries with a weak middle class, other alternatives to the bourgeois revolution came to be developed. Those of the greatest historical significance turned out to be the totalitarian revolutions directed by Communist parties in Russia and China. Their Marxist-trained exponents interpreted their achievement as that of 'permanent revolutions' in the sense envisaged by Marx for the Germany of 1848 — even if the term itself soon became unfashionable because of its early appropriation by Leo Trotsky: they saw them as originally bourgeois revolutions in which the party of the proletariat had wrested leadership from the hands of a weak and wavering bourgeoisie, had won the peasant masses by its determination in carrying out the agrarian tasks of the bourgeois revolution, and had then proceeded to establish its own dictatorial power and implement its own 'socialist' programme. In fact, the industrial working class never established its power in Russia, and did not even play a major role in the Chinese revolution. Instead, both revolutions were led by centralist, totalitarian parties of a type first created by Lenin. These were parties committed to the idea of the historic mission of the proletariat by the Marxian faith of their leaders, but not responsible to the actual interests of the working class nor dependent on its actual will in the sense of being democratic representations of that class; and both resulted not in the establishment of classless societies and the withering away of the state following a transitional revolutionary dictatorship, but in the establishment of a self-perpetuating, single-party dictatorship over a society administered by a privileged bureaucracy.

But while those revolutions were neither democratic, nor proletarian, nor 'socialist' in the Marxian sense of establishing social control over the means of production, for that would presuppose democratic control over state power, they were powerful 'locomotives' of political, economic and social change — of building effective centralised state machines, speeding the growth of industry, creating a collectivised agriculture and, last but not least, expanding national power. They thus established a third alternative road to modernisation: besides the democratic revolution from below and the authoritarian revolution from above, we now know the totalitarian Communist revolution, using a mass movement from below to conquer dictatorial power and transform society from above.

It is the great merit of Barrington Moore's *Social Origins of Dictatorship and Democracy*[1] to have contrasted these three alternative types, or 'models', of development in his examination of the different processes of modernisation in a number of different countries – a merit that is independent of the degree to which one may accept or reject his hypothesis that the decisive causes of the divergent paths towards modernity are to be found in the different types of agricultural social structure prevalent at an earlier stage in the countries concerned.

The Non-arrival of Proletarian Revolutions

When Lenin decided in 1917 to seek to transform the 'bourgeois' democratic revolution in Russia into a 'proletarian' socialist revolution – in spite of Russia's lack of 'economic maturity' for socialism in the Marxian sense and of the minority position of the industrial working class – he did so in the expectation that the seizure of power by his party in Russia would act as a signal for proletarian socialist revolutions in the advanced industrial countries of Central and Western Europe. But those expected proletarian revolutions in industrial societies not only did not materialise then, a fact which forced the Bolsheviks back to the task of modernising backward Russia in isolation; they have not materialised in any industrial country in the more than sixty subsequent years and are, in fact, no longer expected there by the Soviet and international Communists themselves.

To the Communist mind, it may not have proved much that the attempts at Communist uprisings in the years following the end of the First World War were uniformly defeated; for although it is true that the shock at the horrors of that war was profound and the messianic belief in the new Soviet model was then fresh and untarnished by close acquaintance, it is also true that the Communist parties, regarded by Leninist doctrine as necessary leaders for a revolution, had by then been barely created and were as yet inexperienced and untrained in Leninist strategies. It was more serious that the Great Depression of 1929-32, hailed by the Stalinist leadership of the Comintern – however insincerely – as creating an 'acute revolutionary situation', did not even bring attempts at revolutionary mass movements. Among the two nations hit most severely in the greatest crisis ever suffered by the capitalist economies (in both of which the number of unemployed reached at times one-third of the labour force), the United States finally reacted, after much unrest and despair, by democratically electing the reform administration of the New Deal, while Germany produced a totalitarian revolution of the Fascist type, in which an anti-socialist mass movement, helped into power by crucial sections of the upper classes and the state machine, crushed the bitterly divided organisations of the workers, including the Communist Party, without these forces of the left making any attempt at revolutionary resistance.

The next revival of Communist mass movements, in the shape of the French and Spanish 'Popular Fronts' of the 1930s, did not even aim at a revolutionary seizure of power, but at the creation of broad anti-Fascist coalitions whose programme was on no account to frighten away, by social revolutionary action, the bourgeoisie of the leading Western countries from the alliance then sought by the Soviet Union; and when General Franco's uprising produced, as a counter-blow, a spontaneous revolutionary movement in Spain, the Communists under Stalin's orders spent all their energies on the vain attempt to combine an effective military conduct of the Civil War with the stifling of all tendencies towards social revolution, thereby profoundly disrupting the unity of the Republican camp in the process and ultimately isolating themselves in defeat.

Following the low point reached by the Communist parties during the Stalin-Hitler Pact of 1939-41, when they opposed national defence in the countries threatened or overrun by the Fascist Axis powers, it was more natural that they espoused a policy of resistance and national unity at any price after Hitler's attack on the Soviet Union. After the turning point of the war, when admiration for the victories of the Soviet armies and the Communists' own sacrifices had restored their mass influence in many countries, the Communists began to press throughout Nazi-occupied Europe for a leading role in the post-liberation governments, and their strength and experience in partisan fighting seemed to enhance prospects of revolutionary developments in at least a few Western European countries. But the Soviets, who imposed 'revolutions from above' by creating Communist satellite governments in Eastern Europe as far as their armies had marched, instructed the Western European Communists to avoid a violent challenge of the American and British armies and to seek instead to win key positions in democratic coalition governments, even at the price of dismantling their partisan units. The hope was later to transform those coalition governments in an 'East European' manner once the expected Anglo-American withdrawal had taken place. Only in two European countries was a serious effort made at an armed Communist revolution 'from below' — successfully in Yugoslavia and unsuccessfully in Greece, neither of which were industrial societies.

The critical reader may object that in this section an account of the Communist parties' efforts to win power has so far been substituted for a more general history of proletarian revolutionary movements. The answer must be that no working-class uprisings not directed by the Communists have taken place in industrially advanced countries since the insurrection of the German workers in the Ruhr district, which was directed against the military *coup* by Kapp and Luttwitz of 1920 (when the German Communists had not yet become a mass party) and the 1934 revolt of the Austrian socialist workers against the dictatorship of Dollfuss, at a time when the Communists had no mass following. Both movements aimed not at a proletarian dictatorship, but at the defence of democracy against an authoritarian counter-revolution, just as the Italian factory occupations of 1920 aimed at the economic defence of the workers against lock-outs. With these exceptions, the Communists have had the effective monopoly of this type of working-class militancy, apart from Spain immediately before and during the Civil War in the 1930s – and again, Spain was not then an industrial country.

The Communist Retreat from the 'Classical' Revolutionary Concept

By the end of the Second World War at the latest, Stalin and the top leaders of international Communism had ceased to believe in the chances of revolutions of the 'classical' type in industrial societies – in the overthrow of the 'state machine' in advanced capitalist countries by armed insurrection supported by mass movements from below. But Stalin, who was just in the process of engineering the seizure of power by dependent Communist parties in a number of Eastern European countries which the outcome of the war had left in the Soviet Union's sphere of influence, by no means excluded the possibility that the sham coalitions then masking a Soviet-imposed 'revolution from above' in a number of Eastern European countries could, in favourable circumstances, become the models for the direction in which the real coalitions, then formed in continental Western Europe, often with prominent Communist participation, might develop.

The idea that the goal of revolution might be achieved not by an uprising against the state machine, but by getting hold of some of its vital levers through constitutional entry into a coalition government, followed by the use of levers for breaking the constitutional rules, unseating the coalition partners and suppressing the opposition while organising the acclamation of the masses, was, of course, not new. It had first been voiced in the Comintern in 1922 by Karl Radek, who suggested abandoning the opposition to government participation in the 'bourgeois state'. He launched the slogans of a 'workers' government' in Germany and 'workers' and peasants' governments' in the Balkans, meaning Communist coalitions with left-wing socialists in the German, and with democratic peasant parties in the South-East European case. The idea, endorsed by the Fourth World Congress of Comintern and tried out in 1923 by Communist entry into the German regional governments of Saxony and Thuringia under left-wing socialist leadership, was abandoned at the Comintern's next 'left turn' after these governments had been deposed by President Ebert and the Reichswehr in October 1923, and the masses had not risen in their defence.

In the meantime, there arose far more successful examples of a 'constitutional road to power' than Radek's pioneering experiment. Had not the prescription been triumphantly applied by both the Italian Fascists and the German National Socialists? Both Mussolini and Hitler had combined mass mobilisation with the formation of coalition governments as a starting-point for breaking all constitutional rules and establishing their party dictatorships by means of a totalitarian 'revolution from above'. True, the expectation that the 'bourgeois state machine', the Army and police in particular, might carry out the orders of legally appointed Communist Ministers as willingly as they had followed the orders of Fascist ones, could hardly be described as Marxist; true also, there was a difference between the powers of a junior partner in a coalition government and those of its leading party. But at least experience in Eastern Europe seemed to show that in certain circumstances, the prescription might equally work in favour of Communists – at any rate in countries where the army and police had first been purged with the help of the occupying power, and where the growth of Communist mass influence had enabled the party to supply the head of the new government. That is how it had worked out by February 1948 in Czechoslovakia – in the one Eastern European country where the Communist-led coalition had originally been more genuine than anywhere else and where the Soviet troops had withdrawn after less than a year. The Prague *coup* of that date was a perfect Communist version of the totalitarian 'revolution from above'. Despite the differences in the French situation, that is also what must have been in the mind of Maurice Thorez when he unsuccessfully asked for the post of premier in October 1946 after the elections had made the Communists the strongest party in France; and it must have been in Stalin's mind when he tolerated or encouraged the attempt.

This new concept of coalition government as a first stage on the legal road to power for Communists in Western industrial countries was never explicitly proclaimed by Stalin or other authoritative Soviet spokesmen, but it was more than implied in a number of speeches and articles in which Eastern European Communist leaders praised their forms of 'people's democracy' as a model for the coalition strategies of Western Communists – articles then eagerly reprinted in the French Communists' international periodical, *Démocratie Nouvelle*. It was only after those strategies had failed in France and Italy with the break-up of the coalition governments in the spring of 1947, and after the Marshall Plan had for the first time opened the prospect of a consolidation of Western Europe on a democratic, non-Communist basis that the coalition strategy was criticised *ex post facto* at the foundation meeting of the Communist Information Bureau in September of that year. Yet the new militancy of mass strikes and local riots then recommended to the Western European Communists no longer aimed at the seizure of power, but at the more modest goal of wrecking the prospects of economic recovery under the Marshall Plan. The policy was quickly abandoned when it became clear after two years that neither political mass strikes nor Stalin's blockade of West Berlin had been able to achieve that goal.

The next attempt to devise a road to power for the Western Communists was undertaken only after Stalin's death, and this time it was proclaimed by the highest authority from the rostrum of the leading institution of international Communism – by Nikita Khrushchev in his official report to the Twentieth Congress of the CPSU. The 'peaceful' or 'parliamentary' road to 'socialism', which was then for the first time officially sanctioned as an alternative to the Bolshevik model of armed insurrection in the capital and to the Chinese and Yugoslav models of partisan warfare, was later to be bitterly attacked by the Chinese Communists as an abandonment of the revolutionary core of Marxism-Leninism. Now Khrushchev and his supporters had made it perfectly clear that the new strategy was aimed, just like its alternatives, at bringing about the formation of society under Communist Party control: it was 'parliamentary' because it intended to bring the Communists into the government without a previous insurrection, and 'peaceful' in its attempt to avoid a civil war. The examples given at the Twentieth Congress left no reasonable doubt about what was meant. They were the 'peaceful' Sovietisation of Esthonia after its occupation by the Red Army in 1939/40, the 'peaceful' transformation of Eastern Germany into the 'German Democratic Republic' under Soviet occupation, and − most relevant of all − the 'parliamentary' seizure of total Communist power by the Prague *coup* of February 1948. Thus Khrushchev was right in answering his Chinese critics by claiming that he was not abandoning the goal of an eventual complete transformation of the industrially advanced societies of the West under total Communist Party rule; but his Chinese criticis were right in sensing that Khrushchev now believed that in industrial societies with democratic institutions that goal could not be achieved by a proletarian 'revolution from below', only by a Communist totalitarian 'revolution from above'.

In the quarter-century since the Twentieth Congress, however, no industrial country to the west of East Germany and Czechoslovakia has been occupied by Soviet bloc forces, and no opportunity for a Communist take-over like the Prague *coup* has therefore arisen in any industrial society. While many Communist parties in the West shrank to marginal sects, even the traditional Communist mass parties in Italy and France found themselves permanently condemned to a role of sterile opposition without a chance to influence political decisions. Although the consequent frustration had to be accepted by them as inevitable during the prolonged post-war period of Western prosperity, high employment and improving social security, it became intolerable to them as, from the early 1970s, the growing economic problems of the Western world increased their potential of attraction without offering any chance of revolution. To make an effective use of growing mass discontent, it clearly became vital for the Communist mass parties to overcome their isolation and find potential coalition partners; but finding coalition partners seemed no less impossible for parties committed to a doctrine which saw parliamentary coalitions merely as a stepping-stone to its own totalitarian rule.

This urgency to overcome ideological obstacles to the finding of democratic allies must be recognised as one of the two main roots of the spread of 'Eurocommunist' ideas in the West European Communist parties in the 1970s while the other, the growing critical distance of many West European Communists from the evolution of the post-Khrushchevian Soviet Union in general, cannot be discussed within the framework of the present chapter, except to say that it culminated in the bitter rejection of the Soviet bloc intervention against the Czechoslovak Communists' 1968 attempt to loosen the grip of totalitarian rule and to create 'socialism with a human face'. The two roots converged in the eventual recognition that the West European Communists would not find democratic partners unless they clearly rejected the Soviet model of party dictatorship for their own countries and committed themselves to a democratic political system not only as a battleground on which to fight for its eventual overthrow, but as a value in itself, to be preserved even in the process of a socialist trans- formation of the economic system. It was the Italian Communists, more eager for constructive achievements and more flexible than their French comrades, who went ahead with solemn declarations that, when in power, they would preserve the right of opposition parties to exist and would uphold all other political, civil and intellectual liberties. They were first supported by the Spanish Communists, just emerging into the fresh air of democratic legality after a prolonged underground existence under Franco, and finally by the French party. Subsequently all three parties defended their right to this independently assumed new position against Soviet and Soviet bloc criticism which, at the European Communist conference held in East Berlin in June 1976, correctly accused them of having deviated from the essentials of Lenin's doctrine of the dictatorship of the proletariat.

But this commitment to the democratic liberties as ends in them- selves means that the parties concerned, if they adhere to it, are not only no longer working for a 'classical' proletarian 'revolution from below', but also no longer for a totalitarian 'revolution from above'. In fact, they are not working for revolution against the democratic political system at all. In their eyes, the anti-model of Prague in 1968 has destroyed the model of Prague in 1948. The actual conduct of those parties has confirmed the seriousness of the new orientation in the Italian and Spanish case: the Italian Communists have taken a responsible attitude in matters of trade union demands throughout the inflationary crisis, arguing that a worsening of that crisis would en- danger Italian democracy — which would only be to the profit of the anti-democratic right. The Spanish Communists have helped along the difficult transition from Franco's dictatorship to the young democracy now emerging by equally responsible conduct; they have deliberately pursued a constructive policy and restrained violence. By contrast, the conduct of the French Communists, while far from being revolutionary, has been characterised by unrestrained demagogy. They have proved to be more concerned with their momentary electoral strength *vis-à-vis* the socialists than with overcoming their isolation. The depth of their proclaimed conversion to democratic principles must therefore remain in serious doubt. But the mere fact that that proclamation, however tactically conceived, would not have been possible if a serious belief in a future revolutionary overthrow of the democratic system still had a hold over their followers shows that the myth of the coming proletarian revolution, in whatever form, is dead in all the advanced industrial countries.

The Failure of 'Belated' Democratic Revolutions – and their Non-revolutionary Alternatives

We have mentioned above the Marxist expectation that countries that had reached the level of industrial modernity without a democratic revolution, i.e. by a 'revolution from above', would make up for the missed revolutionary experience at a later stage, under proletarian leadership. In fact, attempts at such a 'belated' democratic revolution have been made in several advanced Western countries; but they have not been ultimately successful. However, belated democratic development has succeeded by non-revolutionary means in these and other advanced countries – in ways not foreseen in the Marxian vision.

The most debated case of the failure of a 'belated' democratic revolution is that of the German revolution of 1918-20. Historians are agreed today that it was one of the few great revolutionary mass movements ever to occur in an industrial country. They also agree that, while it was based principally on the industrial working class, the overwhelming majority of its participants aimed not at a dictatorship of the proletariat, but at the democratic revolutionary goal of a parliamentary democracy, made secure by destroying the strongholds of the anti-democratic, authoritarian regime of the past. There is finally a consensus that it ultimately failed fully to achieve that goal, producing instead a weak parliamentary republic, still dependent on vigorous and hostile anti-democratic forces which delivered the country into the hands of National Socialist totalitarianism in 1933.[2] There is less agreement about the causes of this partial, but ultimately decisive, failure of Weimar. While a once influential view held that the Social Democrat leaders had no alternative to their fateful alliance with the Army High Command and the Free Corps because of the seriousness of the Communist danger, most recent German historians take the view, long shared by the present author, that this danger was vastly overestimated by the SPD leadership, considering the small numbers and the poor organisation of the German Communists and the weakness and isolation of Soviet Russia at the time. It has also been shown that the attitude of Ebert and his closest associates was largely determined by a profound lack of understanding for the changes in social power relations needed to make democracy secure. At the same time there is convincing evidence that such understanding was widespread among the mass of their followers, as demonstrated by the vote of the Congress of Workers' and Soldiers' Deputies in December 1918 in favour of a radical break-up of the military hierarchy, and again by the demands of the German trade unions under Carl Legien, after the defeat of the Kapp Putsch in March 1920, for the formation of a joint government of the two Social Democratic parties to carry out a radical purge, in the Army and the high bureaucracy, of the enemies of the young Weimar Republic. The question thus remains why no alternative leaders came forward to implement the mass demand for radical measures to consolidate democracy, and why ultimately these masses themselves refrained from taking further action to complete the democratic revolution.

The case has been regarded by many commentators as the expression of a peculiar German incapacity for revolutionary action, of a tradition of submissiveness to authority deeply rooted in the German national character. But quite apart from this view being contradicted by the mass movement that originally overthrew the Kaiser and by the magnificent general strike that defeated the Kapp Putsch as well as by the armed uprising against the latter in the Ruhr, this hypothesis overlooks that the aimlessness and indecision of the German revolutionary movemen of 1918-20 was not really unique. The Italian mass awakening of the same period, for all its striking differences to the German story, also offers interesting parallels.

The unification of Italy in 1859 under the leadership not of Garibaldi's movement, but of Cavour and the House of Savoy, had been another case of a 'revolution from above'. Indeed, Cavour had in some respects been Bismarck's model. The resulting parliamentary regime, with electoral participation limited by the *Non Expedit* of the Vatican on one side and illiteracy and landowners' pressure in the south on the other, was a far cry from a modern democracy. Italy's participation in the war, bitterly opposed by the bulk of the organised working class, had become wholly unpopular by its end, as the extent of the human suffering became apparent while the expected fruits of victory failed to materialise. The sudden enormous increase in political participation due to the simultaneous radicalisation of the workers and some of the peasants on one side and the appearance of a Catholic mass party, the Popolari, on the other, was bound, in the circumstances, to assume some features of a belated democratic revolution. However, its crucial act, the formation of a broad government of radical democratic reform, which would now have been legally possible, was prevented when the 'maximalist' majority of the socialist party refused, for doctrinaire 'Marxist' reasons, to join a government in a 'bourgeois state'. At the same time, the 'maximalists' had no idea of how that state was to be overthrown in a 'proletarian revolution'. They merely helped to paralyse it, while an equally 'radical' and equally aimless militancy of the trade unions, culminating in the factory occupation of August 1920 in answer to a lock-out in the engineering industry, helped to paralyse the economy. The result is well known: instead of a belated democratic revolution, the first totalitarian Fascist revolution emerged from the crisis of a semi-democratic regime; all the tremendous political and trade unionist activity of the democratic workers' movement and all its heroism in trying to resist Fascist terror proved to have been in vain.

In Japan, the other classical country of the 'revolution from above', there has never been even an attempt at a 'belated democratic revolution'. However, there is still one major crisis in another country that deserves to be examined from this angle: the origin of the French Third Republic in 1871. Historians have been inclined to assume that the tasks of democratic revolution had been completed once and for all in the tremendous revolutionary cycle starting with the events of 1789 and ending with the replacement of the restoration regime by the liberal monarchy of Louis Philippe in 1830. They have tended to overlook that after the failure of the revolution of 1848, the Second Empire of Napoleon III, while continuing to build on the economic legacy of the revolution and indeed speeding up French economic development, had gone back on essential political achievements of the earlier revolutions: universal suffrage for elections to the sham parliament of a plebiscitary, dictatorial regime was no substitute for the essential political freedoms for which the French had fought so long. The fall of the Second Empire by defeat in war, as that of Bismarck's German empire nearly half a century later, thus became the occasion for the rise of a new democratic republic — a 'belated democratic revolution' in an advanced country, and at first sight the only successful one.

But only at first sight, for the Third Republic, proclaimed by Gambetta in response to national defeat, was only consolidated by the Versailles government through its victory over the Paris Commune.

It was thus consolidated under the sign of counter-revolution rather than revolution. For a full quarter-century, it bore the marks of that origin, beginning with the presidency of the defeated Marshal Macmahon, a true precursor of Hindenburg. It was, in the words of Daniel Halévy,[3] a state in which the aristocracy of birth enjoyed a highly privileged standing, in which the Army regarded itself as exempt from democratic control and in which its alliance with the clergy seemed able to hold down all democratic movements of the masses — regardless of the democratic suffrage, the responsibility of government to a two-chamber parliament and the other freedoms enshrined in the constitution. It was, in short, no more and no less a successful democracy than the Weimar Republic. The 'belated democratic revolution' of France in 1871 can therefore be judged no more successful than that of Germany in 1918-20.

Of course, the decisive difference came later. The Weimar Republic, with all its anti-democratic handicaps, had to confront within ten years the worst economic crisis of modern history — and succumbed. The French Third Republic, having survived a quarter-century without such a deadly shock, was finally transformed by internal forces and became the authentic democratic state it had not been at birth. In the decade preceding and following the turn of the century, in which the struggles about the Dreyfus affair and about the separation of Church and state were fought out and won by the left, the dominant position of the anti-democratic hierarchies of Army and Church were broken, and broken for good. What the 'belated democratic revolution' of 1871 had failed to achieve, patient, non-revolutionary struggle, aided by the living traditions of the earlier great revolution, had at last brought about: a viable, modern democracy.

Nor was this to be the last example of the creation of effective democratic institutions in an advanced society without a classical revolutionary process. The collapse of the Fascist dictatorships in Germany and Italy and of authoritarian military rule in Japan owing to their defeat in the Second World War resulted not in 'belated democratic revolutions', but in the emergence of new democratic states by other means, i.e. under the initial tutelage of the victorious democratic powers. True, in the Italian case there were considerable elements both of a 'revolution from above' (in the King's dismissal of Mussolini) and of a 'revolution from below' (in the partisan uprising against the subsequent 'Fascist Republic' in Northern Italy). But even here, co-operation with the continuing monarchy in the struggle to overthrow the last form of the Fascist regime and drive out its German protectors was accepted by the partisans and the anti-Fascist parties directing them; and the post-war abolition of the monarchy took place not by a revolutionary upheaval, but by a peaceful plebiscite, legally conducted by the King's government. The Allied presence assured the legal continuity of the process; the will of the Italians assured the democratic outcome.

In Japan, where there had been no revolutionary stirrings at all, the Americans deliberately refrained from demanding the abdication of the Emperor, but took the lead in drafting a democratic constitution and in initiating a far-reaching land reform. Together with the dismantling of the armed forces, that land reform assured the destruction of the principal anti-democratic forces as thoroughly as the most radical democratic revolution could have done. The result has been a remarkably successful case of the non-revolutionary introduction of democracy in an advanced industrial country with a long-standing authoritarian tradition. One could almost speak of a 'democratic revolution from above' willingly accepted by the people.

In Germany, where Adolf Hitler had been the head of state, no question of legal continuity could arise. Indeed it was the continuity of the state itself that was destroyed. At the same time, the revolutionary impulses were weak in the thoroughly exhausted and defeated nation which was left with little hope, and the occupying powers discouraged them, determined as they were to shape the future political structure of the country in the interests of their own security. In the case of the Western powers this meant that they originally favoured the slow building of a highly decentralised democracy from below. As time went on, the growing self-confidence of the German democratic parties and the sharpening competition with the Soviets forced a quicker pace and a recognition of the need to keep decentralisation within the limits of viability. When finally the East-West conflict and the need for a German partner in the reconstruction of Western Europe under the Marshall Plan made the creation of a separate state in the Western zones of occupation inevitable, the indigenous German democratic forces had grown strong enough to determine its political structure in all essentials. Here, too, the process of constitution-moulding and state-building was now democratic, legal and peaceful. At the same time, the principal anti-democratic forces which a democratic revolution would have had to destroy, the Nazi Party and its war machine, had been crushed by the victors, while the landed aristocracy of Eastern Germany had first been deprived of its political independence by the Nazi regime and had then been dispossessed by the

Soviet occupying power. The heavy industrialists of the Ruhr, weakened by Allied decartelisation policy and trade union codetermination, re-emerged cured from anti-democratic political ambitions by bitter experience. The result has not only been a viable democratic constitution, but a democratic state of non-revolutionary origin which has proved far more immune to internal threats than the earlier product of a failed democratic revolution.[4]

The non-revolutionary rise of three viable democracies from the ruins of totalitarian or military-authoritarian states in industrially advanced countries would have appeared to most contemporary observers as a non-repeatable development arising from the unique situation at the end of the Second World War. Today, however, we are faced with the fact that a non-revolutionary transition to democracy has taken place in two of the three last European military dictatorships that collapsed in the 1970s — in Greece and in Spain, though not in Portugal. In Greece, the military junta was overthrown, after its disastrous foreign policy blunder in the attempted Cyprus *coup*, by the military itself, which then, under popular pressure, embarked upon a gradual transition to democracy culminating in free elections. In Spain, it was King Juan Carlos, designated by Franco himself as his successor, who carried through the difficult process of peaceful and legal democratisation, including the legalisation of democratic parties and finally even the Communist Party, despite the bitter opposition of the entrenched defenders of Franco's dictatorial regime, among them a considerable part of the Army leadership. The achievement of the King and later of the first democratically based government under Suarez in creating a democratic constitution that was overwhelmingly accepted in the face of the immense difficulties of the still unresolved problems of regional autonomy, was clearly facilitated by the reluctant respect of the anti-democratic right for the legitimacy of a monarch who was both designated by Franco and a scion of the traditional Spanish royal dynasty, as well as by the determination of the left, including the Spanish Communists, to avoid a repetition of the horrors of the Civil War. However, both the young democracies of Greece and Spain have had to pay a price for their non-revolutionary birth which the democracies arising out of the Second World War have been spared: in contrast to the latter, their creation has been dependent on the consensus of the same military hierarchies which had previously been the pillars of authoritarian, anti-democratic regimes; hence they have been unable to destroy a force which might once more turn anti-democratic in a future crisis. Both thus remain burdened with the problem which the French Third Republic only solved after a long time, and on which the Weimar Republic foundered.

Causes and Consequences

It appears, then, that modern industrial societies are remarkably resistant to the kind of revolutionary change envisaged by Marx. They have not produced a single 'proletarian revolution' in a century. Nor have those which had not undergone a democratic revolution before reaching the industrial stage been able to produce a fully successful 'belated' democratic revolution of the classical type. This waning of classical revolutions in the industrial world is far too general a phenomenon to be explained by the peculiar conditions of any one country or the peculiar characteristics of any one nation. In fact, it is more general than the basis of Marx's own generalisation about the 'locomotives' of history.

How, then, are we to explain the apparent fact that those 'locomotives' have been taken out of service in the industrial societies of our time? Disappointed would-be revolutionaries, like the late Herbert Marcuse, have presumed to find the reason in the supposedly unlimited capacity of 'late capitalism' for ideological manipulation. But this view ignores the fact that we are by no means faced with an incapacity for major political and social change in modern industrial societies. Indeed the last section has listed a number of major examples of changes in a democratic direction that have been no less far-reaching and profound than revolutionary changes of the classical type. What is missing is merely the familiar *form* of the democratic revolutionary process — the irresistible surge of the fury of the masses sweeping away the old order, which used to inspire the enthusiasm or the fear of the onlookers.

Now there is indeed an obvious connection between this alteration of the form of major political and social change and the arrival of the industrial age. It lies in the enormous increase in the importance of the functions, and therefore of the functioning, of public administration in the daily life of the people. A state order that expressed itself in the holding down of the masses by biased laws backed by force or in foreign wars could be happily overthrown in time of crisis. A state which depends on the safe transportation of vital supplies, the prevention of epidemics, the schooling of the children, the safe functioning of an immensely complicated division of labour may be burdensome and in need of major change, but the continuity of its functions is needed by all.[5] In the Spanish Civil War of the 1930s, people on both sides feared their enemies and the extent of killing and destruction. In the Spanish transformation of the 1970s, people feared a new civil war as much as a national catastrophe. And they avoided it, while achieving major change by other means.

If this analysis is correct, it becomes comprehensible why revolutions, in our time, are in the main confined to 'Third World' countries. In the advanced industrial countries, the only revolutions still likely to be acclaimed by the masses in a crisis are those that take place not against the state machine, but with its help, like the Fascist revolutions in Italy and Germany and the Communist Prague *coup* of 1948. Yet those can hardly be said to have advanced the course of history. Conversely, a number of major structural changes in the social and political order, which at other times would have required a violent revolution, have been achieved in advanced societies by other forms of 'liberalisation' and 'democratisation'. That argument applies not only to the above examples from the Western capitalist world and to its future; it also applies, in the author's conviction, to whatever prospects may exist for an eventual liberalisation of the Soviet regime and the states of the Soviet bloc. Unlikely as such a liberalisation may appear today, its achievement by revolutionary upheaval is the least likely method of all. For in our industrial (or 'post-industrial') age, the 'locomotive' has become an outdated means of historical transport.

Notes

1. J. Barrington Moore, Jr., *Social Origins of Dictatorship and Democracy* (Boston, 1966).
2. See F. L. Carsten, *Revolution in Central Europe* (London, 1972). For an important recent contribution, see H. -A. Winkler, *Die Sozialdemokratie und die Revolution von 1918/19* (Göttingen, 1979).
3. D. Halévy, *La Republique des Ducs* (Paris, 1937).
4. See R. Löwenthal, 'Bonn und Weimar', in *idem, Gesellschaftswandel und Kulturkrise* (Frankfurt, 1979).
5. For an earlier statement of this argument with special reference to Germany in 1918-20, see R. Löwenthal, 'Die deutsche Sozialdemokratie in Weimar und heute', in *idem, Gesellschaftswandel.*

APPENDIX: F. L. CARSTEN'S WRITINGS

A. Articles

'Die Judenfrage in der Auseinandersetzung zwischen dem Kurfürsten Friedrich Wilhelm von Brandenburg und den Landständen', *Tijdschrift voor Geschiedenis*, LIII (1938), pp. 52 ff.

'Die sozialen Bewegungen in den Pommerschen Städten vom 14. Jahrhundert bis zur Reformationszeit', *Tijdschrift voor Geschiedenis*, LIII (1938), pp. 366 ff.

'Der Bauernkrieg in Ostpreussen 1525', *International Review for Social History*, III (1938), pp. 398 ff.

'De sociaal-historische grondslagen van Pruisen', *Verslag von het vierde congres van Nederlandsche Historici*, The Hague, 31 October 1938, pp. 18 ff.

'Die Staten-Generaal und die Stände von Cleve um die Mitte des 17. Jahrhunderts', *Tijdschrift voor Geschiedenis*, LV (1940), pp. 14 ff.

'Slavs in North-eastern Germany', *Economic History Review*, XI (1941), pp. 61 ff.

'Medieval Democracy in the Brandenburg Towns and its Defeat in the Fifteenth Century', *Transactions of the Royal Historical Society*, 4th series, XXV (1943), pp. 73 ff.

'The British Court at Wiesbaden, 1926-1929', *Modern Law Review*, VII (1944), pp. 215 ff.

'The Origins of the Junkers', *English Historical Review*, LXII (1947), pp. 145 ff.

'Historical Revision: East Prussia', *History*, XXXIII (1948), pp. 241 ff.

'The Great Elector and the Foundation of the Hohenzollern Despotism', *English Historical Review*, LXV (1950), pp. 175 ff.

'The Resistance of Cleves and Mark to the Despotic Policy of the Great Elector', *English Historical Review*, LXVI (1951), pp. 219 ff.

'British Diplomacy and the Giant Grenadiers of Frederick William I', *History Today* (November 1951), pp. 55 ff.

'Prussian Despotism at its Height', *History*, XL (1955), pp. 42 ff.

'Was there an Economic Decline in Germany before the Thirty Years' War?', *English Historical Review*, LXXI (1956), pp. 240 ff.

'The Failure of the Weimar Republic', *History Today*, VI (1956), pp. 318 ff.

'From Scharnhorst to Schleicher: the Prussian Officer Corps in Politics, 1806-1933' in Michael Howard (ed.), *Soldiers and Governments* (London, 1957), pp. 73 ff.

'The Estates of Württemberg', Anglo-American Conference of Historians, *Bulletin of the Institute of Historical Research*, XXXI, (1958), pp. 21 ff.

'The German Generals and Hitler', *History Today*, VIII (1958), pp. 556 ff.

'A Note on the Thirty Years' War', *History*, XLIII (1958), pp. 190 f.

'Die deutschen Landstände und der Aufstieg der Fürsten', *Die Welt als Geschichte*, 1 (1960), pp. 16 ff. Reprinted in *Die geschichtlichen Grundlagen der modernen Volksvertretung* (Darmstadt, 1974), pp. 315 ff.

'The Great Elector', *History Today*, X (1960), pp. 83 ff.

'Rosa Luxemburg', *Survey*, 33 (1960), pp. 93 ff. German version in L. Labedz (ed.), *Der Revisionismus* (Cologne-Berlin, 1965), pp. 68 ff.

'The Causes of the Decline of the German Estates', in Album Helen Maud Cam, *Study presented to the International Commission for the History of Representative and Parliamentary Institutions*, XXIV (Louvain, 1961), pp. 287 ff. German

version in: *Historische Zeitschrift*, 192/2 (1961), pp. 273 ff.
'The German Estates in the Eighteenth Century', *Receuils de la Société Jean Bodin pour l'Histoire comparative des Institutions*, VIII (1961), pp. 227 ff.
'L'échec des libéraux allemands de 1860 à 1866', *Rasegna Storico Toscana*, VIII (April-December 1961), pp. 295 ff.
'Bismarck and the Prussian Liberals', *History Today*, XI (1961), pp. 760 ff.
'History under Ulbricht', *Survey*, 37 (1961), pp. 90 ff.
'The Court Jews: a Prelude to Emancipation', *Yearbook of the Leo Baeck Institute*, III (1958), pp. 140 ff.
'The Reichswehr and the Red Army', *Survey*, 44/45 (1962), pp. 114 ff.
'Die Reichswehr und Sowjetrussland, 1920-1933', *Österreichische Osthefte*, 6 (1963), pp. 445 ff.
'Reports by Two German Officers on the Red Army', *Slavonic and East European Review*, XLI (1962), pp. 217 ff.
'Die Entstehung des Junkertums' in R. Dietrich (ed.), *Preussen: Epochen und Probleme seiner Geschichte* (Berlin, 1964), pp. 57 ff.
'Nationalrevolutionäre Offiziere gegen Hitler', *Aus Politik und Geschichte, Beilage zur Wochenzeitung Das Parlament*, 15 July 1964, pp. 46 ff.
'August Bebel', *Survey*, 55 (1965), pp. 141 ff.
'What German Historians are Saying', *Encounter* (April 1964), pp. 106 ff.
' "Volk ohne Raum": a Note on Hans Grimm', *Journal of Contemporary History*, II (1967), pp. 221 ff.
'A Bolshevik Conspiracy in the Wehrmacht', *Slavonic and East European Review*, XLVII (1969), pp. 483 ff.
'Die faschistischen Bewegungen: Gemeinsamkeiten und Unterschiede' in *Fascism and Europe*, an International Symposium (Prague, August 1969).
'The Historical Roots of National Socialism' in E. J. Feuchtwanger (ed.), *Upheaval and Continuity. A Century of German History* (London, 1973), pp. 116 ff. German version in *Deutschland, Wandel und Bestand* (Frankfurt, 1973), pp. 110 ff.
'Arthur Rosenberg: Ancient Historian into Leading Communist', *Journal of Contemporary History*, VII (1973), pp. 63 ff. German version in *Geschichte und Gesellschaft*, Festschrift für Karl R. Stadler (Vienna, 1974), pp. 267 ff.
'New "Evidence" against Marshal Tukhachevsky', *Slavonic and East European Review*, LII (1974), pp. 272 ff.
'Revolutionary Situations in Europe, 1917-1920' in C. L. Bertrand (ed.), *Revolutionary Situations in Europe, 1917-1922: Germany, Italy, Austria-Hungary* (Montreal, 1977), pp. 21 ff. German version in D. Stegmann, B.J. Wendt and P.C. Witt (eds.), *Industrielle Gesellschaft und Politisches System*, Festschrift für Fritz Fischer (Bonn, 1978), pp. 375 ff.
'Rivoluzione e Reazione nell'Europa Centrale (1918-1920)' in *Rivoluzione e Reazione in Europa 1917/1924*, Convegno storico internazionale (Perugia, 1978), vol. II, pp. 135 ff.
'Interpretations of Fascism' in W. Laqueur (ed.), *Fascism: a Reader's Guide* (London, 1976), pp. 415 ff. Revised version by Pelican Books, London, 1979, pp. 457 ff.
'Faschistische Bewegungen in Österreich, mit einem Vergleich zu Deutschland' in K. Bosl (ed.), *Die Erste Tschechoslowakische Republik als multinationaler Parteienstaat* (Munich, 1979), pp. 43 ff.

B. Books

The Origins of Prussia (Oxford, 1954; German trans. 1968)
Princes and Parliaments in Germany from the Fifteenth to the Eighteenth

Century (Oxford, 1959).
Reichswehr und Politik, 1918-1933 (Cologne-Berlin, 1964; English trans, 1966)
The Rise of Fascism in Europe (London, 1968; German trans. 1968)
Revolution in Central Europe, 1918-1919 (Berkeley-Los Angeles, 1972; German trans. 1973)
Fascist Movements in Austria: From Schönerer to Hitler (London, 1977; German trans. 1973)

NOTES ON CONTRIBUTORS

Volker R. Berghahn, Professor of History, University of Warwick, Coventry, England.

Gunnar C. Boehnert, Assistant Professor of History, University of Guelph, Ontario, Canada.

Karl Dietrich Bracher, Professor of Contemporary History and Political Science, University of Bonn, West Germany.

Henry Cohn, Senior Lecturer in History, University of Warwick, Coventry, England.

John Hiden, Senior Lecturer in European Studies, University of Bradford, England.

James Joll, Stephenson Professor of International History, London School of Economics and Political Science, England.

Martin Kitchen, Professor of History, Simon Fraser University, Burnaby, BC, Canada.

Richard Löwenthal, Emeritus Professor of Political Science, Free University, Berlin.

Barbara Marshall, Lecturer in History, Department of History, Philosophy and European Studies, Polytechnic of North London, England.

Wolfgang J. Mommsen, Professor of History and Director of the German Historical Institute, London, England.

George L. Mosse, Bascom Professor of History, University of Wisconsin, Madison, Wisconsin, USA, and Koebner Professor of History, Hebrew University, Jerusalem, Israel.

Hartmut Pogge von Strandmann, Fellow, University College, Oxford, England.

Anthony Polonsky, Lecturer in International History, London School of Economics and Political Science, England.

Michael Riff, Queen Mary College, London, England.

INDEX